SAGE was founded in 1965 by Sara Miller McCune to support the dissemination of usable knowledge by publishing innovative and high-quality research and teaching content. Today, we publish over 900 journals, including those of more than 400 learned societies, more than 800 new books per year, and a growing range of library products including archives, data, case studies, reports, and video. SAGE remains majority-owned by our founder, and after Sara's lifetime will become owned by a charitable trust that secures our continued independence.

Los Angeles | London | New Delhi | Singapore | Washington DC | Melbourne

Advance Praise

Armed forces is undoubtedly the best institution for management training. One learns to be a leader, constantly facing challenging situations in a hostile environment, often with inadequate resources, and coming out a winner. This experience when applied to the corporate world can work wonders. And that is what this book is all about, inspiring managers to take charge of VUCA situations during planning and execution. The numerous examples taken from military life make for an interesting read. The author has very appropriately woven his experiences in the army with the requirements of the modern-day industry to chart a course for success.

—Lt Gen. (Dr) A. K. S. Chandele, PVSM, AVSM
President, Institution of Electronics and
Telecommunication Engineers
Former Director General, Electronics and
Mechanical Engineers, Indian Army

Conflict and corporate environment are characterized by volatility, uncertainty, complexity, and ambiguity in a highly dynamic and competitive context. The author has hands-on experience of conflicts and corporate culture. He correlates military and corporate life artfully in this book, offering a rich, pragmatic, and fascinating account. His style is innovative, refreshing, lucid, and captivating. His deep insights not only make the book an interesting read but also serve as a guide to leadership and skill development for achieving competitive success.

—**Maj. Gen. B. K. Sharma, AVSM, SM, and Bar (Retd)**
Deputy Director (Research) and
Head, Centre for Strategic Studies and Simulation,
USI of India, New Delhi

A thorough book for all aspiring managers endeavoring for an in-depth understanding of each stage of the project life cycle. The author has sequentially crafted the chapters with perfect understanding of what is expected in planning and execution so that each stage is devoid of a VUCA issue. This book will ensure that new generation managers are conscious of the waste and losses and become the future force multipliers in their respective companies.

—**Dr Sanjeev Prashar**
Professor, Marketing
Chairman, Executive Education and Consultancy,
Indian Institute of Management, Raipur

It is often said, "plan for uncertainty and hope for certainty." The essence of this profound thought is well captured by the book. He distils years of experience from the armed forces and synthesizes it with his focused and penetrative analysis of life in the corporate world. In doing so, the book attempts to break the shackles that we as leaders and managers at times tend to create around ourselves. It outlines in an easy-to-understand language, with a cross-pollination of examples, the means to stay ahead of the curve. The author's suggestions provide an insight into the potential pitfalls of a project cycle and the means to defeat them at every level of leadership, from functional to oversight and hands-on to visionary.

—**Colonel Vivek Chadha (Retd)**
Research Fellow, IDSA

This is a book targeted at armed forces veterans who aspire for a second career in the corporate world. The book will also serve as a guide for managers in the corporate world to dealing with VUCA effectively. The book imbibes best practices of the armed forces as applicable in the corporate world which they can relate to easily. It is highly recommended that all officers and other ranks who are retiring read this book to understand how various departments work and function.

The experience we gain in the armed forces is immense and our skill sets are unique. When we enter the corporate world, we should contribute in a valuable manner in whatever role we have been assigned. The ethos and values of the armed forces continue to remain our guide in whatever field we choose. The leadership qualities of the armed forces personnel stand out, and these have been amply highlighted by various examples in the book. I compliment the author for his detailed research and articulation while bringing out this book.

—**Maj. Gen. Jagatbir Singh, VSM**
Director General (Resettlement)

Compliments to the author for bringing out a book that highlights the dilemma and challenges faced by professionals who are involved in managing or executing projects. Effective project management is a key capability for any organization that is trying to grow in these uncertain times. This book has been able to draw upon the techniques and real-time stories about the Indian Army and connect them aptly to the real-time challenges being faced currently by many organizations. The author has been practicing many of the concepts shared and has also been passionately spreading the techniques about managing uncertainties through the various training programs that he has been conducting at Thermax. This book would be very useful to anybody involved in the business of managing or executing projects.

—**B. C. Mahesh**
Executive Vice President and
Business Unit Head, Thermax Power

My compliments to the author on publishing a coveted book on project sustenance in the dynamic scenario. Strategically thinking, endogenous and exogenous factors are responsible for any company to become a growing entity. Research and development is a critical factor for the ever-changing market dynamics. Let us not forget that well-established companies such as Kodak and Nokia are losing market share in no time. Utilization of internal and external resources, competitive products, substitute products, adoption of modern technology, and change management are the key factors in the success of a firm. I wish that the book is well accepted and applied by managers and they derive maximum benefit out of it.

—**Deepak Pande**
CEO, Suljhan Consulting

What is your plan B? Executives at all levels are learning the importance of this question as they steer their organizations through the challenges posed by the VUCA world. This book by Col. Bakshi illustrates in a simple and effective manner the what and how of plan B. Focused execution is at the core of ensuring success and a refined approach, same as presented in the book, will surely help the professionals reach their goals in a definitive and effective manner.

—**Shishir Joshipura**
Managing Director, SKF India Limited

The parallels between military and management thinking have long been known, with frequent allusions to strategies, tactics, and campaign. Col. Bakshi hammers these home with examples from his own career and their implications for management in an easy, how-to manual. This will be a useful compendium for fresh entrants to management careers.

—**Dr Shreekant Sambrani**
Economist and Management Consultant, Formerly Professor,
IIM Ahmedabad and Founder-Director, IRMA

The thought itself of writing a book on this subject is laudable and on top of it to make it an interesting read is a great effort of immense dedication. The book is infused with experience, knowledge, and wisdom. The basic principles of success are the same in all projects with the core requirement being the speedy and timely completion of the task with high quality standards delivered at least cost.

An army man is a trained professional, a master of all of the above, with an ingrained *tadka* of loyalty, dedication, integrity, and forthrightness with a very high sense of responsibility/accountability. It is ironic that the nation, the public sector, the corporate world, and all other enterprises have neither realized the worth of this huge disciplined human resource of lakhs and lakhs of veterans nor been able to utilise/exploit them. That is only one side of the story. Equally at fault is the poor adaptability of the dedicated veteran to the totally alien working environment of the corporate world. While learning new tricks of the trade is easy, the "unlearning" of the hardcore values that he imbibed during the service period, is the more difficult part. Most veterans are capable of the most difficult of the tasks, but this simple process of adapting to the corporate work culture seems an uphill and herculean task. It is so because the service values get absorbed in your blood and become a part of your persona. But then there are success stories of the likes of Colonel Wahi, who gave ONGC its growth and character, and many others. It is possible with a little serious and conscious effort. This is where this book will come handy, which is a very well-meaning, benign effort, outlining many relevant aspects and methodology for this transformation. A lot of space has been dedicated to strategy, careful and detailed planning and preparation, and stages right through the journey of the project, from drawing board to the turn key phase. Insha Allah, this will be a guiding light to the veterans who aim for a corporate career. My compliments to Colonel Vikram Bakshi for the thought and its culmination into this lovely treatise.

—**Brig. (Retd) Vijay Saxena**
Senior Vice President, D S Green Agrotech Pvt Ltd

Very useful compendium of time tested techniques in project management and troubleshooting. A must read for all project managers. The book is a simple and easy to follow step-by-step guide to success for every project manager.

—S. K. Soni
Former Operation Head Power Division Thermax and
General Manager, Project Rohan Builder

The FORWARD-LOOKING MANAGER IN A VUCA WORLD

The FORWARD-LOOKING MANAGER IN A VUCA WORLD

VIKRAM BAKSHI

Los Angeles | London | New Delhi
Singapore | Washington DC | Melbourne

Copyright © Vikram Bakshi, 2017

All rights reserved. No part of this book may be reproduced or utilized in any form or by any means, electronic or mechanical, including photocopying, recording, or by any information storage or retrieval system, without permission in writing from the publisher.

First published in 2017 by

SAGE Publications India Pvt Ltd
B1/I-1 Mohan Cooperative Industrial Area
Mathura Road, New Delhi 110 044, India
www.sagepub.in

SAGE Publications Inc
2455 Teller Road
Thousand Oaks, California 91320, USA

SAGE Publications Ltd
1 Oliver's Yard, 55 City Road
London EC1Y 1SP, United Kingdom

SAGE Publications Asia-Pacific Pte Ltd
3 Church Street
#10-04 Samsung Hub
Singapore 049483

Published by Vivek Mehra for SAGE Publications India Pvt Ltd, typeset in 10.5/14 pt Adobe Caslon Pro by Diligent Typesetter India Pvt Ltd, Delhi and printed at Saurabh Printers Pvt Ltd, Greater Noida.

Library of Congress Cataloging-in-Publication Data Available

ISBN: 978-93-866-0231-2 (PB)

SAGE Team: Manisha Mathews, Sunil Koli, Megha Dabral and Rajinder Kaur

**This book is dedicated to my Father
Late Colonel R. S. Bakshi**

*He commanded the EME Battalion in Operation Pawan in
Sri Lanka, apart from taking part in 1965, 1971, and Punjab and
Northeast counterinsurgency operations.*

*He was the most gentle soul I ever came across in my life,
leaving a lasting impression on whoever came in touch with him.*

*Thanks Dad for teaching me the most valuable lesson of my life—
to practice patience when things go wrong,
but be resilient to seek the goal even under VUCA conditions.*

Thank you for choosing a SAGE product!
If you have any comment, observation or feedback,
I would like to personally hear from you.

Please write to me at **contactceo@sagepub.in**

Vivek Mehra, Managing Director and CEO, SAGE India.

Bulk Sales

SAGE India offers special discounts
for purchase of books in bulk.
We also make available special imprints
and excerpts from our books on demand.

For orders and enquiries, write to us at

Marketing Department
SAGE Publications India Pvt Ltd
B1/I-1, Mohan Cooperative Industrial Area
Mathura Road, Post Bag 7
New Delhi 110044, India

E-mail us at **marketing@sagepub.in**

Get to know more about SAGE

Be invited to SAGE events, get on our mailing list.
Write today to **marketing@sagepub.in**

This book is also available as an e-book.

Contents

Foreword by Tapan Misra ix
Acknowledgments xiii

Introduction 1

1. Strength of Character and Leadership 6
2. Countering VUCA with Disruption 26
3. Anticipate VUCA with Advance Information 36
4. Orientation to Avoid VUCA 50
5. Strategic Planning for a VUCA Future 62
6. Tactical Planning 80
7. Operational Planning to Prevent VUCA 143
8. Execution in VUCA Conditions 176
9. Monitoring and Control 200
10. The Hybrid Leader 227
11. Closing of the Project 253
12. Technology to Help in Countering VUCA 268

Bibliography 280

Foreword

Many organizations like ISRO have been part of several successful projects right from their inception. There are many factors that stand out for their success, but one of the most important aspects which is also behind the genesis of this book is how organizations such as ISRO deal with VUCA that enables to prevent delays and cost overruns in projects.

VUCA stands for Volatile, Uncertain, Complex, and Ambiguous conditions which suddenly halt a project or an operation and which can have serious fallouts. One can imagine the number of issues that are covered by the ISRO team in exploring unknown space, but these are surely dealt first by anticipating the issues that may result in a serious condition. Thereafter, preparing better conditions in advance to prevent such VUCA issues or making resources available for timely correction at a later date is needed to prevent a project from going astray.

VUCA is a term that originated from the armed forces, and like space endeavors, there is an element of risk in armed forces operations; nobody knows what is going to happen next. If officers, managers, or teams are not prepared for it, they may end up losing lives also. That is why this book *The Forward-looking Manager in a VUCA World*, written by an ex-army officer Lt Col. Vikram Bakshi, is of so much relevance to the corporates and business houses also. In today's world, there is a competition among all companies to deliver fast without losses. This book is, hence, a lifeline for many managers to understand the methods of and tools for planning in advance to prevent a situation that may bring a loss to their company.

With VUCA as a backdrop, this book discusses inspired planning and relentless execution using the top to bottom approach. The book covers the life cycle of the project, how planning is done at the strategy level with the inception of an idea from the top management, then how it involves functional heads of the departments (HODs) at the tactical level to coordinate their responsibilities with each other. The operational level gets down to site or real execution team planning, covering issues of the execution more in depth. The action plan is the steps of the execution to be finally done keeping the strategy, tactical, and operational graduated plan in mind.

In short, this book caters to all levels of managers from a young graduate to a senior manager to the top management to understand all topics and tools. Anytime you need some guidance on any of the topics in a project, use this book as your pocket mentor. It is a comprehensive guide for doing projects in a real world by detailed planning and fast-track execution along with monitor and control and contingency planning.

The USP of this book is that it not only provides a practical approach to planning or execution at all levels, but it also provides many aspects of leadership in each chapter. The book has true case studies woven around project management topics which reflect the varied range of leadership that is needed in various situations. The real stories of heroes of the armed forces and corporate world who rose in difficult times are truly stunning. The riveting business and life lessons are refreshing, forcing readers to think about many sensible concepts and how to use them. The prime benefit of this inspiring management book is the true stories from the armed forces, how diverse VUCA situations were overcome by selfless service, duty performed, and ultimate sacrifice of officers and men of the armed forces in the line of duty.

Definitely, this a masterpiece and a must-have for all business houses and project companies. This is a great book which will not only change a manager's perception of life on how to embrace uncertainty but will also guide him/her with many disruptive tools and methods from the armed forces and corporate world alike on how to respond to a VUCA situation. This book will surely help managers and veterans alike to become forward-looking managers. It is so much a prerequisite today to understand how and why a project or company can come in troubled waters and how to prevent that by preventing VUCA situations.

A must-have for all those dealing with projects and operations of any nature. Happy reading!

Tapan Mishra
Director, Space Applications Centre,
ISRO, Ahmedabad

Acknowledgments

> *Be grateful for whoever comes because each has been sent as a guide from beyond*
>
> —Rumi

I wish to firstly acknowledge many writers and contributors of articles whose work I have referred to at the end of the book.

However, there are certain things we cannot learn from books, but only from interacting with people. I humbly wish to acknowledge these contributions in shaping my thought process while writing the book.

I learned foresight planning and rapid execution to counter VUCA issues by witnessing the leadership style of a few senior officers such as Brigadier P. S. Sajwan, Brigadier S. S. Narula, Major General B. K. Sharma, Brigadier Vijay Saxena under whom I served.

Similarly, I also wish to mention Mr T. Remesan and Mr K. C. Chakravarthy who were my project sponsors for a greenfield project. They were foreseeing and timely resolving all issues when I was dealing with the execution part as a project manager, and we delivered the project before baseline schedule and with cost savings.

I must mention Major General S. S. Suhag, Brigadier J. N. Nayar, and Colonel Gyanendra Singh who helped me learn the importance of processes to prevent a VUCA condition. Similarly, I must mention

Mr A. G. Kshirsagar for his guidance in a brownfield project. We got a gold award in the Quality Circle Forum for the Six Sigma processes in the turnaround of a consolidation plant of boiler products.

I also recall two Director Generals of EME (Corps of Electronics and Mechanical Engineers), namely, Lt Gen. N. B. Singh and Lt Gen. Ajay Chandele who exhorted to do quality engineering work that prevents a VUCA rework or any fallouts later.

I observed the importance of employee relationship building and customer-centric culture from our corporate leaders of Thermax, namely, Mr B. C. Mahesh, Mr Sunil Raina, Mr Umesh Barde, Mr Kirtiraj Jilkar, Mr M. L. Bindra, and our MD, Mr M. S. Unnikrishnan. The ethical ethos is guided by our company founders, the Aga family.

Project culture is also about getting trained in new skills. After leaving the army, I joined the Info Dynamic team, and special thanks to R. V. Singh and other project managers who helped me in this transition to telecom projects from my automotive background. I later shifted to the boiler manufacturing industry, and thanks to many colleagues in the Heating Division of Thermax for the knowledge shared. Bhavik, Savli team, and Chakan Unit also deserve a special mention for all the knowledge on projects, supply chain management (SCM), and logistics.

I subsequently got to learn all about Power Plant Projects Thermax under my ex-boss Mr S. K. Soni who also helped me with tips for the book. I must thank a few more gentlemen for insight in related knowledge areas in my transition. Mr Sanjeev Vichare (Safety and Enterprise Resource Planning [ERP]), Mr Nitin Saraf (Material Management), Mr Abhay Kulkerni (Processes), Mr Sanjay Goel (Operations), Mr Devendra Bora (HR), Mr P. Harisai (site work), and Mr Parag Damle (ERP).

I have learned a lot from my Father, Colonel R. S. Bakshi. He used to calmly deal with unforeseen problems because of his fineness and understanding. I also wish to thank my family, especially my mother, my wife, and my son, who encouraged me for the new challenges in life. I must also mention my veteran friends Major Sandy Verma, Colonel Rahul Kapahi and Lt Col. Puneet Khanna and other mates, for being there when I needed them most in VUCA conditions of life.

The project is also about teamwork. I want to thank all my colleagues, course mates, juniors, seniors, soldiers, and blue-collar workforce in the army and corporate world who are very much in my heart and part of memories. Special thanks to one and all for all your help and support. A warm salute!

Introduction

*Everything about yesterday has
gone with yesterday.
Today, it is needed to say new things*

Armed forces is one profession in which chaos and danger lurk at every step. Next is the project management industry. Both jobs are temporary in nature, beginning with a definite start and an inevitable end. Events in both are ever-changing, dynamic, flexible, and require quick response and fast decision-making.

In the last decade, it has been noticed that many large MNCs in projects and operations were either shutting down operations or running at losses. They were giving their market dominance away to new disruptive players. Everybody blamed the recession for the downtrend.

The real reasons were also within the enterprises ways of working. Losses were happening due to their inability to deal with problems in time. Managers were not able to do forward-thinking which resulted in delayed decision-making and ill-prepared teams.

VUCA

I found this chaotic situation of the business world similar to a military VUCA situation where a problem comes up suddenly, and there is no immediate solution.

VUCA stands for volatile, uncertain, complex, and ambiguous. It finds its origin from wartime military situations in counterinsurgency operations where an unknown enemy has to be tackled suddenly.

- **Volatile.** It means the working condition is laden with immediate, unexpected problems. We can easily predict the problems and deal with them if there is a strategy in place.
- **Uncertain.** Being unclear about the present situation and future outcome, it becomes hard to know whether a change will bring a positive or negative result. We call it Fog of War.
- **Complexity.** The situation has multiple factors and interconnected issues that signify the multiplicity of critical decision-making factors.
- **Ambiguity.** It is a lack of clarity facing the unknown.

The term VUCA has now been adopted in the corporate world as well. It is because the companies find similar situations of survival during times of turbulence. There are many surprises and unexpected turn of events that can delay the business results.

A project manager can face many VUCA conditions in his/her project that are not anticipated and can slow down the project. It can impact the schedule, delay the deliverables, and cause cost overruns. It can also snowball into the delayed integration of other activities, making the project a nonstarter even before it gets off the ground. All subsequent planning and execution will fail.

COUNTERING VUCA THE ARMED FORCES WAY

Managers today have no choice but to keep pace with constant changes in business to drive growth. Today countering VUCA in business is as much a necessity as it is in armed forces.

VUCA conditions require a new set of rules and methods, and we can learn from armed forces how to deal with these conditions.

Corporate houses have to encourage new rules of decentralized leadership and armed forces unconventional warfare. There are many underlying themes of the way armed forces address VUCA conditions timely.

- **Learn from past battles.** Undertake an aftermath analysis of past operations in armed forces to avoid facing the same VUCA problems in the subsequent operation.
- **Think like the enemy.** Assess how the enemy will react and prepare counteractions based on the VUCA problems that may arise.
- **Progressive elaborated planning.** In the armed forces, the battle plan at the strategy level gets translated to the tactical level, then to the operational level, and finally to real actionable steps. It is like a rolling waveform with series of successive iterations as more and better information is available. For example, the planning for a surgical strike by India in Pakistan started at the army headquarter but became more detailed and elaborate at the lower levels.
- **Quick and flexible execution.** During the terrorist attack on the Taj Hotel, Mumbai, the terrorists had held up several hostages. However, the National Security Guard (NSG) team contained the situation by adopting quick drills. The team not only killed the terrorists but also rescued the hostages.
- **Fallback plan.** The action team also has secondary and alternative options as a fallback plan. If things go wrong as per Plan A, the team shifts gear from Plan A to Plan B; winning remains the sole purpose. In the Kargil War, the small teams changed directions many times while climbing the ridge but they kept the enemy at the top in sight.
- **Reserve for contingencies.** A commander never utilizes all his resources at one go. There is always an emergency reserve to handle any VUCA response from the enemy.

WHY HAS THIS BOOK BEEN WRITTEN?

This book has been written to help managers understand VUCA. In each chapter, it correlates many aspects of armed forces and the corporate world to deal with VUCA problems.

In armed forces, a leader leads the fight with the enemy against all the odds and situations. Similarly, in a project, the project manager should take ownership of the situation and lead the team by example.

Chapter 1 deals with the leadership needed now in VUCA conditions. The companies that aspire to emerge as winners have to imbibe economy of resources, lean structure, efficient processes, and accountability values. They have to learn to integrate people, system, and technologies to convert plans to actions without VUCA effects.

Chapter 2 deals with VUCA, disruption, and resources, processes, and values (RPV) in detail. Teams should be able to foresee problems in order to prevent the VUCA situation. They should also be able to execute boardroom plans effectively at the ground level.

Chapters 3–7 deal with planning as an elaborative process, with different stages of strategic, tactical, and operational plans complementing each other.

Chapter 8 addresses the process of execution, that is, how the actual act of work is to be done. The implementation team needs to be trained through drills to follow detailed plans promptly.

Chapter 9 discusses monitoring and controlling aspects. It is important that the execution of a plan aligns with the baseline schedule, cost, scope, and quality; therefore, there is a continuous need to monitor the ground situations and develop alternatives for the evolving requirements.

Chapter 10 deals with planning in forwarding location and its implementation. The companies need to adopt the art of decentralized planning and implementation so that the responsibilities and decision-making can be shifted to the hybrid teams. This saves a lot of time, and the leaders at all levels believe they have a strong involvement in the success of the company.

The book advocates forward-thinking in VUCA situations, that is, thinking proactively rather than reactively. It emphasizes the use of effective leadership skills and encourages creative teams to resort to replanning and fresh execution when things go wrong.

The book is for every mid- and senior-level manager who wants to establish himself/herself in the corporate world. The book will also be useful for armed forces Veterans who are about to take a plunge in the industrial and corporate arena as they will be able to use their armed forces experiences and tools discussed here.

ADOPT RACE ATTITUDE TO OVERCOME VUCA

Companies today are not only expected to deliver within the schedule and with quality and low cost but deliver faster, better, and cheaper. This book also discusses developing the RACE attitude which means rapid delivery, absolute work, class quality, and economic work.

I invite readers to understand how to use some of the armed forces and corporate disruptive methods to achieve RACE results. As an author, I hope the readers from armed forces and corporate world alike will get benefitted from the best practices in the armed forces.

I look forward to meeting and interacting with you and also welcome suggestions to improve the second edition. Please do send inputs at vikrambakshi67@gmail.com. Happy reading to all you future Generals, the chronicles of a project leader.

CHAPTER 1

Strength of Character and Leadership

> *We have three hundred tons of brain power, how can we motivate our people so that those three hundred tons move in a particular direction.*
>
> —Goran Lindahi

A FLASHBACK FROM THE NATIONAL DEFENCE ACADEMY

It was many years ago at the National Defence Academy (NDA) that Brando won the final bout of the boxing match, not because he was good but because his opponent had lost deliberately, as the winner of the boxing semifinal bout was to be up against R. S. Gill, the reigning boxing champion of the Academy and the Mike Tyson of NDA.

Brando had no experience of boxing before he joined the Academy, but a senior got him into boxing to put his stubborn streak to test. When others would give up exhausted, Brando would stare back in defiance,

FOR YOUR BUSINESS SHELF

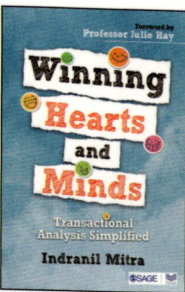
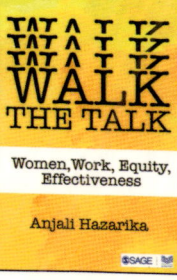
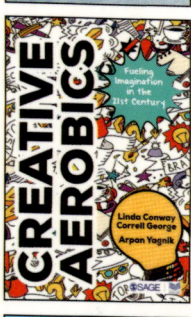

www.sagepub.in

SHAPING TODAY'S MANAGEMENT THOUGHTS

indicating his indomitable spirit. As a matter of fact, Brando knew he would have to use his strength and maintain his cool and calm in the face of the brute force he anticipated from R. S. Gill in the finals. He knew that he needed to be more resilient and gritty to survive the technicalities in the first two rounds.

The boxing bout started; Gill charged, Brando ducked and got a lot of nasty jabs. The first round was over; Brando felt a rage building up inside him, seeking vengeance. The second round was a repeat of the first except that Brando was holding up to the reigning champ. The round ended with a lot of bruising and bleeding for both the boxers.

The third round was tough with a lot of battering on both sides. The punches continued from both the opponents. Although Gill won on technical points, Brando as the underdog became the crowd's favorite, and Gill never forgot that fight. This boxing competition gave Brando some important life lessons. Brando overcame his fears, learned to persevere against all the odds, and discovered the resilient side to himself. That is what the Academy teaches its cadets.

LEADERSHIP

In the year 2016, Veteran Colonel (Brando) had completed 21 years of service in the army. Since he was always keen to take up challenging projects, he grabbed an opportunity to show his prowess in project management. The Colonel wanted to see all his team members as managers cum leaders. He knew that in today's volatile, uncertain, complex, and ambiguous (VUCA) environment, leaders would be called upon to deal with multifaceted emerging threats and situations. The following qualities are essential to effectively handle VUCA problems.

Persistence and Resilience

The most important trait is the "never say die" attitude in the face of a tough problem. Whether in the army or at the workplace, people experience enthusiasm, obstacles, near-collapse state, resilience, and a range of emotions.

Persistence, resilience, and willpower must be the foundation of a person's character, and that helps to sustain the momentum against all VUCA problems. In armed forces, it is called "maintenance of tempo" in the face of odds.

Adaptive Leadership

The pace of change in the current working environment is faster than our ability to respond, and new circumstances are rolled out before we get used to the old ones. It is hence imperative that leaders at all levels must adapt to changing conditions rapidly.

A team leader should ensure that his/her members do not lose the objective or the purpose. At the same time, he/she should be open to new ideas and thought processes and analyze various alternatives available.

Keep the Distant Objective in Sight

At the NDA, one needs to pass many physical tests before going to the next term. One such test was clearing a 9-feet ditch which Brando did with aplomb most times till once he fell and hurt his ankle. Following this episode, Brando was filled with an irrational fear when in full battle gear, with a rifle, he had to jump in the air and cross the ditch 9-feet wide, 5-feet deep.

To overcome his absurd anxiety, Brando decided to practice on his own. He remembered that his PT teacher had asked him to take the leap of faith in the air, focusing on the far side of the ditch. He did just that and landed much beyond 10 feet of the outer edge and did it again and again and again till it became a habit.

There will always be issues that slow down the short-term goals. However, it is important that the leader is able to rise above these small obstacles and look at the distant goals or the bigger picture.

Thinking on Your Feet

Once in a battle, a Junior Commissioned Officer (JCO) reported to a young Major that the enemy had surrounded them from all directions. The Major did not panic but said, "Good we can now attack the enemy from any direction."

In armed forces, one is ready for a counterattack by anticipating enemy actions. Troops move at a rapid speed to counter any volatile action by the enemy.

Similarly, in the case of projects, it is important to remain calm, composed, and have a positive quick thinking attitude with preset drills and alternative plans to tackle VUCA issues that will inevitably come.

Team Work

In a war, there is always an unspoken commitment of team leaders toward each other and no soldier is ever left behind.

During the war, a soldier who was safe inside a trench saw his friend in almost dead condition ahead in the no man's land with enemy forces firing at his friend and others. His senior advised that if he goes there, he will also get killed. Still the soldier crawled and went ahead and came back reporting that his friend had died. However, his friend's last words were "Jim I knew you would come for me." The soldier did not let down his friend's trust in his last moments—that is what mattered.

This team spirit is engrained in training while running the famous cross country or endurance runs after camps at NDA—25–30 km run over wild terrain and mountains with full battle gear and rifle in hand. The team carries weak runners with them, and at times the mates' rifles too. However, the key to winning is that all the runners have to come in as a team in the least amount of time, leaving no stragglers behind.

Similarly, when a project is going astray, the leader has to keep his/her team together. Some members are cooperative, some resistive, some neutral, some assist, and some are threats. However, a project leader is expected to maintain the overall enthusiasm in the project so that all members can individually deal with any volatile situation that arises.

Resource Management

One needs to use resources to the optimum and get results the first time without having to rework.

In the army, the firing instructor would say: "Hold the trigger, steady your breath, watch the target and unleash a single shot of death. One Shot One Kill."

The learning was to save resources and to use them economically. A soldier may never get a second chance as the enemy might shoot him if he missed the first time.

Similarly, in projects, to prevent a volatile situation of resource paucity, one has to use resources economically and at the right moment to facilitate completion.

Discipline and Punctuality

It is better to be disciplined and punctual than to react to volatile situations.

In NDA drill classes, discipline at drill square meant synchronized movements, proper dress code, and timings in academic classes. It is the same for projects where timing and discipline are of utmost importance.

Create Leaders Under a Leader

There is always a great need for junior leaders to be under a leader at every level, who could make the difference in dealing with VUCA issues in time and appropriately. In a VUCA environment, the traditional concept of centralized command control and micromanaged issues will only further compound the problem.

Normally, there are two kinds of organization we come across:

1. **Hierarchical organization.** It is similar to many corporate project companies, where there is one boss and others are required to follow his/her instructions. There is no decentralization in decision-making.
2. **Non-hierarchical organization.** Armed forces work in a non-hierarchical leadership within three domains. The leadership is at individual, group, and organization levels, and that means we have leaders under a leader to get things done.

In armed forces, there are non-commissioned officers and JCOs under officers as junior leaders. In the same way in projects, a leader can be the supervisor or site incharge or a coordinator or a project manager. Like the JCOs play a crucial role of a bridge between men and leaders, a supervisor plays a role between engineers and workers in a project.

It is always the junior leadership and young officers that make things move in the organization. They are owners of their individual sub-teams and share the same objectives and unit mission in the process of achieving organizational success.

A decentralized decision-making process would have self-driven junior leaders at all levels. It helps in cutting out the waiting time of unnecessary approvals and decision-making.

Dealing with a Volatile Situation

In the Kargil War, the enemy was sitting atop the mountain. The company commander of the Indian Army was tasked to lead the company assault on the mountaintop early morning. The artillery firing had started to soften the enemy defense, and the young major peered through the fog of war and missed seeing the enemy's light machine gun (LMG) on the side bunker.

The young major lined up his troops in assault line with bayonets fixed. He ordered his troops to start climbing up to capture the hilltop in assault formation. With a war cry, the troops lined up in the straight assault formation and started rushing up the slope. He assumed a sure shot victory as they were many in number. The situation, however, soon turned into a slaughter with the enemy LMG opening up and killing his few men in rapid gunfire.

In such a volatile situation, the young major had to not only maintain his resolve to reach the top but also change tactics.

If a leader maintains his vision and a sense of purpose, he can find ways to overcome the volatile situation.

In the Kargil War, the same company commander soon realized that they should not attack the enemy with large forces but use small teams of four to five soldiers and send them on their own, finding their way to the top so that they do not show a big target to the enemy LMG. He also moved with his four to five soldiers to neutralize the LMG post with a grenade and directed his artillery gun to blast the LMG post.

The small teams reached the mountain using their own route with fewer casualties, and the young officers who led the attack were able to hoist the battalion flag on the peak.

A volatile situation can be best countered if the team has a vision. It will ensure that each team member takes charge of the situation with commitment and dedication. The officers of the Indian Army shared the vision to evict the enemy from our post. This vision motivated and led soldiers to cripple the enemy with their actions.

Everyone remembers how Capt. Vikram Batra, with his small team, captured peak after peak. His famous words in Hindi were *Yeh dil maange more* which he used with a TV news reporter. It means "this heart desires more" (it is a famous Pepsi ad slogan). After every win, he would reinforce the vision to capture the next peak, keeping the message alive. He, thus, prevented a volatile situation initiated by the enemy to break the morale of his team.

Clearing the Uncertainty

One might remember the movie *Border* which was based on true war events of the Indian Army unit holding out against the Pakistan attack in the Battle of Longewala.

There was uncertainty in the air as the aircraft could not fly at night due to lack of night flying capability. There was hence a total lack of information whether the aircraft will reach in time to support ground troops when the Pakistan armor tanks attacks the Longewala node.

Major Kuldip Singh Chandpuri, the company commander of 23rd Battalion Punjab Regiment was uncertain about the air support to help his unit against the enemy tanks. He, therefore, simply led from the front, moved from one trench to another, ascertaining every information on how to deploy his guns and position his troops. He made the best use of ground cover to overcome the lack of aircraft support by deploying his troops in critical points to defend against Pakistani tanks.

It is a great story where a VUCA situation was overcome by personal leadership taking charge of the uncertain situation on the ground. The army tanks were held off until early morning when the Indian aircraft reached and blasted the enemy tanks.

Similarly, in projects, there will be occasions when there will be lack of information. The project manager, therefore, will find it hard to know what is happening or predict what the future will look like.

In such an uncertain situation, the basic aim should be to develop an understanding of the situation.

> **Lead from Trenches.** The leader must spend time with blue-collar forces in the trenches and should not shy away from asking about the signs of failure or success based on how the work is going. It helps in better understanding of the events and prevents unpredictability.
>
> **Realistic.** The ground realities have to be clearly understood by gathering all possible information even if it is a difficult truth. It helps to connect all the dots.

Gut Instincts. The project manager needs to act in a vacuum trusting his instincts and skill sets to prevent rude surprise. At times, experience and lesson learned from a similar situation in the past may also come in handy.

Lead in a Time of Crisis. In a combat situation, the action takes place "in the front." Strong leaders get there despite the fact that it can be a dangerous place, and they listen to their "frontline commanders." All best project leaders have one thing in common: They lead from the front and share the same burdens as their team members and also bring a sense of awareness of problems faced by the team.

Solving a Complex Situation

On April 17, 1970, the spacecraft Apollo was crippled because of an electrical fault[1] *one of the oxygen tanks exploded, and it was losing oxygen. Going to the moon was out of the question and getting the aircraft back to the Earth was a challenge in itself.*

The first message received from the spacecraft to Earth was not a panic or long worded message but a simple one, "Houston, we've had a problem." The astronauts or the flight directors did not show any sign of panic or hopelessness. Instead, they focused on managing the situation to the best of their ability without getting emotional.

The second reaction was to get a clarity of what exactly was to be done. The mission control team had to get the team back to earth. There was interrelatedness of all things from an Earth station to the spacecraft, and everyone was connected to each other to test and implement the solution for each aspect as it came. One individual in the scheme of things could have risked the whole mission if he/she was not clear about what was to be done. However, the mission crew jointly got the team back, and it was called a successful failure.

---

[1] https://www.nasa.gov/mission_pages/apollo/missions/apollo13.html

How does leadership help to solve complex situations?

- **Contingency plan.** All leaders have a backup plan, and they are prepared with their preplanned response to save time and control losses.
- **Quick decision-making.** Leaders have to prevent analysis paralysis in situations that are not black or white but gray. They should be able to take quick decisions through confusion and chaos. All operate with joint ownership of success like the mission crew of Apollo.
- **Information sharing.** Leaders should create an environment that promotes the exchange of knowledge and ideas among individuals and departments. Transparency of results should be displayed not to hound people but to address their problems. Avoid short term solution and over-reliance on quick wins.
- **Shared vision.** There has to be a common goal and vision shared among all leaders. Managers must drive all towards a common objective instead of developing a narrowed vision to build their own success.
- **Micromanagement versus autonomy.** Complexities occur when a leader snuffs out collective wisdom and sharing of ideas. Hence, there should be more autonomy with transparency and accountability. Use micromanagement only in the critical task, and not in all matters as it results in the breakdown of trust and creates diffidence in team members.
- **Priority issues.** In a complex situation, clarity is important. Leaders have to see through the web of such complexities and filter out the priority issues that need immediate attention.
- **Agents of change.** Leaders should act as catalysts for change. They must be able to tap the strengths of the people and work towards a common purpose. They should also be knowledgeable and lead by example.

Overcoming an Ambiguous Situation

The demonetization that occurred in October 2016 in India was a classic case of an ambiguous situation. The Government of India announced the withdrawal of all ₹500 and ₹1,000 banknotes and they could not be used as legal tenders anymore.

The government claimed that the action would curtail the shadow economy and crack down on the use of illicit and counterfeit currency to fund illegal activity and terrorism.

However, the situation became very volatile as people were not ready for this change. The scarcity of cash due to the failure of timely printing of new currency in large amounts led to chaos. Most people who were holding old banknotes faced difficulties. They had to exchange limited notes and wasted critical time due to endless queues outside banks and ATMs across India. This led to confusion and chaos that could have been avoided.

There was uncertainty on the additional tax when people had to shift to new digital ways of making payments. However, the move turned out to be a blessing in disguise and is expected to bring a paradigm shift in the economy. It will curb black money and promote a cashless economy.

There was also a lot of hype from both the media and the opposition which made the situation even more complex. The suffering of the people standing in the queues and deaths reported depicted the failure of connected agencies to cope with the situation.

So what was ambiguous about the whole exercise? There was mass interpretation with many versions. There was no proper response and many inappropriate changes of ruling by the RBI regarding withdrawal facilities and rules and timelines. This caused a lot of disorder in the system creating stress among common people and banking institutions. A lot of unbanked villages and small-scale industries were severely hit due to the currency crisis. There were also many industries which were significantly affected.

The lesson learned is if management is venturing into an ambiguous situation, they should be analytic, amply clear on defining the results, and also have an action plan on how to endure during the tough initial days. One should go in more details, peel layer after layer to understand the full significance and impact of the events and plan accordingly to plug the gaps. They have to train themselves in analysis tools to have a foresight of future and be less ambiguous.

Effective Team Management

Project managers must display the following characteristics for effectively managing teams.

- **Servant leadership for leading teams.** In armed forces, the welfare of soldiers comes foremost. If you take care of your soldiers, they will follow and also take care of you. As Field Marshall W. Chetwood said at the Indian Military Academy:

  > The safety, honor, and welfare of your country come first, always and every time. The honor, welfare, and comfort of the men you command come next. Your ease, comfort, and safety come last, always and every time.

- **Welfare.** A project leader always cares for his/her people and provides a conducive working environment. It is important to realize that "wars may be fought with weapons, but people win them."
- **Safety.** In armed forces, officers never "order" or ask a subordinate to do something that they wouldn't do themselves. The officer-to-men casualty ratio in the Indian Army is the highest, and that is because our officers believe in leading from the front when they are crossing a minefield.
- **Being ethical.** The last word is ethical leadership. There will be times when VUCA situations tempt us to take a wrong path, sell our souls, deceive our seniors and teams with lies to promote our low-performance work, or take credit of our juniors' good work, overlook their welfare, and think of ourselves. A VUCA will multiply only if not addressed head on. For that one has to face it and correct it.

I remember a letter written by Gen. K. Sunderji which is relevant for every leader and manager not only in armed forces but also in the corporate world. Let it be a guiding light for all.

A word about him—he was a brave chief and a visionary in his field. He was responsible for getting us out of our cocoon of defense mind frame and think out of the box to be in a responsive mode to tackle any VUCA situation across the border. His famous Brass Tracks exercise is so relevant even today.

His letter must be read by every leader in the corporate world and armed forces, again and again, to imbibe the critical values needed to lead a team amidst difficult VUCA times.

That famous letter for all leaders and managers from General K. Sundarji as follows:

> General K Sundarji, PVSM, ADC
> Army Headquarters, New Delhi-110 001
> 1 Feb 86
>
> Dear Brother Officer,
>
> 1. It is imperative that we have a totally combat effective Army to support the revitalised India of tomorrow in her rightful place in the world. This involves getting the "man-machine mix" just right, improving the quality of both and placing them in a structure which will be effective in the battlefield milieu of the Nineties and the early decades of 2000. It is an exercise as exciting as it is challenging and I am fully confident that we will succeed.
>
> 2. Briefly mentioning the "machine," we have thus far modernised only by discrete changes of weapons systems and equipment. We were also dependent mostly on imported equipment, which apart from not being designed to suit our exact requirements, were also not "state of the art" and at least a generation behind those used by more modern armies. Much of this has changed and is fast changing. Our R&D has come of age and having had a close look at the scene for some years, I can assure you that we are on the verge of take-off. There are still some problems of translation of R&D into production, but these are also being solved fast. Therefore,

the time has now come for us to take a total look at technology, threats, tactics and organisations in order to restructure our Army and develop doctrine for the future. This is in hand, and want each one of you to be involved in the process.

3. However, no amount of modernisation of arms, equipment, tactics and organisations can produce results unless we have the right kind of man in the right state of mind, manning the system. And that is what this letter of mine is about.

4. The fact that the Army is one of the national institutions which has, comparatively speaking, weathered the post-Independence years and yet remains effective, should not make us complacent. Field Marshal Cariappa used to say, "Good officers–good Army; bad officers–bad Army." This is as true today as it was then. We should, therefore look at ourselves first and be not only frank but hypercritical. As a whole, the Corps of Officers has lost much of its self-esteem, pride and elan; it is becoming increasingly careerist, opportunist and sycophantic; standards of integrity have fallen and honour and patriotism are becoming unfashionable. Paradoxically, all this is happening, while in the narrow sense, professional competence has been going up at all levels since 1947. Broad-based though our intake has become, our young officers have proved in every action which they have fought, that they are brave and lead from the front—our officer casualty ratio in every action testifies to this. Where then are we going wrong?

5. First, let us look at ourselves—the senior officers; most of us are senior to some of the others and so this includes almost all of us. We have obviously NOT set the right example. Many of us have not professionally kept ourselves up-to-date, doctrinally or technologically; we have felt that we have "got it made," and rested on our oars; we do not read enough; we do not think enough, and some of course, have been promoted well beyond their capability! In the practise of our profession, we have not insisted on standards being maintained and turn our eyes away from irregularities (living in a glass house?); we have not been tolerant of dissent during discussion and encourage sycophancy (a result of our having "switched off" professionally?) we have not been accepting any mistakes (due to hankering after personal advancement?), thus encouraging our juniors to either do nothing worthwhile or to oversupervise their juniors, who in turn are not allowed to develop professionally or mature as men.

This leads to frustration. Finally, some have perhaps unthinkingly developed a yen for 5-star culture and ostentation which flows from new-rich values in our society, where money is the prime indicator of success and social position. This adoption of mercenary values in an organisation like the Army which depends for its elan on values like honour, duty and country above self is disastrous for its elan and for the self-esteem of the individual in it. And once we start thinking of ourselves as third class citizens, it is not long before our civilian brethren take us at our own valuation, and some of them perhaps not without a touch of glee!

6. I am not suggesting that woefully inadequate pay and poor compensation packages for hard and turbulent service conditions, and being forced to live slummily with a poor quality of life do not prevent the development of elan and self-esteem. They do. It is also a fact that the overall compensation package of the servicemen is poor and has deteriorated rapidly over the years. So is it a fact that the present dispensation is inequitable as far as the armed forces are concerned as compared to their peers in other government services. These facts have been brought forcefully to the notice of the Pay Commission and the Government and I will continue to press hard for a fair and equitable deal. I would also like to add that all my contacts with the authorities so far have convinced me that they are sympathetically aware of our problems. The Prime Minister himself is aware of the psychological problems caused by the unwarranted and continued degradation of service officers in the Warrant of Precedence. He has ordered that this problem be analysed and put up to him. But to tell you all this is not the purpose of this letter; I want to dwell on what we can do, in-house, to increase the elan and self-esteem of the Officer Corps.

7. The bed-rock of elan is the professional competence of individuals and leaders, and the faith, confidence and pride in the effectiveness of the group—the section upwards, to the Army as a whole. In developing professional competence, I would like to emphasise developing an active technological curiosity without which one cannot cope with the battlefield of tomorrow. I want that we read more and seriously, think more and seriously, discuss more and seriously and write more and seriously about professional matters. This last, has been inhibited by our exaggerated and self-defeating system of security classifications and centralised clearance requirements. I intend putting this right speedily. As regards

developing group effectiveness, we have to do much more towards making our training mission-oriented, interesting, competitive and effective in spite of the various constraints of which we are well aware. We should certainly avoid training for training's sake which not only gets to be boring but moves further and further away from the realities of battle conditions. Let us not get to the mentality of the British Colonel of the regular army who is said to have remarked on 11 Nov 1918, "Thank God the war is over; now we can get back to some serious soldiering!"

8. All of us talk about "Officer Like Qualities" and about being officers and gentlemen. I am not sure whether to many of us these terms means the same thing. Being a gentlemen does not mean Westernisation and becoming a poor imitation of a "White Sahib;" it does not mean a tie and a jacket or the ability to handle a knife and fork just so! It refers to the "Sharafat" that is ingrained in the best of Indian culture; of honour and integrity; of putting the interests of the county, the Army, the unit and one's subordinates before one's own; of doggedness in defeat; of magnanimity in victory; of sympathy for the underdog; of a certain standard of behaviour and personal conduct in all circumstances; of behaving correctly towards one's seniors, juniors and equals. I am very concerned about the increasing sycophancy towards seniors which unless checked will corrode the entire system. Much of this, I realise, is due to the pernicious system of recompense and financial advancement being totally linked to higher ranks. These are of necessity limited due to functional compulsions, and which notwithstanding cadre reviews, are microscopic compared to prospects of our peers in other Government services. And finally, prospects of promotion in rank, being totally dependent on the reports of the seniors. I am hopeful that the introduction of the "Running Pay Band," which would offer equitable prospects without being fully tied to ranks, would break this vicious circle and help us to develop strong backbones and guts. I would like to make a point regarding those officers who are unfortunate not to be cleared for promotion to various selection ranks. Barring a very small minority, the bulk of them have not been cleared, not because they are not good, but because the system functionally cannot absorb them in a higher rank, and generally it is a difficult choice. In any of the civil services, these officers would have passed through their respective selection grades with ease. The fact that they are retained in the Service up to the ages of 50, 52, 54 or 56 depending upon their rank, is not an act of

philanthropy, but because the Army needs them for a vital function. They are not discards or deadwood; they are the salt of the earth and are required to lead companies, squadrons and batteries in war and it is at this level that actions are won or lost and fill equally vital positions in the various higher ranks at which they have got blocked. A running pay band will recompense them for the job they continue to do well and also restore their self-esteem.

9. On the symbolic and psychological plane, I would like to see much less of obsequious and compulsive "sirring." A "Sir" on the first meeting for the day ought to be adequate, followed up in later conversation by "Major" or "Colonel" or "General" as the case may be. I am not suggesting familiarity or impertinence—seniors ought to be treated with due respect and courtesy but cringing must be avoided.

10. On the part of the seniors, there is an unfortunate tendency today of more or less sticking to one's own rank level even in social intercourse and not mixing adequately with junior officers. This must be put right. We cannot afford to have a caste-system within the Officer Corps. In dealings with peers and juniors also, courtesy, consideration and good manners are equally essential. There is none so disgusting as a person who boot-licks the senior, boots the junior and cuts the throats of his peers. I also notice that of late there has been a regrettable communication gap developing between officers and men. I attribute this primarily to selfishness on the part of the officers and not caring enough about the men. This must be corrected. At all levels, we must insist that we live up to the Chetwodeian motto.

11. There is a lot that we can do to improve our quality of life. The standards of officers' messes in all areas have deteriorated badly. Dust, dirt and grime, sloppily turned out mess staff, chipped and cracked crockery, unpolished furniture and silver etc., are more and more in evidence. A pseudo-plush decor is attempted, with expensive and garish curtains and upholstery, wall-to-wall carpeting and so on; these cannot compensate for lack of care, attention to detail and maintenance of standards; nor can aerosol room fresheners substitute for fresh air and cleanliness. Messes are generally run down and seedy on a daily basis and though special efforts are made to spruce them up for special occasions (generally following the aerosol route) the lack of standards still comes through. This must be put right by the painstaking method of insisting on standards. We must keep the messes traditional without opting for a 5-star decor. The standard of food is generally poor and lacking in variety, not because the ingredients are not available but because of lack of attention to

organisation and poor training of cooks. With free rations, there is no reason as to why we cannot spend a little on training our cooks and modernising our kitchens. While on the quality of life, I must mention that by custom and usage of service, some privileges do go with added responsibility and senior rank, and I am sure that none would grudge these if used sensibly. However, in some cases senior officers tend to get delusions of grandeur and overdo their privileges on a Moghul style. This is bad and must stop. Otherwise privileges themselves might be withdrawn.

12. We must encourage our officers to make full use of the opportunities that the Service provides of developing a wide range of interests. We serve in all parts of the country, including inaccessible areas, to get where civilians have to invest in money and effort. We have the advantage of infrastructure available country-wide. Apart from opportunities for all kinds of adventure activities, interests in astronomy, photography, fishing, wild life, bird-watching, conservation and so on can be cultivated with little expense. There is a lot going for life in the Service and we must make the most of it.

13. Let us all resolve that we will:

(a) Shed the dead weight of mediocrity and strive for excellence, each one in his own sphere.

(b) Hold fast to all that is best in our traditions and the finest in values, while doing away with the useless and meaningless.

(c) Avoid ostentation.

(d) Not sell our souls for a good ACR and promotion.

(e) Constantly enhance and update our professional competence.

(f) Sensibly decentralise authority and responsibility.

(g) Permit maximum initiative to our subordinates, and accept a fair quota of honest mistakes as necessary payment for their professional growth and maturity.

(h) Encourage dissent and new ideas at the policy formulation and discussion stage and insist on implicit obedience in the right spirit, post-decision, at the execution stage.

(j) Cultivate a justifiable pride in ourselves, our units, formations, the Army and the Country.

(k) And finally, live up to the motto:

"The safety, honour and welfare of your Country come first, always and every time. The honour, welfare and comfort of the men you command come next. Your own ease, comfort and safety come last always and every time."

14. Before I close, a word to our professional cynics! I can almost hear some say, "Well, we have known all this for quite a while but what's been done? I'll believe that something is going to be done when I see something happening on the ground!" As a people, thus far, we have generally been waiting for initiatives from on top; for neatly gift-wrapped solutions from "authority;" we have waited for the "Sarkar" or "Bhup Singh" or whoever, to do it. I put it to you, that YOU have to do something about it too. We have everything—the brains, the bravery, the technology, the skills, the ability—all we have to do is to get YOU moving and "Get our Act together" and there is no stopping us!

God Speed!

Yours sincerely,
General K Sundarji

TAKEAWAYS

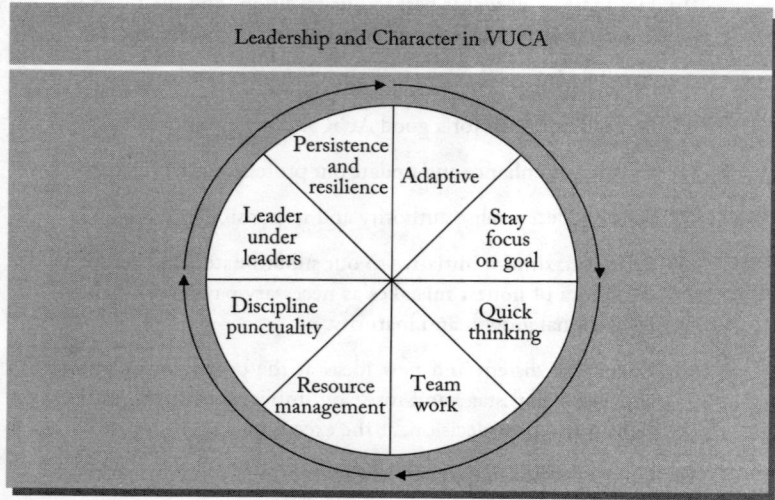

Strength of Character and Leadership

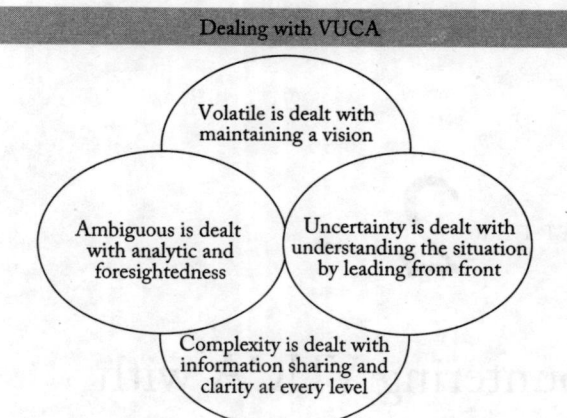

CHAPTER 2

Countering VUCA with Disruption

Open your eyes but for this world is only a dream

—Rumi

FLASHBACK: VUCA CONDITIONS IN ARMED FORCES

He was a young major in 2002 posted in Jammu and Kashmir in a counterinsurgency formation. He remembered his first outing, on hard intelligence, they had surrounded a village where three terrorists were hiding in a house. Over there, rules for the operation were different and dictated by all four conditions of VUCA.

Sweat was trickling along his spine; his muscles were alert, eyes were scanning for any suspicious eye movement among the crowd. They had assembled all villagers in the open ground for a head count. A few of the villagers were shouting anti-India chants. He knew one wrong move now and all hell will break loose. The situation was becoming volatile as *the crowd was becoming resistive. There was an unknown enemy hidden among villagers ready to shoot him and his team.*

The situation was becoming more complex as he and his men had to enter the house doing house drill search operations. The terrorist hiding behind the door may use a civilian as a hostage and shield, and crossfire will result in casualties. Meanwhile, the chanting crowd was making the situation more ambiguous. They could not be considered as enemy even if they were shouting anti-India slogans and threatening to surround and pelt the team with stones.

It is hard to know the whereabouts of an enemy amidst a crowd. One needs to be vigilant and plan ahead before the terrorist strikes. Similar is the situation in projects, and they can be dealt with forward-thinking.

VUCA PROBLEMS IN PROJECTS

Some of the VUCA problems that will come up in any project are:

- Project work obstructed due to material not reaching in time.
- Delayed approvals from the manager leading to delays in work.
- Insufficient workforce.
- Material-handling equipment not reaching in time resulting in delays of subsequent work.
- Sudden change in the ground situation causing rework.
- A team member falling sick or leaving, leading to disrupted timelines.
- Several design revisions due to bad quality.
- Increase in the project scope against initial estimates.
- Excess material dumped/sold as scrap.
- Material lost in rain/fire/theft resulting in cost of added labor to catch up with lost work and time extension issues thereby leading to the client holding the payments.

Effects on Project Cost

- Delayed schedule due to rework or incomplete work. This increases the cost of project along with penalties from a customer. Every cost adds up to losses if it is not justified.
- This cost overrun or catering for an additional charge to adjust such losses increases the overall cost of the project. This increased cost also causes established companies to lose market dominance to competitors.
- New and small companies earn more profits than established companies and also take away orders as they are able to better manage VUCA situations. For such lean companies, it is all about saving that additional cost that might get spent unnecessarily to correct VUCA issues later.
- By identifying the VUCA problems in advance, one will have time for an appropriate response at a lesser cost and an overall less budget.

THE RISE OF NEW SMALL COMPANIES

Managers of established companies are not trained or held accountable to do a project in a lean way for a number of reasons. These managers incur a substantial cost to react to unpredictable VUCA conditions. They are more used to just passing through one storm to another that is brewing. There is nobody to have a firm control of the rudder to steer the team through to calmer waters. Losses and delays are the accepted norms. In other words, such companies which could not handle VUCA by forward-thinking suffer losses. These companies also lose orders by getting their business disrupted by new players in the market. The prime reasons are that such companies cannot give a competitive bidding to get new orders because they are not confident of doing a project faster, better, and cheaper.

The new companies are catching up with large enterprises by taking advantage of the disruptive processes and technologies. Their leaders follow a nonhierarchical setup and prepare teams to be lean, mean, and fast movers. There is no room for silos or departments; quick decision-making is the order of the day to keep pace with operations.

So it is a double whammy for the conventional established project companies. They suffer from their own internal VUCA issues as well as external disruptions by lean competitors who work smart. These conventional companies have no choice but to preempt new competition before they themselves get disrupted. Such companies have to now learn to reduce the cost of project implementation by improving their own response to VUCA issues.

INNOVATIONS

Innovations are new ideas, devices or methods. These are of two types: sustaining innovations and disruptive innovations.

Sustaining Innovative Companies

These companies sustain themselves by improving their existing products to the next level on dimensions historically appreciated by customers. Clayton in one of his write-up "Seeing What's next" also discusses sustaining products with examples such as airplanes that fly farther, computers that process faster, cellular phone batteries that last longer, and televisions with incrementally or dramatically clearer images are all examples of this.

It is not sufficient for companies to sustain innovations in order to keep their business growing. They are catering only to niche customers. It is more important to decide what the mass customer wants, otherwise the business will have to sooner or later wind up.

Kodak, Nokia and Blackberry mobiles have shut shops. All these three companies were technology-driven, had a loyal customers' base, were great brand names, and had strong balance sheets. However, they failed to realize that both Apple and Samsung had disrupted the market in an innovative way. These companies started providing a better digital camera at a very competitive price which affected the sales of Kodak. Both Apple and Samsung were also pitching directly to the consumer, projecting their mobiles as a fashion-buy. They also provided a lot of applications in iOS and Android catering to a mass customer base that significantly affected Nokia and Blackberry. Now Nokia and Kodak are trying to bounce back by bringing in some disruptive changes in their product business.

Disruptive Innovation Companies

It is the new buzz word. Disruptive innovation is a term coined by Clayton Christensen, a leading expert on innovation and growth. It means a process by which a product or service takes root initially in the simple application at the bottom of a market. It then relentlessly moves up in the market eventually displacing established competitors.

There is a new segment of players in the market that are constantly striving to innovate their products and services to attract the customer. They have unique ways to approach the markets or even create new markets of their own.

Apple, Samsung, Uber, Netflix, Google, and Skype gave customers value for their money in their respective lines of product or service. Manufacturers are already adopting 3D printing in many ways. There are fully automated factories and sensors-fitted devices monitoring labor. The project industry is also crying out for the product cycle to be better, faster, and cheaper. Disruptive processes could resolve the triple constraints by providing better time, cost, and quality.

The entrant attackers or disruptive innovators serve the least demanding customers as well as those not served. On the other hand, those companies that refuse to change, will get displaced. The future of many such traditional established companies is now in jeopardy and their sustenance will depend on their ability to adapt to this creative era that is ever-evolving.

RESOURCES, PROCESSES, AND VALUES (RPV)

What prevented the established companies from shifting to disruptive innovations and processes?

It is the RPV of an enterprise that is not able to match with the business needs in these changing times. For companies to be disruptive, they need to change their outlook on resources (what a firm has), processes (how a firm does its work), and values (what a firm wants to do).

- **RPV suits sustaining innovations.** The RPV theory defines an organization's strengths as well as its weaknesses and blind spots. Established organizations successfully tackle sustaining opportunities with their RPVs. They have existing resources, established processes, and set values. RPV, in this case, enables them to prioritize what are the business growth areas in their improved product offerings. RPV is a strength there.
- **RPV is a hindrance in disruptive innovations.** On the flip side, RPV is designed only to make improvements in expensive products and not products that are cheap, convenient, and simple to use. Unlike sustaining innovations, disruptive innovation means to deliver a product useful to the customer at a low price without incurring a loss.

Owing to RPV factors, the traditional established companies are unable to adopt disruptive innovations. The future business model will, hence, run at lower margins than the current business model. There needs to be an overwhelming change in every organization's RPV. The million dollar question is can a team/group disrupt itself to work or deliver a product in an innovative way with little cost.

Disrupt the Disrupters

How can the traditional established companies then defeat the unconventional lean new players at their own game?

There is very less distinction between the four stages of VUCA. However, since it is here to stay, it is better to deal with VUCA as an ally. The conventional way of working and tools will not help to counter VUCA. To reestablish market dominance, one has to forgo the traditional tools of planning or execution.

Disruptive Tools

The working environment is continuously changing and to be on the top of the game, companies need to adopt many disruptive tools:

- Project companies need to train people at every level, particularly those at the bottom, to perform at a rapid pace.
- Planning and implementation have to be synergized to be able to take into account possibilities of disruption.
- Taking stock of losses, resources, and lessons learned is essential.
- Just like in the army, the first plan is only as good as the first contact with the enemy. Plan A must always be accompanied with a backup Plan B.
- The team should have hybrid members who are thinkers and doers at all levels; they should do planning and implementation simultaneously.
- There must be a culture of ongoing vigilance in the working to provide alerts as and when required. In the rapid changing world, companies will have to work with more situational awareness of what can go wrong. They will have to recognize a pattern that can go awry.
- Holistic thinking combined with tacit knowledge, and trusting experience can help resolve VUCA issues.

PARADOXES

When disruptive innovations emerge, they paralyze established players. The start-up companies, however, are less vulnerable to disruptions as they don't have much baggage to carry.

However, over a period of time, start-ups grow and acquire more people and processes. Eventually, they too fall into the same trap of RPV and start focusing on sustaining products like the big business players.

At the same time, established companies realize their mistakes and start aiming to be more lean and disruptive. So the cycle of disruption and sustenance catches up with all in the end.

As John Rice, Vice Chairman of General Electric (GE) and panelist at The Economist Summit, once said:

> We have to be an agile dinosaur. We have to go through a process to rethink how we want the company to be in the 21st century. We cannot remain attached to the factors that contributed to our success in the 20th century. We have to change.

The established companies could disrupt these small businesses by doing a project with more creative planning and relentless execution. It is not just innovation that causes disruption, disruption can also be brought in by preventing late delivery, rework, bad quality, and anything that may result in cost overruns.

RACE CULTURE

These disruptive tools advocate RACE culture. RACE is an acronym for resolving triple constraints in the project. RACE culture is adopted by the armed forces and by the organizations that have embraced best practices in the corporate world.

Rapid Work

- We work with speed, but that does not mean we compromise on quality.
- We achieve the speed rate by a simple operating plan understood by every soldier in the ranks or every team member in a project. Every member has a sense of direction during execution.
- The speed and guidance of the actionable operating plan matches with the tactical plan and the commander's or team leader's strategic intent.
- The fast work also advocates walking across the organization solving issues one-on-one with departments. That is the best way to counter delays due to bureaucracy and prevent complicated approvals.

- If we face a VUCA situation, we respond fast to unexpected conditions.
- Teams are small and every member is in a multitasking role aiding quick decision-making.
- Continuous monitoring of logistic and other resource support function for rapid execution. Nothing is left to chance.

Absolute Scope of Work

- We get to complete work with absolute integrity.
- We make sure all work is covered in planning and is connected.
- The scope covers the expectations of all stakeholders.
- The subcontractor hired is accountable with clear milestones.
- Work processes are defined in standard operating procedures (SOPs) to prevent any rework or unfinished work.
- We accommodate requests but avoid changes in scope from the client.

Class Quality Work

- It is there in every aspect of the project and product scope deliverable.
- There has to be quality from start to finish. Whatever we do is without defect and avoids rework that can add to the cost.
- The work should also look aesthetic. Each element of the complete system should be in coherence with each other. Our work should have the same sustaining quality even after we leave the workplace.
- We have measurable quality metrics to set standards and benchmark.
- There should be transparency in the process; any glitches should not be covered up but addressed before proceeding to the next phase.
- Lessons learned from the earlier projects should be remembered, and mistakes should not be repeated.

Economic Cost

- In simple words, we treat cost as a constraint.
- Total transparency in overspending is paramount. We can then identify the cause so as to control cost overruns. Over budget and wasteful spending demands accountability, probity, and lessons learned.
- Our resource cost is under control as we work in a small but the best team.
- We avoid cost overruns due to overwork and rework. That also prevents snowball effect of more losses.
- We also do not believe in penny-wise pound-foolish syndrome. We avoid losses by spending a little on the preventive measures.

TAKEAWAYS

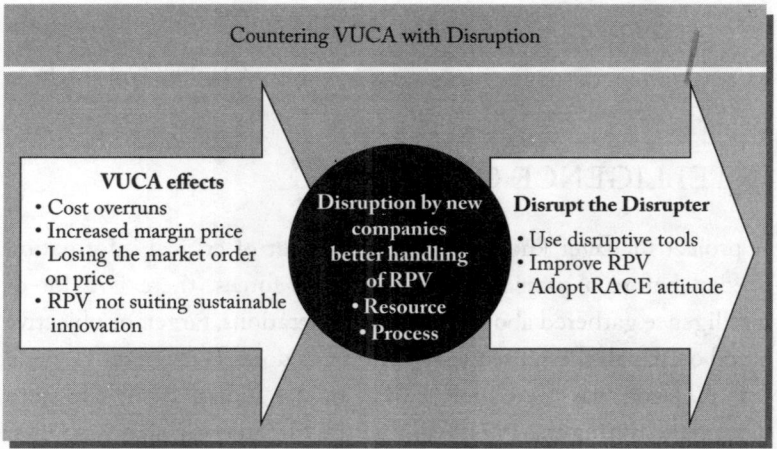

CHAPTER 3

Anticipate VUCA with Advance Information

> *We tend to meet any new situation by reorganization and attribute to this the illusion that progress is being made.*
>
> —Charlton Ogburn, Jr

INTELLIGENCE GATHERING

A project manager knows that there is a lot of critical information needed before a project starts. In armed forces, there is a lot of intelligence gathered about the area of operations, target, or objective based on which the subsequent planning is done. Lieutenant General J. F. R. Jacob was the Chief of Staff of the Indian Army's Eastern Command during the 1971 War, and the Indian army planners under his leadership had found information about the enemy terrain and operations. This activity started many months before the Great War, and it led to solving critical issues. The war was a success primarily because of advance thinking and detailed planning.

Excerpts from the Writings of Lt General J. F. R. Jacob

The crackdown (by West Pakistan on East Pakistan) took place from March 3rd to the 26th. The Indian Government was very concerned about a large number of refugees that kept coming in. At the beginning of April, General (S. H. F. J.) Manekshaw the army chief, called up Lieutenant General Jacob to say that the Government required the army to move into East Pakistan immediately. Lt Gen. Jacob told him that it was not possible because there were mountain divisions and no bridges and there were many rivers between Dhaka and India, very wide and unbridged.

The monsoon was about to break; the divisions were not trained in riverine warfare, there was no transport (mountains divisions have very little), and it was not possible to move in. Gen. Manekshaw said that the Government was accusing him and the army of being cowards. Lt Gen. Jacob said, "You tell them that it's not you, it's the Eastern Command that's not moving."

"When the bloody hell can you move by?" he asked.

"If you give me the bridges and other stores required and the time for training, not before 15th of November," Gen. Jacob replied.

"Why?"

"By 15th of November the ground would have dried up, and we should be able to move," replied Gen. Jacob.

After that, Manekshaw went to Mrs Gandhi and the cabinet and briefed them.

Lt General Jacob shares how the Indian Army visualized and prepared for war before it started:

So, we knew a war was coming, and I made a plan to capture East Pakistan. I knew that the Pakistanis would defend the towns, so the main strategy of that plan was that Dhaka was to be our final and principal objective since it was the Geopolitical and Geostrategic heart of then East Pakistan. In each of the other sectors, for instance, in the Jessore sector, we selected objectives like communication centers. So, we decided to bypass the towns and use subsidiary tracks and head straight for Dhaka. We never wanted to capture any town, because capturing a town takes a long time. I knew the war would be short; I knew the UN was bound to intervene, so we couldn't spend time capturing towns. You see how much the time Americans took to capture the town of Fallujah in Iraq?

So, the strategy was to draw them to the border, use subsidiary tracks to bypass the towns and defenses and head for Dhaka from all directions. The main problem was logistics, which was critical in winning that war. So, in May 1971, even before we received any orders from anyone, we started building up the logistics in Tripura for one corps, throughout the monsoons, before any orders arrived from Army HQ. Similarly, C in Tura and other places, we got the Borders Roads Organisation to make the roads, made hospitals airfields, etc. In May, I sent a plan to Army HQ giving Dhaka as a principal objective and allocation of troops. HQ sat on it for some time, and it was only in August that General Manekshaw and his Director of Military Operations K. K. Singh turned up and gave us the following plans.

ESSENTIAL INFORMATION BEFORE A PROJECT STARTS

On the lines of intelligence gathering in army operations, the following information should be gathered in project management to anticipate VUCA issues.

- **Understanding local operating conditions.** The project manager needs an assessment of the prevailing operating conditions listed as follows:
    - Political stability and local labor union influences
    - Details of the payments and worker facilities as per work rules
    - Weather conditions that could affect work and logistics
    - Local holidays and festivals which may cause work to stop temporarily

- Customer working style and profile
- System requirements and training facilities available to be ready for work
- **Gathering business and product information.** The project manager must gather details about the product and purpose of the project. If a company wants to take up a large-scale project outside India in order to open its doors in the Southeast Asian region, the project manager should know the business need and the drivers behind the project.
- **Statement of work.** The project manager should have a broad description of deliverables of the project. This is also included in the product scope description and the characteristics.
- **Assessing the technical parameters of the project.** The project manager should also understand the characterization of the project which includes:
  - Site description with plot plan layout
  - Site survey and soil investigation/data
  - Individual power plant system, equipment, and design
- **Understanding of project commercials.** The project manager should try to prevent penalties by the customer and should be in touch with the sales team for details on the following:
  - Preparation of commercial brief and exhibits
  - Complete set of contract documents
  - Owner organization and owner interfaces to approve changes, etc.
  - Potential areas of risk in the schedule, cost, quality, and scope
  - Details of performance guarantees, bonuses, and liquidated damages (LD)
  - Owner obligation for space, administration, security, etc.
  - Critical paths and milestones

- Payment provision and documentation procedures
 - Project insurance and documentation
- **Codes, standards, specifications, regulations, and process.** The teams must understand the following:
 - SOP and procedures to follow till product commissioning.
 - List of materials and component required in the project.
 - Detailed instructions/operation sequence in the project.
 - Estimated timescales and costs involved in all phases.
 - Quality control requirements.
 - Evaluation yardstick of the finished project.
 - Responsibilities to comply with health and safety requirements.

ESTABLISHING A VIGILANT CULTURE

In this regard, first let's discuss Samsung Note 7 mobile case study to analyze the failure of a vigilance system in place.

Samsung Note 7 was slated to be in competition with Apple's latest products. Note 7 was launched with much fanfare; however, due to some manufacturing defect in the battery, the entire business plan of the company went for a toss. A manufacturing defect in the phones' batteries had caused some of them to generate excessive heat, resulting in fires.

Owing to this situation, Samsung had to carry out a thorough investigation of its production and design processes. Ultimately, the defect was found to be in the battery terminals.

However, failure of vigilance in manufacturing led to unwanted negative publicity. To date, Samsung Note 7 mobiles are not allowed on airplanes. It is important to avoid similar situations of failure even in the smallest component of a project. It could arise due to some error in the process from supply to its installation and lead to cost overruns, negative publicity of the brand, loss of trust among consumers, and loads of rework.

In war conditions also, there is a constant vigilance against the enemy by all means of surveillance. It helps to plan a step ahead of the enemy with fewer surprises and losses.

Project teams at every level should be aware and keep a vigil on the weak spots in their area of responsibility so that they are able to improve by anticipation of adverse events.

Project managers should get a correct perspective on how the competitors are working with better speed in projects at a lesser cost. It would also help them in improving the critical areas they may have missed out.

A vigilant work culture should be established at every level to monitor and anticipate VUCA events. It comprises of the following:

- **Encourage outspoken mavericks.** Managers must encourage employees who are considered outspoken or mavericks to speak up about emerging issues. This would establish a trust culture within the team and encourage them to honestly observe and provide truthful feedback. It would also help them foresee early signals of what is going wrong.
- **Vigilance system.** The organization becomes vulnerable to disruptive rivals who see and take advantage of these early, easily missed signals. The project teams must watch, evaluate, and respond to such weak signals. These signals can come from anywhere in the business environment and are difficult to interpret but will indicate that a storm is coming.
- **Catching early signals.** The junior managers in the organization should have the ability to "see around corners" and attend to first signs of threats and potential opportunities. These signs are often an indication of new serious threats and opportunities. If a team develops a superior peripheral vision capability, they will then determine how well they can sense and act on these often-confusing messages.
- **George day seven steps.** George Day in his book *Peripheral Vision*, describes seven steps to help set up an alert vigilance

system against VUCA issues and external disruptions by other companies:

Step 1: Scoping is where to look for a VUCA issue.
Step 2: Scanning is how to look for a VUCA problem.
Step 3: Interpreting the data that indicates something wrong.
Step 4: Probing is what to explore more carefully.
Step 5: Acting on the insights by building some counter-measures.
Step 6: Organizing is how to develop vigilance.
Step 7: Leading is making an agenda for action in resolving the VUCA issue.

TRAINING FOR THE PROJECT

Many lean companies have internal training programs in all fields that help nurture new employees and enable old employees to upgrade their skill sets. For example, Thermax Ltd has a full-fledged learning development program which even trains the trainer to prepare them with critical training skills.

Training is ongoing throughout the period even when a soldier or an officer is not on active duty. It is impossible to think that a new operation or a project can be commenced without basic training or refresher orientation of the subject involved.

Refresher Training

The project team should have a similar refresher training before the onset of the project. The aim is that all team members should get oriented for the challenges they are getting into and be ready for them.

- **Reading contracts.** It is imperative to read and understand the commercial documents for purposes of claim avoidance or seeking an extension of time unnecessarily.

- **Extension of time (EOT).** This clause can have the following variables to seek more time for completing a project:
    - Suspension of the works by the customer
    - Variations due to act or omission of the contractor
    - Force majeure conditions
- **LD.** Leaders need to ensure that they do not fail in their commitments. Otherwise, they will have to pay to the customer by way of LD for unjustified delays.
- **Tracking EOT.** The project team members should be able to keep track of EOT by maintaining the following documents from the start of the project till its closure.
    - Notice requirements for customer
    - Potential insurance claims in force majeure cases
    - Any work that is done on holidays, and overtime
    - Union issues that cause delays
    - Problems of space, water, or electricity
    - Site access not allowed in time or the start date
    - Permits not given timely
    - Delays due to the customer and their impact on schedule and cost
    - Changeover procedure and change notification for schedule and cost causing delays
    - Approval of customer and baseline changes causing delays
- **Tracking LD.** To prevent LD clauses, the project team should take note of the following as the project progresses.
    - Commencement and completion dates
    - LD amount and trigger points
    - Caps on liabilities and indemnities
    - Entitlements to extensions of time
    - Timely filed insurance claims
    - Steps during force majeure

- **Understanding codes, TR, standards, specification, and RPs.** The project manager should explain the different project-related aspects to team members from time to time.
  - Codes provide a governing set of rules for design, material, fabrication, assembly, installation, inspection, examination, testing, repair, and alteration of products. An example is the ASME Boiler and Pressure Vessel Code.
  - Technical regulations are mandatory government requirements that define the characteristics and the performance needs of a product, service, or process in view of public safety. An example is the Occupational Safety and Health Administration (OSHA) that provides rules for personnel safety on job sites.
  - The standards documents establish engineering or technical requirements for products and practices. An example of standards is ISO 9000—a quality standard used the world over. Standards are indicated alongside specifications. These show specific quality norms for materials, components, or services.
  - Recommended practices provide guidelines or written practices for performing operations or functions. They also help to identify additional skills and professional competencies in the working environment.

LEARNING FROM PAST PROJECTS

We have seen the movie based on the real incident of the Titanic disaster. It is one of the most compelling examples of how things can go wrong due to management and human error. There was nothing wrong with its engineering, design, architecture, or technology. Everything that was needed to prevent a disaster was there.

It is a good example to learn from history how a VUCA situation could not be anticipated in time due to a host of reasons. The iceberg warnings went unheeded, the iron rivets were too weak, the binoculars were locked up, and so on. The ship management had also failed to assess the magnitude of the disaster, so they ignored placing the required number of lifeboats on decks as it would have looked crowded.

What we can learn is that poor management is the leading cause of disaster in most projects, however unsinkable or well-planned they are. The management staff of Titanic was overconfident that nothing could go wrong with the ship and that they would be able to beat its schedule arrival time.

In armed forces, the team learns from history by reading about many campaigns only to learn from past failures. In fact, there are compulsory promotion exams on military history that help in conducting future battles.

The example of Hitler and Napoleon is the best to explain what happens if one ignores history.

Both Hitler and Napoleon had attacked Russia. The two invasions were separated by a century, and still, they have so much in common. Hitler did not learn from the mistakes Napoleon made 100 odd years ago. Russia's size, abundant manpower, and harsh winters had defeated any external enemy, and the supply chain of the attacker was stretched beyond its endurance. Napoleon and later Hitler both attacked Russia in winter months. However, both failed to make adequate preparations for winters and long campaigns, which resulted in heavy defeat for both of them.

It is, hence, equally important that before planning for a project, one reads up about previous such projects and learns from history to avoid blunders. All successful projects or failed projects teach us something.

As a project manager, it is better to discuss with old-timers how execution strategies can be analyzed from their previous projects. It will provide insight into the challenges in resource and people management.

LEARNING FROM CURRENT PROJECTS

Project managers must establish a culture of learning from any issues that crop up during the implementation of a project.

We keep reading how a particular automobile manufacturing company has recalled some of its cars from a particular batch for correction of some components or assemblies. One of the latest instances is in Japan where a million cars of a particular manufacturer were recalled to correct defects in the inflator and propellant devices. It shows how companies monitor products even after sales and ensure customer satisfaction by maintaining current engagement with them.

WAR DIARY AND ATR IN PROJECTS

A debriefing report after a project is concluded is essential. In the armed forces, there is a culture of maintaining a war diary and an action-taken report (ATR) to learn about issues that cropped up during the assignment through observation and insight.

An officer is required to keep a war diary in which all events that took place and the lessons learned are recorded on a daily basis. The officers also maintain an ATR after every engagement. The situation report or ATR is sent every day to the formation headquarters with details of the military action.

As a matter of fact, the objective of feedback is to sustain, enhance, and increase the project preparedness. All soldiers or workers are collectors of positive (sustain) and negative (improve or change) information. Debriefing and retraining of the lessons learned are essential for improving on subsequent projects for all operating teams. Maintaining a site notebook primarily has two advantages—it allows the use of best practices and helps anticipate problems for subsequent projects. Project managers should also encourage their juniors to start making ATR after every milestone so that they can learn from their mistakes and improve their performance.

FUTURE FOCUS AND CONTINUOUS UPDATE

A regular focus on how the market segment is behaving and what the customer is up to is essential. It helps in being ahead and dealing with surprises. An example could be the telecom war between Reliance and other telecom companies.

Reliance industry has led a competitive telecom war always thinking of future and continuous upgrade of technology. In 2002 they offered a combination of CDMA and WLL technologies that provided a lot of freebies and cheap services. It was unheard of that time to get unlimited free incoming calls and cheap billing and so as expected it created jitters among other telecom operators and was lapped up by the public.

Exactly after 14 years, Reliance has caused similar disruption by introducing Jio. Reliance has again triggered a market war. In September 2016, they inaugurated a free voice and data plan and extended the freebies till mid-2017. This has strongly hit the profitability of other players and disrupted the market for them. The other companies were forced to do something radical to come out of this disruption. Vodafone and Idea responded with an unexpected merger and put up a stiff competition for Reliance in the telecom war.

In the armed forces, there is a constant update about any new development that the enemy is undertaking during a war. At the same time, there is a continuous update of new technology in weapons and warfare that needs to be inducted into armed forces. Before a war, there is a holistic assessment of any technology to be procured that will help during wartime.

During projects, teams should be encouraged to pay more attention to the changes that would define the expected future. The intention is to get everyone in the organization to look at the periphery or at new processes or methods that are taking shape in the market. It also involves understanding new technology, channels, and consumer behavior.

In best of corporates, there are sessions on "creative future" where diverse groups look at how a customer or supplier or contractor is changing, and the technology is developing.

Just like soldiers in armed forces learn everything about the enemy first to be victorious, it is important to find out the best practices and work processes adopted by other companies. The following table is helpful in looking at these aspects holistically.

Companies	Essential resources	Critical processes	Key values
What do we lack and our weakness			
What do our competitors lack or their weakness			
Best practices adopted by our competitors			
How can we adopt or improve			

Source: Author's own work.

HOW IS RACE METHODOLOGY BEING ACHIEVED?

We are achieving RACE results by following the disruptive methods such as gathering information, setting up a vigilance system, and learning and training the teams.

- **Rapid work.** It is being achieved by identifying all VUCA issues in the business case and statement of work and by trying to find the solution for it.
- **Absolute work.** It is ensured by analyzing information about engineering and technical requirements much in advance so that subsequent planning does not miss out any scope of product or project.
- **Class quality.** It is ensured by codes, specifications, and standards that can be followed up with suppliers and manufacturers. The team also learns from old lessons and what competitors are doing to set new standards for quality.
- **Economic cost.** The team should also understand the contracts and issues of LD and time extension claims.

TAKEAWAYS

To conclude, it is important to gather as much information as possible about past, present, and future possibilities before the start of a project. It sets the tone for future planning as has been discussed in the following chapters.

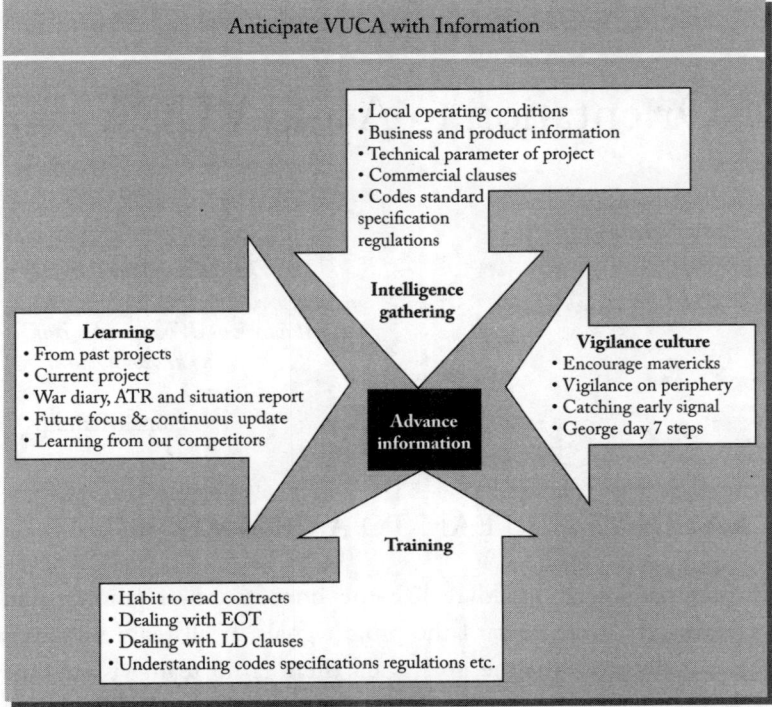

CHAPTER 4

Orientation to Avoid VUCA

> *What I have done is build the most beautiful buildings in the best locations. What good is it if no one knows about it?*
>
> —Donald Trump

LEADING THE TEAM TO A COMMON GOAL

Project managers should realize the importance of guiding and orienting the team toward the project goals. If all team members are not aligned with the goal, then there is no team vision. The lack of understanding of a common goal can lead to VUCA issues emerging from lack of coordination. The team gets disillusioned and does not look forward to achieving the objective. It would then be just a job.

There are many such stories where leaders take charge and make things happen and inspire their teams. One example is the legendary Kapil Dev leading India to World Cup victory in 1983. I was a young kid, but I still remember the three events in the World Cup that gave me the belief that we could win.

In the group match, which was unfortunately not recorded, India was struggling against Zimbabwe at 17 for 5 when Kapil Dev walked in and made a blazing 175 runs. He smashed fours and sixes and it was an absolute pleasure to read in the newspaper the next day about his achievement.

The vision for winning the World Cup had begun. The next event was the semifinal where the whole team showed motivation and ambition. Significant contributions from Gavaskar, Srikant, Mohinder Amarnath, Yashpal, and Sandeep Patil helped in chasing England's score of 213 runs.

I knew we had won when, in the final match with West Indies, India was struggling to defend a paltry score of 183 and Kapil Dev turned tables by taking Vivian Richard's wicket with a spectacularly timed running catch.

Now, that happened because Kapil Dev had dared to dream the impossible—winning a World Cup dominated by West Indies, England, and Australia. Even when the chips were down in the match against Zimbabwe, Kapil Dev did not lose sight and took charge of the situation and guided his team with a common vision to win the World Cup.

Another factor is the *Junoon* (obsession). It is essential for all leaders to create something new; it comes from their own heart. A leader must first set his/her heart on any task he/she undertakes. This reflects on the team members who realize that they are going on a new mission, a journey that will be a change for the good.

In every battle, there is a strong emphasis on leaders building up a belief that they are going to win. There is a vision of achieving glory for the country, followed by a mission of the battle, and objectives to be attained. The aim of the battle is what everybody focuses on.

In a similar way, for a project team orientation, every team member must understand the objectives, and they should put their best efforts into the project. For that the team has to have a joint vision, mission, and aim that will keep reminding them to stay on course. But before that there is something more needed—a clarity of priorities amidst various scenarios that may affect the dream.

SCENARIO BUILDING USING INFLUENCE DIAGRAMS

The first step in team orientation is the team thinking ahead about all possible scenarios and determining the most plausible one. It may be a decisive factor, and if we prepare ourselves, it will help in achieving our objective. Accordingly, the orientation of the team and future planning will get modified.

Just before the start of a cricket match, factors such as weather, pitch conditions, or key players from the opposite team not playing determine the various scenarios which may affect the winning chances. Based on this, the match strategy is planned, for example, how many spinners or pacers to keep, what order to play in, etc.

Let us discuss another example of scenario building in a team.

General Pervez Musharraf was coming to the Agra summit for peace talks with the Indian Government. There was a scenario building exercise to prevent another backstabbing like the Kargil War when the Lahore Summit had happened. The Indian Army was asked to be alert at LoC and the border areas, to counter any surprise attack by Pakistan while General Musharraf talked about peace in Agra. There was no trusting the Pakistan Army anymore.

The Army was also asked to deploy defenses at short notice in a nodal point defense in deserts to prevent any enemy ingress when peace talks were going on.

Nodal Point is like a hub deployed with defensive forces and all weapons and tanks that protect the open area and main axis coming from the border.

Influence Diagrams

Influence diagram (ID) is used to depict many chance scenarios leading to war. It also interrelates the political factors with the military factors in the war-gaming scenario.

An ID depicts a decision by a rectangle, chance scenario by an oval, the objective is a hexagon, and function a rounded rectangle. The ID depicting a simple war situation is explained in Figure 4.1.

Orientation to Avoid VUCA   53

Figure 4.1. Influence Diagram for a War Situation

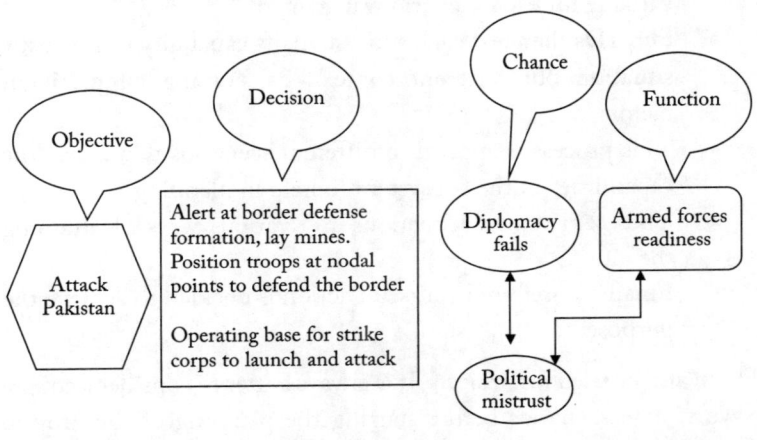

Source: Author's own work.

The Strike Corps of the Indian Army were put on an alert, and so they had a battle plan ready to strike deep into Pakistan territory. In the case of a worst possible scenario, the Pakistan forces try to sneak while Pervez is being welcomed at the Agra Summit. That time the Indian war campaign across Pakistan will start by our attacking Strike Corps forces passing through our defenses. At the same time, our defense formation at the border would also stop the Pakistan forces that might try to come in.

The brigade defensive formation were asked by Corps Headquarter to predict from which all axis the Pakistan Army would also come in, as and when the war started. In line with this, the brigade units were to plan to lay the defensive minefield and obstacles to increases defense posture.

In a similar manner more sub-IDs are then made by lower formation units for their respective defensive and attacking positions to achieve their aim under different scenarios.

Thus, ID is a useful tool to assess various scenarios:

- ID breaks down the analysis of the situation mainly to determine the existing situation and decide the purpose to be achieved.

- ID helps in capturing the relationship between the primary variable for each scenario war-gamed.
- Sub-IDs then test each subsystem, its capability in a realistic situation but different context, considering all pertinent factors.
- This process is applied to different scenarios that assess the capabilities of the subsystem to help in planning.
- The team draws deductions and various ways of attaining the aim.
- Finally, a preferred course of action is decided to achieve the purpose.

ID can also be used for projects. It is always better to consider a couple of worst case scenarios before starting the planning of the project. Think of what all can go wrong that may take the complete project in a different direction. The following ID assesses priorities in various scenarios discussing numerous chances/possibilities (see Figure 4.2).

Figure 4.2. Influence Diagram for a Project

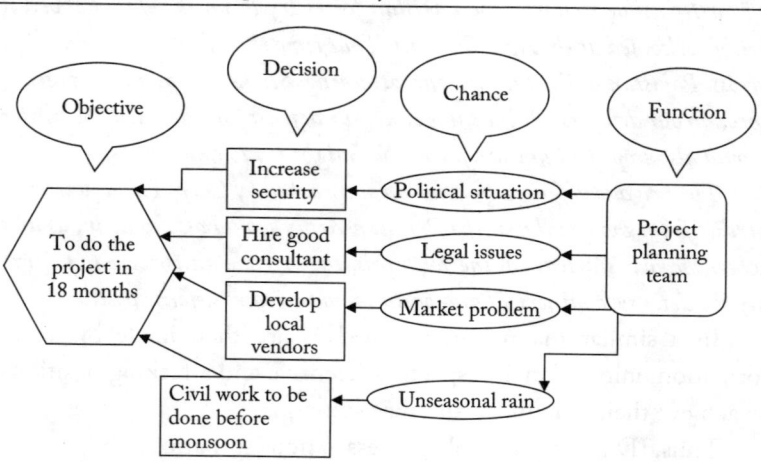

Source: Author's own work.

Depicted in ovals shape are the chances/possibilities, and they have been discussed as follows:

- **Political situation.** There could be a situation where a project manager wants full appreciation done of the political situation where the project is to be done. The area is susceptible to many terrorist attacks, which would amount to risking the team.
- **Laws are not clear.** In a situation where the team is unfamiliar with the local laws and the legal system is different from that in India, they would need a thorough briefing of country laws and traditions so that they do not hurt the sentiments of the local population.
- **Market problems.** Getting complete familiarity with the market rate for procurement, contractual labor, and machine handling vendors are required.
- **Monsoons and unseasonal rain.** Unseasonal rains or natural calamities can delay work or delivery of materials or equipment.

Accordingly, a priority scenario has to be confirmed and a decision has to be taken on guiding the project planning based on the most likely scenario.

PRIORITIZING SCENARIOS IN PROJECTS

In the armed forces, before the project planning, the team gets down to real policy planning. They do a lot of scenario building. For example, the planner thinks of the most likely route the enemy will use to attack and plans a counterattack accordingly. In the planned counterattack, there is the main attack plan, a contingency backup, and a subsidiary plan.

Likewise, the project team should think about the probability of a possible ugly scenario happening during the project life cycle and plan for its best solution. They should also prepare for the next possible scenario that can happen.

The aim is to have a primary plan in place. The contingency plan intends to deal with critical uncertainties. The team can influence the future by managing risks more effectively and make the project more profitable. The plan also allows a rough estimation of resources, timelines, and other driving forces.

In the examples mentioned earlier, the project manager should discuss and find with the team and management the worst scenario which cannot be controlled or managed. For example, the site operations of a project could be severely affected due to monsoon and unseasonal rain.

The initial planning must, therefore, revolve around the monsoon months to ensure that maximum work is done either before or after monsoon and keep the weather monitoring alerts to foresee unseasonal rains. Now, with the scenario decided on which project planning will be based, a vision has to be formed in the next step.

VISION

Creating a vision for each project helps anticipate possible future events and developments with imagination and wisdom. ISRO has been leading India's success story with its vision in space technology. Their vision statement is as follows: "Harness space technology for national development, while pursuing space science research and planetary exploration."

Vision is always created with the aim to foresee the accomplishment of the entire campaign from start to finish. A vision helps in achieving the perfect results regardless of the task. It is not one odd battle or one action that will decide the war, the vision for the execution ensures a sense of continuity.

Some examples of vision in armed forces are as follows:

- ***The vision for the Strike Corps.*** It had been developed to attack Pakistan.

- *Win the battle.*
- *Capture Lahore...by this time.*
- *With minimum casualties.*
- *With the lowest loss of our tanks.*
- *Do not trouble civil population while advancing.*
- *Treat enemy soldiers fairly as per Geneva Convention of POW.*
- *Ensure that administrative supplies/medical facilities also move up.*

- **The vision for the defense formation.** *It was developed to stop the enemy attack. Each unit of the formation also had their vision according to the role given.*

Project Vision

In a similar way, the project manager must develop a vision for the project. Visionaries thrive on change and being able to draw new boundaries. The project team can follow these steps for developing a vision.

- **Step 1.** It involves mapping the project. Write the name of the project in the center of a large sheet of paper. Identify every aspect of the project that the team can think of.
- **Step 2.** Start with "wouldn't it be great." The point is that identifying ideal scenarios lead the project in new directions and to heights never achieved. The key to this method is that once we have identified the best vision, our planning will take a much different approach.
  - Wouldn't it be great if we had a complete list of all legal requirements of the project with an indication of the regulatory body and contact person for each?
  - Wouldn't it be great if the project was completed with no labor stoppages or slowdowns?

- Wouldn't it be great if all overtime costs could be eliminated?
- Wouldn't it be great if all the equipment necessary for this project were in working condition on the days scheduled for use?
- Wouldn't it be great if there were no accidents during this project?
- Wouldn't it be great if no OSHA inspections were requested during this project?
- Wouldn't it be great if all subcontractors completed their work as per schedule?

- **Step 3.** Ask your team now to imagine themselves walking into work while the project is underway. All team members must visualize the best possible outcome for each stage of the project.
- **Step 4.** The team makes a vision board. This board can be kept in the war room for daily inspiration so that the team can read the vision board and feel motivated.

THE MISSION

It is a description of how we are supposed to function and what are the work values and future results.

For example, ISRO's mission is "design and development of launch vehicles and related technologies for providing access to space."

In the armed forces, each formation and unit establish their mission from the vision of their task to be accomplished. A mission focuses on the purpose of each unit through a statement describing the reason for its existence.

As an example, my engineering unit in army had this unit mission: "To provide support to fighting units in the battle zone by repair and recovery of damaged equipment and vehicles as far forward as possible in the battle zone. 100 percent equipment availability for war."

I had got this mission statement written on my troop's caps and signboards outside the headquarters to remind the team that they need to support the fighting arms to win the battle.

Project Mission

In a similar manner, the importance of the mission is all about undertaking a remarkable journey together. It could be a single statement printed on a T-shirt or cap or stationary head or letterhead or coffee mug, or put up on a noticeboard in the war room.

For a corporate project, the mission could be as simple as getting a bonus check for a project from a customer for timely or effective completion of a project.

OBJECTIVES

Objectives can be developed after the vision and mission are defined. The more precise the definition or description of the activities, the better will be the understanding of the team members, and achieving results from the process could be easier.

One of the objectives ISRO developed from its vision and mission is "Promotion of Space Technology."

Objectives are predetermined based on the unit's role and responsibilities. Objectives must be SMART, that is, specific, measurable, achievable, realistic, and timely. Objectives must be clearly defined so that the tasks become goal-oriented and unproductive and unsystematic tasks can be avoided.

Project Objectives

In the same way, the objectives of the project should also be determined.
- **Specific.** What to achieve by when.
- **Measurable.** Information obtained should be measurable.

- **Achievable.** The objectives should be achievable and not unrealistic.
- **Relevant to the mission.** It should fit in with the overall vision and mission.
- **Timely.** Timeline by which they will be achieved.
- **Challenging.** It should be stretched beyond routine.

AIM

From objective comes aim which is usually a single line. It is a single simple sentence like "aim is to attack enemy company at a bridge and capture it by D plus 2."

His engineering unit aim: "To ensure all equipment readiness handed over to all units by D minus 1."

Project Aim

As for the project, the aim is "The team must complete the work in… months within laid down baseline performance parameters."

HOW IS RACE CULTURE BEING ACHIEVED?

- **Rapid work.** A more detailed brainstorming of what can go wrong in various scenarios. Scenario building gives us enough time to prioritize VUCA issues and plan for it.
- **Absolute scope.** A shared vision, mission, and an objective will provide an aim for the project. All these align with the complete range of work to be done.
- **Class quality.** A clear vision helps in thinking about quality right from the planning stage.
- **Economical cost.** A clear objective and aim will help focus on the actual deliverable and control scope creep and additional cost.

TAKEAWAYS

It is important to orient the team in a common direction before commencing project planning.

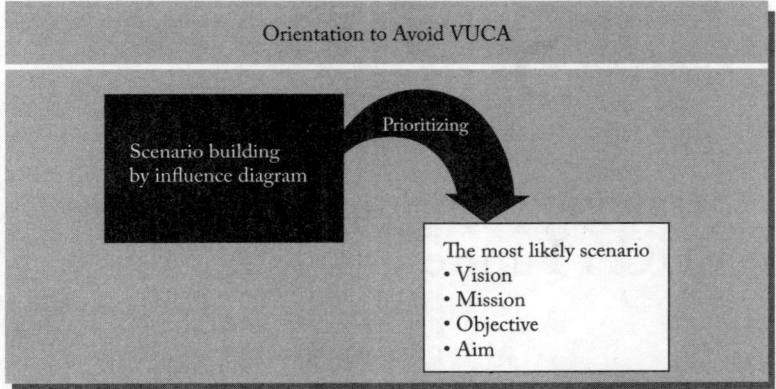

CHAPTER 5

Strategic Planning for a VUCA Future

We try a bunch of stuff; we see what works, and we call that our strategy

—Dennis Bakke

STRATEGIC PLAN IN VUCA

A strategy plan provides a direction in the life cycle of the project. The challenge is an uncertain future. How does one plan for a project that could get laden with unexpected problems? Companies are highly automated today with processes and ERPs but they are still not able to close important milestones in time. Obviously, there is something wrong with strategic planning.

The project team members are focused on what the team should do for them instead of making a strategic plan about what they should do to support the fighting team. In armed forces, the focus of the strategic plan is to defeat the enemy, but nobody forgets the soldier who fights, so all aspects of the strategic plan are to muster resources as per requirement and in time to the battle location.

A project manager should be conscious of the fact that his strategic plan should evolve around people. It would be people who would sense the VUCA issues and not his IT systems or processes; these resources would fall into place automatically once people in majority are tuned to the overall plan instead merely being the followers.

A manager should, therefore, invest in people, stakeholders, suppliers, contractors, workers, and involve them in his strategic plan. He should understand their requirements and evolve the scope of the work to align with their expectations.

The story of Amul is the story of the brand that revolved around people, the key resources. It started with the basic stakeholder, that is, the farmer at the grassroots level who provided milk to the dairy cooperative society to be processed at the milk union at the district level and was then marketed at state milk federation. The Gujarat Cooperative Milk Marketing Federation provided access to the centralized marketing and quality control facilities which were the missing links in the dairy economy. Amul has become one of the most known and respected brands in India today because every person in the process chain worked towards building the brand.

Another example of why strategy should be focused on people involvement is of the famous Dabbawalas in Mumbai. They are no executives and they do not have advanced GPS systems or ERP to manage their timings or perform quality checks on the tiffin delivery process navigating the heavy traffic of Mumbai. They pick up tiffins from the most obscure streets of Mumbai and deliver them in time to offices. Although, they are gradually getting into the use of mobile communication and online orders but their success lies in their immaculate planning, self-belief, and commitment toward their job.

A FLASHBACK OF STRATEGY PLANNING

The young officer was dozing under a jeep after a good lunch and chilled beer. He was waiting to go home after a grueling six-month training exercise in the desert stay.

"*Sir, there is an urgent call from the HQ,*" *a soldier came running from sand dunes to his jeep. The young major rushed to his tent to attend the call from his commanding officer (CO).*

"*Hi Young man,*" *the voice of his CO was crystal clear.* "*A few terrorists have attacked the Parliament; there were a couple of fatal casualties of among deployed security forces in the Parliament. They have killed the terrorists, but since they were Pakistan sponsored, the Indian Government has decided to launch an all-out offensive as retaliatory measures,*" *said the CO.*

The Higher Formation HQ orders have come that the Strike Corps was ready to be launched into the Pakistan territory. Their brigade was in defense role and was to be deployed along the frontier to prevent enemy ingress.

His CO Colonel J. N. Nayar continued, "*the Brigade Commander, Brigadier Vijay Saxena, called me to attach you in his Brigade Headquarter. His staff officer in Q branch is admitted to the hospital, and it will be a while he reports back to Brigade HQ. You're second in command in the company and can coordinate the deployment of your company when you are doing the duty of staff officer in Brigade HQ.*"

Within minutes his Brigade Commander, Brigadier Vijay Saxena came online asking him to move to Pitthewala Brigade Headquarter Node. He was to join hands with the GSO2 and do the strategy planning.

He did the planning in the following manner.

Reconnaissance of Project Site

A defensive battle entails gathering of information from all human sources and surveillance equipment deployed to determine which inroads on the border should be protected. It would also decide where the battle of the forward zone would be fought with the enemy to delay them as much as possible and cause maximum attrition.

With the same concept of gathering information in mind, a project manager should perform regular assessments to develop a better understanding of the scope of work involved with customers and locals. A project site assessment should be able to cover the following:

- Assess the site condition, soil content, and geology aspects
- Verify the surrounding and space availability
- Check the availability of electrical power, water, and communication
- Understand the effects and duration of seasonal climate
- Check the transportation services availability and cost
- Understand the compliances of governmental regulations
- Assess communications and connectivity facilities
- Check on the availability of labor
- Coordinate the arrangements for housing and food for the team
- Liaise with local doctors for medical services or hospital

ESTABLISHING A WAR ROOM

War room or sand model room or ops room is a room at a military headquarters where maps showing the current status of the battle and deployment of troops in combat are maintained. The staff officer assigns time and place for all stakeholders to assemble in the brigade war room to discuss the scope of operations and how to manage them.

Likewise, a project manager should use his office as a strategic planning room. It would help the team to have review meetings on an everyday basis, and the information can be presented on the charts as a daily update. Daily briefings and debriefings in this room will help keep tabs on the progress of the project.

IDENTIFYING THE STAKEHOLDERS

At the start of any operation, the staff officer in the headquarter identifies all units, currently attached or those that are likely to be posted in their area of responsibility, so that he knows about all the stakeholders needed to prepare the strategic plan.

The staff had to coordinate the requirements of all stakeholders for the defensive strategic plan at brigade orbit. It was essential first to identify the concerned stakeholders and then assess their needs and impacts to make a phased plan broadly. Who are these stakeholders?

- *The enemy who always attempts to ingress into our territory.*
- *The basic fighting unit of our forces carrying out a platoon deployment, at the right place with the right amount of ammunition.*
- *The supporting teams that would provide surveillance and supportive fire to the platoon soldier.*
- *The service element to provide the soldier with a timely administrative backup.*
- *All that planning for a soldier to fight the enemy in the most likely area of ingress would finally dictate the strategic location of his units and deployment at a higher level.*

Project System

Similarly, a project manager should emphasize the need to identify the project system and stakeholders. A project system has the following elements:

- **System.** A system is a framework of interconnected parts or objects or components. No part acts in isolation and it gives a unified whole to perform a particular purpose or project. This reduces the risk of erroneous interpretations and decisions.
- **Nodes.** A project system has a structure like functional departments with mutual relationships. We call them nodes or parts. A well-organized project system provides better control of diversity, variability, and uncertainty among all nodes. All individual functions contribute to the whole system. They achieve results in the form of a secure exchange of energy, matter, and information.

- **Stakeholders.** The heads or concerned people from these nodes who add value to the project are called stakeholders. Links establish the interconnectivity and interaction between nodes or stakeholders. It allows them to function as a system—to behave in a specific way (accomplish a task or perform a function). Project systems are also open and act as stakeholders as they interact with the outside environment like suppliers and contractors.
- **Stakeholder register.** It is good to list down the stakeholders with their roles and responsibilities in a chart as follows:

ESTABLISHING COMMAND, SUPPORT, AND ATTITUDE OF STAKEHOLDER

Before the commencement of any war operations, the command and control of all units operating in a formation are established. Some are in direct control of the formation, some are only for administration, a few are in support, etc. It helps to create linkages so that there is no confusion during the battle between the units directing orders and the ones complying with them.

Table 5.1. Stakeholder Register*

Stakeholder introduction	Command & control	Key role in project	His expectation from project	Performance feedback to improve Further
Name and contact with email id/with position in concerned department/ location	Under command/ Direct support of other department/ Indirect support from other department/ Dual reporting	Work to be done by him/ her impact or influence	Support needed from others Interconnection with other deliverables for his deliverable	KPI (Key performance indicators) Areas of improvements with solutions

Source: Author's own work.
Note: Attributed to armed forces and Project Management Institute teachings.

Likewise, a project manager can have a clear visibility of the command and support structure if his/her team is able to identify all nodes, links, and their relationship with each other (refer to the stakeholder register Table 5.1 on the previous page).

- **Voice of supportive tasks.** The project manager should identify a particular area of influence and area of responsibility for each stakeholder as it would ensure that they do not clash with each other's roles and responsibilities. It would also help each stakeholder to focus on giving the manager a correct decision, thus, acting as the voice for the supportive task.
- **The voice of intent.** The project sponsor will decide what is possible for the organization, regarding resources and expenses released for doing the project. He/she will be the one where the buck stops or if the project manager needs any help.
- **The voice of the customer/user.** The project manager should be able to understand what is needed in reality by correctly interpreting the customer contract. It would be good to have someone on the team who understands customer requirements well and can guide the project manager and the project team with respect to the final product requirements as per the customer. That way the project manager will stay true to the contractual obligations.
- **The voice of experience.** A project manager should identify senior and experienced managers to help him/her with how the project will work in reality and to subsequently plan for it.
- **The voice of design.** The functional heads will help the manager to explore various possibilities in the areas of design engineering, procurement, construction, and other support functions.

Visualize the Stakeholder's Attitude

It is important to separate the stakeholders on the basis of their responses. The aim is to use a different yardstick of collaboration based on their attitudes although everything must be finally synchronized within the system. It is good to categorize the stakeholders as allied, cynics, fence sitters, etc.

STAKEHOLDER FOR LOCAL INTELLIGENCE

In any battle, a lot of information also comes from the local villagers, agents, shepherds, etc. They are the real source of all information about the enemy and how and when they build up with tanks and infantry in the area of ingress at the border.

Similarly, in projects, we tend to overlook many unknown supporters and mavericks, the fixers, the movers, and shakers. They are the source of the latest real updates. These are the people who also chase issues for us, behind the scene where things get sticky. They are the unsung heroes. The project team should look at everything, listen to everyone, and know how to reach these people. They should search for nuggets of gold everywhere and look at the potential assets that can help them.

The team should also walk through the production floor and talk to the factory workers. Everybody should ask themselves how a particular individual can help in the long run or what can push the delivery on priority?

STAKEHOLDER TO MANAGE/CONTROL RISK

In armed forces, the enemy forces deployment are assessed by the planners to start planning for their own resources and implementation. After that the respective commanders at all level also reassess any particular strength of the enemy and how to counter/manage the risk of enemy action.

Notably, the same risk is always there in any project. The project team needs to have an overview of things that can go wrong in each phase of the project. The aim is to identify the possible VUCA issues and the broad advanced measures that can be taken to reduce the risk.

It is hence better to identify those stakeholders and leaders who will be able to counter such risk. They could be experienced managers or worker or a reliable supplier, etc.

FORMULATING THE SCOPE OF WORK

In the armed forces, the staff officer lists out the requirement of work needed to be done. These are broadly under three categories. "G" matters related to operations, "Q" matters related to logistics supporting the operations, and "A" aspects are related to administration of forces during the operations.

Project and Product Scope

A project manager should do similar requirement gathering and connect the list with the originators by a traceability matrix. A requirement is simply a feature that a product or service must have to be useful to its stakeholders.

As shown in Table 5.2, the team must gather requirement from all concerned to have an idea of product requirements and project management. The product scope defines the type of product, service, or results for the customer. The project scope refers to all work done to get the product range.

- **Requirement gathering technique.** The team first conducts a brainstorming session of all stakeholders to gather requirement for the product and project. They also invite experts to contribute and interview some senior experienced people who had done this kind of project earlier.
- **Requirement traceability matrix.** The team also connects the requirement to the originator for making it traceable through a grid. It helps to link elements from origin to the objective throughout the software project cycle so that no part of scope is left out.

- **Requirement documentation.** The project team segregates various requirements for the ease of follow up and also ensures its completion.

Table 5.2. Understanding Various Requirements*

No.	Type of requirement	What it will achieve
1	Business requirement	It will help in aligning during the project so that business goals are met. It also defines the working rules and guiding principle for how the work will be achieved.
2	Stakeholder requirement including customer, supplier, subcontractors and internal functional heads	Their expectation, impact, and communication will help in aligning all stakeholders to do the project.
3	Product requirement	Functional and nonfunctional parameters. Technical and standard compliances to be met. Training requirement needed. Specific project work needed for product installation.
4	Project requirement	What will be the project support needed and what all project work has to be done to meet the deliverables for the product.
5	Resources requirements	Specific needs in people, equipments and material.
6	Information and intelligence requirements	Past records of similar projects, any debriefing, etc. Any lesson learned in archives and current/future status of related information of the project.
7	Quality	Performance parameters to be met compliance and acceptance criteria.
8	Transition	How the transition of handing over of phases of projects will be done to next stage of stakeholders.

(Table 5.2 Continued)

(Table 5.2 Continued)

No.	Type of requirement	What it will achieve
9	Miscellaneous	What are the dependencies, assumption, and the constraint in meeting requirements?
10	VUCA and risk mitigation	Any specific additional work needed to be done to mitigate any VUCA issues.

Source: Author's own work.
*Note: Attributed to armed forces and Project Management Institute teachings.

FINALIZING THE ORDERS FOR TASKING

For war preparations in the army, a detailed list of direction with the responsibility of each unit and time by which it should be completed are issued. The scope of work is discussed in detail for overall coordination. Specific individual units are also tasked to implement their missions. A few examples are:

- Corps of Engineer company to coordinate the mine laying.
- Armed Squadron and Mechanize company to fight the forward zone battle.
- Air defense detachment to site the radars to track enemy movement.
- Ground Liasion officer (GLO) to coordinate air strikes on enemy tanks. They brief pilots on situation on ground and helped them to identify own forces and enemy forces by maintaining bomblines on operation maps.
- A liaison officer to coordinate Strike Corp passing through the defensive brigade to attack across the border.
- All other individual infantry units also make a defensive plan.

Scope Baseline

Likewise, as shown in Table 5.3, the project managers should finalize the product and project scope statement. The project team can develop the baseline scope from requirement documentation. Scope baseline defines work, guides project team, confirms in scope/out of scope, and sets stakeholders' expectations.

Table 5.3. Management of Scope with Team as Agreed with Customer*

Product scope	Description of the product
	Business benefits
	Baseline characteristics to be met for customer satisfaction
Project scope	Baseline of project work finalized with customer to achieve product scope
	Project scope to be defined in different phases of work like Civil, Mechanical, Electrical, Commissioning, etc.
	Phases of work to be broken down as individual task assignment and mission
Completion criteria	Defines satisfactory deliverable (and their characteristics)
Dependency linkages	Information and support from other links and other stakeholders
Out of scope	Scope work that is not to be done by anybody till approval
Area of responsibility in work	There is full authority to plan and conduct operations; for which a force, or component commander bears a certain responsibility. Identify all such work for leaders/stakeholders.
Area of influence in work	Like in armed forces it is the work by any leader who can directly influence operations by his and team capabilities under his own command or control. Identify that work limit.
	It avoids interference and confusion in each other work
Area of interest in work	Like in armed forces, it is that work which is out of our influence but is in enemy/or other territory and if not done will jeopardise the complete operation. Identify such work that needs to be also monitored so that timelines are met for all.

Source: Author's own work.
**Note:* Attributed to armed forces and Project Management Institute teachings.

A BROAD GENERIC PHASE-WISE PLAN

In the armed forces, a rough war plan is drawn describing various phases of the battle that will take place. The brigade has to give a plan to the division by integration and coordination of all units. Although the plan sums up to a single formation plan, it involves deployment of all arms and services. The brigade will bid for any additional resources needed and draft a battle phase where the role of each unit is linked to each phase with timelines and resource strength.

Phases of the Project

In a similar way, a project manager also develops and visualizes the first holistic picture of the project.

- **Scope work is divided into phases.** It is mainly to separate the project into various phases and put the critical convergence timelines for an early deliverable in each phase of the project. There is an identification of different key work streams. It also correlates with the primary key deliverable of their function which is critical to the project and in the absence of which a project cannot proceed.
- **Phase-wise milestones collaboration.** The stakeholders in consultation with the project team broadly identify their functional milestones that will converge with other departments. This allows the project team to have a combined broad, high-level project plan where all stakeholders finalize the phase-wise dates of convergence with another departments.
- **Phase-wise collaboration of functions.** The project team finally links all departments to coordinate time and cost to prevent any miss outs or rework by any department.
  - Engineering team to provide milestone of engineering drawing release as per phases of the work breakdown structure (WBS).
  - Procurement team to match the delivery of items as per the design drawing version and WBS.
  - Visibility of work being done at ends to be maintained and photographs with quality inspection reports dates to be fixed.
- **Customer aspirations.** The interim deliverable as per contract provision is also identified in each phase.

- **Individual tasking.** It enables to have a priority-aligned structure with all its elements and their deliverables. It is better to have a RACI chart depicting what each stakeholder has to do. RACI stands for responsible, accountable, consult, inform.
- **Input and output in each phase.** Project requirements are considered as data that are processed by the project team into products or services as outputs for each step.

  It is better to identify and group teams as per RACI to have clear roles and responsibilities.
- **The phase-wise role of stakeholders.** The project teams identify how each stakeholder will collaborate and connect with others in each phase (see Table 5.4). The following questions should be answered during this exercise:
  - What will the stakeholder produce?
  - What resources will he/she manage?
  - Who does he/she need to connect with?
  - What is the command/control structure?
- **Planning quality package-wise in each phase.** The project team also discusses with the customer and all stakeholders the quality policy with quality matrices to follow in the project deliverable. The team confirms that the quality checking processes are established. The suppliers also submit the maintenance manuals of products in each phase, that is, from factory till erection and later commissioning.

Table 5.4. Allotment of Role and Responsibilities to Team*

Task decision	RACI	Who	What	When	Input from earlier phase	Output to next phase
	Responsible					
	Accountable					
	Consultant					
	Informed					

Source: Author's own work.
**Note:* Attributed to armed forces and Project Management Institute teachings.

- **Balancing the budget at each step.** Project managers also consider the following factors that may impact the cost of each step while doing the project:
    - The bigger the project with various products and equipment, the more engineering would be required, thus increasing the cost. The only way to reduce cost is that the engineering should be correct the first time and not cause any rework in any phase.
    - The location also increases cost, particularly when environmental issues are there. More cost is required for a product and project which does not cause any pollution.
    - In geographical terms, the logistic cost will be more in the remote areas. In urban areas, the land price for the use of labor colony or warehousing will be more.

LOGISTIC SUPPORT

Before the start of a battle, the individual needs of all interested parties are also identified to make an impact on a large defense layout. All concerned parties give out their strategy plan about how they will deploy as per the task.

- **Assessing engineering support.** Coordinate engineering support from corps of engineers, electrical and mechanical engineers, and signals.
- **Planning procurement for ammunition and fuel and ration/supplier/water.** All units to send indent demand for ammunition, fuel, rations, and other supplies for processing to the Army Ordnance Corps (AOC), Army Supply Corps (ASC), and other supporting units.

Project Support

Likewise, the project manager should discuss broadly with functional heads how they will coordinate back support in each of the following phases:

- Logistics
- SCM material and supplies delivery
- Store and site office
- Communication
- Safety
- Transportation
- IT
- Administration

MANAGEMENT BY COMMITMENT

All stakeholders should commit to updating the strategic plan with the latest situation. They must continue discussing various scenarios and plan changes if any. The staff officers should seek progress and all should stick to timeliness.

That is to say, the strategic plan is the first plan to be established within the first few days. The team should focus on the broader and high-level section of the scope that is critical to the project's success. It also requires a high level of coordination between interdependent contributors and functions.

Even in a project, the commitment by all stakeholders allows sharing and creating adequate conversations between the different contributors about what is critical for the project. It provides a great experience in team building. It is better to have an updated convergence plan posted on walls of the project team premises for internal communication. This is helpful for the team to gain confidence.

FINALIZING THE STRATEGIC PLAN

The strategic plan concludes when the final battle orders for all stakeholders and units are rolled out. The teams start making their individual tactical plan that is presented to the formation commander in subsequent days.

Project Charter

Similarly, in the case of projects, all the information from various teams would be used to conclude the strategy planning with a proper project charter.

- Business case: justification/needs/requirement
- High-level product description
- Vision
- Mission
- Measured objective with milestones and success criteria
- How each objective will transit to the next phase
- Stakeholder list and requirement
- How they will be linked together with their respective deliverable
- Communication and feedback system
- Resources required
- An outline of plan made by each stakeholders for their own departments/functions.
- High-level risk and VUCA issues
- Vigilance system
- Project approval requirement
- Assigned project manager
- Organization structure: name of project sponsor and project manager with list of all other stakeholders

HOW IS RACE METHODOLOGY BEING ACHIEVED?

- **Rapid delivery.** Identification of all stakeholders and explicit allotment of duties will ensure that work is delivered in time with proper responsibility and accountability. The work is divided into phases with each step having a visibility of timelines and schedule and the resources are also allotted accordingly.

- **Absolute scope.** The requirement gathering is a great exercise also involving the stakeholders including the client. It helps in identifying a proper scope statement with complete product deliverables and project processes.
- **Class quality.** For each phase of work during the project, a clear set of quality governance structure and matrices can be defined.
- **Economic cost.** It involves the integration of delivery with cost in each phase. Other factors that will have an impact on price are also discussed.

TAKEAWAYS

The strategic plan is primarily focused on stakeholders and their requirements to prevent any VUCA surprises in any phase of a project.

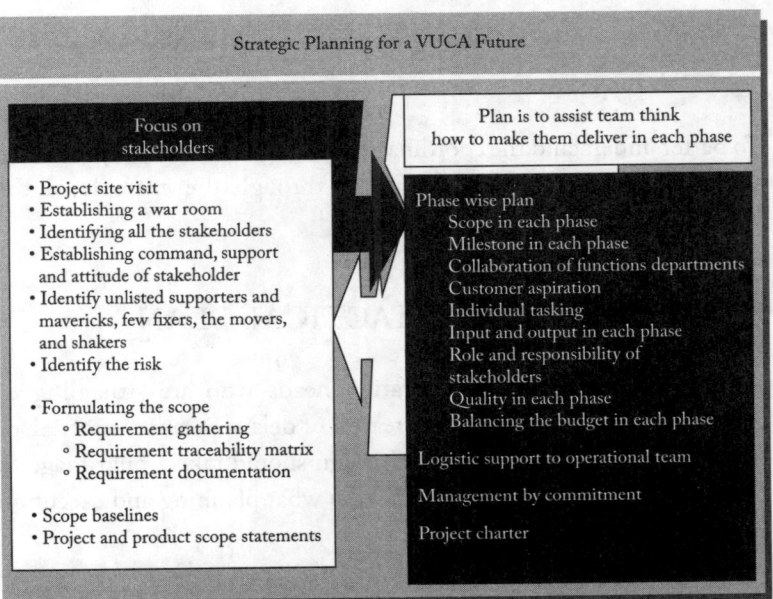

CHAPTER 6

Tactical Planning

> *There is no mistake; there has been no mistake, and there shall be no mistake*
>
> —Arthur Wellesley

To better understand the coordination among functional departments and different stakeholders, let us go through the example of the Kumbh Mela.

THE KUMBH MELA—TACTICAL PLAN

All project managers and operation heads who are struggling to close their projects for the petty reason of delays in labor, material, or equipment, or due to incomplete design should take a pilgrimage to the Kumbh Mela in Allahabad to learn what planning and execution in project are all about.

The Kumbh Mela of 2013 was the largest peaceful assembly of people in human history. Within a span of 5–6 months, an entire mega-city was built for this mela and was later dismantled on Ganges River. The city was there for 3–4 months, and it just vanished within a month after the event. This highlights the importance of modular construction along with the speed of putting up the structures and dismantling them.

The scope of the work in the mela was by no means small. It was like any other engineering, procurement, and construction (EPC) project or service/IT project. It involved the following tasks that were no less than the work in putting several power plants together.

- A city was to be developed on an uninhabited flood plain which was under water till the work started. All the soil works and flood measure works were to be completed by September-end of the previous year after monsoon ended and river water receded from the banks.
- The team had to make the main road and connecting it with bylanes. They also setup bridges wherever needed. By December-end, the team had created temporary roads and divided the city into sectors and grids. That allowed distribution of space for accommodation and other structures to come up by January-end.
- Side-by-side drainages, sanitation, power grids, railways, bus transportation, fire tender, and all civic amenities were set up. The city also developed a helipad, hospitals, police and army security against terrorist threats, shops, hotels, hostels, and accommodations for tourists.
- The management team was catering to more than a million tourists coming and going through a vast network of special railway and bus services.
- They also had to cater for logistics, water, food, tents, storages, and other basic amenities along with erecting communication towers for the occasion.

No wonder a Harvard study made 2013 Kumbh Mela a case study worth emulating and highlighted that it was organized better than the Commonwealth and Olympics games. It is important to know what made Kumbh Mela such a great success. The following factors, along with managing the scale of mobilization in quick time, contributed to the success.

- There was a common vision of every team member of the organizing committee. This aspect of vision has been covered in earlier chapters.
- There was an ownership of mission in every individual such that he/she was aware of his/her responsibility and understood that if anything went wrong in his/her work, somebody will have to suffer losses.
- Every functional manager or any executive did real brainstorming to arrive at the steps and actions to be undertaken by his/her team. The planning was so meticulous that nothing was left to chance or to be resolved later. Every possible wrong scenario was worked out as a VUCA condition that was covered with an automatic response later.
- There was a total decentralization of decisions to manage contractors, subcontractors, material-handling equipment, and a commitment from all the workers to complete the arrangement for the city. It also involved dismantling the city without traces of waste or dumps of degradable material that spoiled the environment.
- There was also a sense of divinity in the work that was being undertaken. It was like a city that was created out of nothing and that went back to nothing. A moksha was attained by the city itself, which was the reason why pilgrims came to this city of Kumbh.

BASIC INGREDIENTS OF A TACTICAL PLAN

Having seen the tactical planning of Kumbh Mela, it is also important to understand what are the factors involved in a tactical plan:

- Identify the scope of work
- Break the scope of work

- Identify how quality is achieved
- Ensure that execution is within the planned cost of resources
- Communication
- Administration
- Team management
- Risk management

DISRUPTIVE THINKING AND BRAINSTORMING METHODS

In a tactical plan, the challenge is to make the stakeholder think in detail about their contribution and role in the project in each phase. It helps to solve problems and gaps that may exist between them. Every step is visualized on the sand model, and pros and cons of each maneuver are discussed. The project manager should then invoke the stakeholders to start imagining how they will contribute to the overall plan. Each department identifies its center of gravity where they must focus. There are some disruptive thinking tools which are discussed as follows.

- **Marline process.** It is a group-based, reverse planning activity where the end goal is described first and is ideal for iteration planning. The functional teams start with a picture of victory in advance.
    - We start by describing the final solution with all the system components and success criteria completed. We create the image of a successful deliverable.
    - Next, we get the team to list all the technical attributes that must be in place to support this.
    - Then, moving backward, we brainstorm each successful step that occurred to produce the desired outcome.
    - We then ask the team about the risk in various support functions and try to solve the VUCA situations much in advance. The aim is that we should be able to see

the solutions to the potential VUCA roadblocks that may occur.
- ○ Backward planning helps to identify a missed-out step. By starting from our original objective, how it is was being achieved, and slowly moving back each step gives us another starting point for planning and more opportunities for team input.

- **Remember the future in action.** As in the marline process, a project manager must engage the project stakeholders in imagining how the future will unfold.
  - ○ All will think of a future event as one that has already occurred. We presume the release or iteration to be complete, and we ask them to describe what happened for it to be successful.
  - ○ Here we ask the probing questions to get a satisfactory result with no issues. This enables us to be more efficient in our thinking and decision-making, and we are able to select the best options in our plan.
  - ○ The purpose of "marline" and "remember the future in action" is not to try and predict the future. It is to better understand the stakeholder's definition of success. We try to foresee the possible issues and develop steps to overcome them.
  - ○ Having visualized and generated consensus on what "done" looks like, the team is better positioned to move towards the goal mindful of the issues and extra steps that might be required.

- **Reverse brainstorming.** The project team should first identify the problem or challenge clearly and write it down. Each team member should then reverse the statement by asking, "How can I possibly cause this problem?" or "How can I attain the negative effects?"
  - ○ The idea is to brainstorm the reverse problem to generate opposite solution ideas. The brainstorm ideas must be

allowed to flow freely and no idea should be rejected at this stage.
  - Once the team has brainstormed all the ideas to solve the reverse problem, it should change these into solution ideas for the original problem or challenge.
  - The team should now start to evaluate these solution ideas to develop a potential solution or at least the attributes of a possible solution. The teams must always solve problems by combining brainstorming and reversal techniques.
- **Orchestrated immersion sessions.** It involves immersing the stakeholder team members, especially EPC team members, in an educational experience.
  - There is a relaxed alertness due to the elimination of fear of failing in challenges. This challenging environment is created in part by using the guided discovery process where the team members are asked to use creative thinking techniques and extract answers on possible problems. The moderator uses leading questions and not just gives them the answers to problems.
  - The essence of organization immersion is that the team learns to browse things in new ways in which a shift in the sensory activity capacities takes place, for example, seeing the order and collaboration in some sorts of "messy" lecture rooms and getting new skills for real-world performance. For this, the body, brain, and mind should all be engaged in the learning. The whole person learns, which requires a constant combination of academic content and practical experience.

In any operation or start of the battle, the risk is identified, assessed, analyzed, and evaluated, and the planning starts accordingly. Adequate response and resources are catered in tactical planning for risk mitigation. Similarly, the project manager must do a full risk management so that once he gets down to planning, he incorporates all the risks and uncertainties in his plan that affect his schedule and cost factors.

RISK IDENTIFICATION IN PROJECTS

Some of you would have seen many movies based on real stories of climbing Mt Everest. The latest blockbuster is *Everest*, where the risk of weather is ignored and the climb in final summit ends in tragedy. There are similar risks in technical terms or internal organization risks which are to be assessed to prevent a tragedy.

A project manager should broadly discuss the risks in each phase during strategy planning as shown in Table 6.1. The project team should organize a brainstorming session while developing a tactical plan to study what all can go wrong. It is also good for the team to study the Project Management Body of Knowledge (PMBOK) notes which have more details about the subject.

Table 6.1. Risk Categorizing

Technical risk	Project management risk	Organizational risk	External risk
Technology	Communication	Stakeholders issues	Contractors/supplier
Interface	Schedule	Approvals	Labor/Material handling equipment
Product SCM	Funds		
Quality	Logistics		
	Site management		

Source: Author's own work.
Note: Attributed to armed forces and Project Management Institute teachings.

Qualitative Risk Analysis

The team should also prioritize the identified project risks using a predefined rating scale. Risks are rated based on their probability or likelihood of occurrence and their impact on the project objectives.

- **The chance of its happening.** The probability of each risk can be accessed and assigned a rating.

Probability range	Natural language expression	Numeric score
91% through 99%	"Very likely" to occur	5
61% through 90%	"Probably" will occur	4
41% through 60%	"May occur" about half of the times	3
11% through 40%	"Unlikely" to occur	2
1% through 10%	"Very unlikely" to occur	1

- **Impact assessment.** The team can assign color codes to the risks. The risks capable of highest impact can be assigned the color red, the ones with standard impact can be yellow, and those less impactful can be set in green.

Effect on the project	Example	Natural language expression	Numeric score
Project failure (It indicates that minimum acceptable requirements have not been met)	Schedule adjustment > 2 months cost impact > 40%	Very high	16
Significant cost/ schedule increases. Secondary requirements may not be achieved.	Schedule adjustment > one month cost impact > 20%	High	8
Moderate cost/ schedule increases, but essential requirements would still be met.	Schedule adjustment > 2 weeks cost impact > 10%	Medium	4
A little cost/ schedule increase. Requirements would still be achieved.	Schedule adjustment > 1 weeks cost impact > 5%	low	2
No effect on the project.	schedule adjustment < 2d cost impact <5%	Very low	1

- **Risk score.** The team must ascertain the risk in totality by considering both the probability of its occurrence and its impact on the project. It should plot the ratings on the risk impact/probability chart. A higher matrix score indicates a higher level of risk.

	Impact on project	Very low	Low	Medium	High	Very high
The probability of occurrence		1	2	4	8	16
Very likely	5					
Probably	4					
May occur	3					
Unlikely	2					
Very unlikely	1					

The project team should seriously focus on risks that are very likely in nature and have high impact.

- **Update.** The team should prepare prioritized list of risks and ascertain the safety measures with increased alertness. It involves the ranking and prioritizing of risks along with grouping them into respective functions. It is also better to list down the short-term and long-term risks separately.

Quantitative Risk Analysis

It is very important to quantify each risk and assess its impact on the project. When a team delays a project, it should not be analyzed subjectively but quantitatively. For example, there is a 50 percent chance that the team will delay the task by four weeks. Some tools that can help to quantify the risk are discussed as follows.

- **Sensitivity test.** The team can use tornado analysis to determine which risk factor they should focus more on.
    - The x axis of a tornado diagram in Figure 6.1 plots a range of our primary concerns like the cost or duration

of any activity. The y axis in Figure 6.1 plots the various factors for which values are to be determined. Each factor reflects the range and width of each bar that indicates the impact on cost.
  o The graph identifies those risk factors which are high in terms of both their impact (and leverage) and uncertainty. The team should focus on big bars in charts that indicate VUCA issues to save time and cost.

Figure 6.1. Tornado Diagram

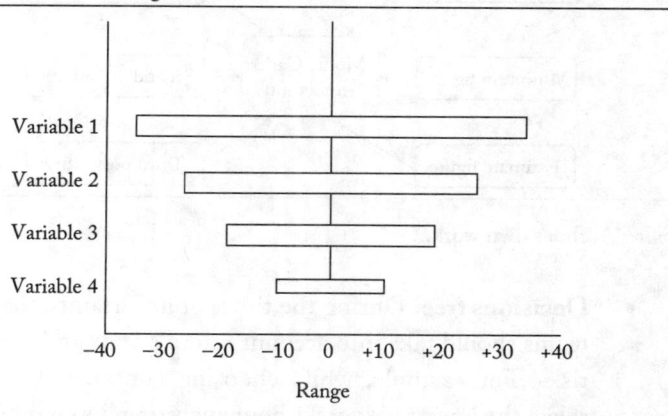

Source: Author's own work.
Note: Attributed to Project Management Institute teachings.

- **Three-point estimate.** The three ranges x, y, and z use three estimates—pessimistic as x value, optimistic as y value, and most likely as z value—for determining cost and schedule period to have more realistic figures of duration and amount.

    Expected value = (Pessimistic + 4 (Most Likely) + Optimistic) / 6.

    $$\frac{x + 4y + z}{6}$$

- **Modeling and simulation.** The Monte Carlo technique in software is used to perform simulations of the project uncertainties. It helps to determine many possible models based on inputs. For example, as seen in Figure 6.2, a project manager provides as inputs the minimum, maximum, and estimated range of days required for the completion of each task. The model runs the simulation on these ranges and gives an estimate of when the project will finish.

Figure 6.2. Monte Carlo Simulation

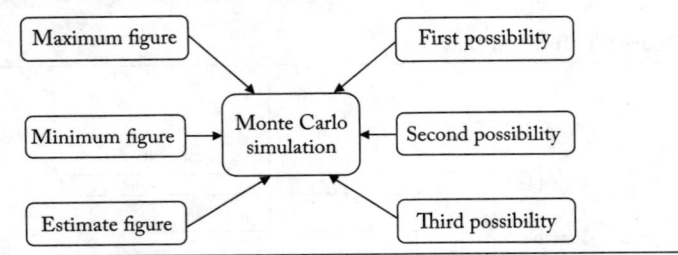

Source: Author's own work.

- **Decisions tree.** During the times of uncertainty, the project teams should take into account future events and the related risks. For example, while choosing contractors, we often select the lowest bidder without analyzing his credibility and the pain it may cause later. So, we use a decision tree with a flowchart of nodes. The node is an uncertain event and has two or more alternatives or possible outcomes.

    A decision tree is used in decision analysis to help identify a strategy most likely to lead to a goal.

    At times of uncertainty, the project teams should consider the future events and their related tasks to arrive at a decision. For example, as seen in Figure 6.3, while choosing a contractor, one should analyze the credibility, strength, and competencies of the bidding companies rather than just price.
- **EMV.** The expected monetary value analysis can be used to determine the cost of all the decision paths in the project. We assign each path a probability of occurrence along with

Figure 6.3. Decision Tree with Two Alternatives at Each Stage

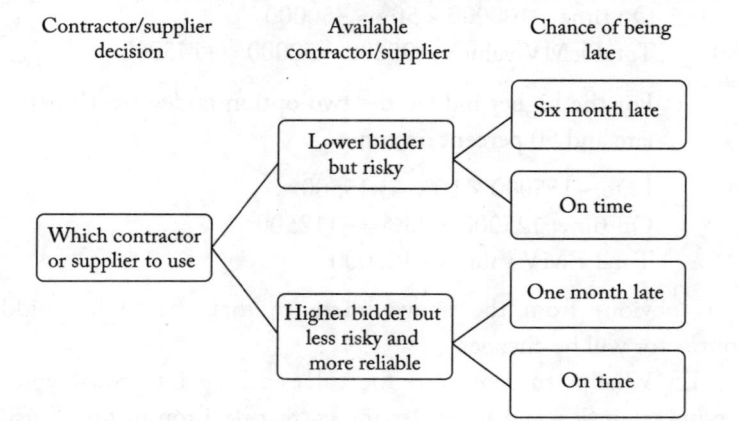

Source: Author's own work.
Note: Attributed to teachings of Project Management Institute.

the monetary value of the impact of the risk. The expected monetary value (EMV) formula is probability multiplied by impact. This value is positive for opportunities (positive risks) and negative for threats.

This can be explained by a decision-making tree.

The lower bidder quotes ₹100,000 for his work, and there is a 50 percent probability that he will deliver the work late by 3 months. The customer has assigned ₹1,000 per day as late charges making it 90,000 for 3 months. So the total cost arrives at ₹190,000.

The higher bidder quotes ₹125,000 and has a 10 percent probability of delivering the work 1 month late. The penalty for delay is the same, that is, ₹1,000 per day. So the total cost arrives at ₹155,000.

Now, using the EMV formulae to determine who is better, we determine EMV value of each chance node.

The lowest bidder has two option nodes, that is, 50 percent late and 50 percent on time.

Late: 190000 × 50% = –95000
On time: –100000 × 50% = –50000
Total EMV value = –95000 – 50000 = –145000

For the higher bidder, the two option nodes are 10 percent late and 90 percent on time.

Late: –155000 × 10% = –15500
On time: 125000 × 90% = –112500
Total EMV value = –128000

It is obvious from the above inference that the higher bidder contractor will be cheaper.

EMV helps to determine the values taking into consideration the uncertainties, and identifies the correct decision in the decision matrix tree.

The cost of the project is always monitored on VUCA issues by EMV calculations. For example, a project faces three common causes or occurrences for the months of October to November which are as follows.

There is a 30 percent probability that the project would get delayed due to unseasonal rainfall in October, and it will cost ₹50,000 as penalties levied by the customer if the work is not completed according to the work breakdown structure (WBS) in that period.

There is a 50 percent probability that the project would get late during the Diwali period as the labor will go on extended holiday, costing ₹30,000 as penalties.

The probability that the steel prices would drop is 50 percent. This would result in the benefit of ₹75,000 in the material cost. Calculating EMV (minus) for threats and (plus) for opportunities,

EMV = – 30% × 50000 – 50% × 30000 + 50% × 75000
= +7500 in October

The reduction in steel prices have saved us in the month of October but more than that our monitoring of the future market of material value allowed us to compensate the losses which we would have otherwise suffered due to rain and fewer labor delays.

Types of Risk Response

Once the risk is qualitative and quantitatively assessed, the team must evaluate the risk response and back it as follows.

- **Agreed response.** There is a certain risk on which a response is planned. The plan is most likely to be effective against the risk and all team members agree to it.
- **Avoidance.** It entails eliminating the risk or any uncertain condition and protecting the project objectives from its impact.
- **Transference.** It shifts the consequence of a risk to a third party, together with ownership of the response. It, however, does not mean that the risk is eliminated.
- **Mitigation.** It reduces the probability and consequences of an adverse risk event to an acceptable threshold. The team takes early actions to lessen the likelihood of the occurrence of a risk and its impact on the project. Preventive measures are more effective than trying to repair the consequences.
- **Acceptance.** In a situation when a project team is unable to identify any suitable response strategy, they must learn to deal with the risk and plan to face the challenge strongly and effectively.

Alternative Plans

The team must develop specific actions to enhance opportunities and reduce threats to the project's objectives.

In any battle plan, the leader prepares in advance for the emergency response strategy. Likewise in project a project manager calculates the management reserve and contingency reserve, discussed as follows, based on the estimated cost of each activity.

- **Contingency reserve.** It is the cost or time reserve that must be added in our future planning to manage identified risks or "known–unknown" (known = identified, unknown = risks).

This is an estimated reserve calculated by using the expected monetary value (EMV) and the decision tree method. The project manager controls it to solve any identified risk that may occur.
- **Management reserve.** It is calculated to be included in future planning and to manage the unidentified risks. It is also termed as "unknown–unknown" (the first unknown stands for unidentified, and the second unknown is the risk that we are not aware of). It is a random figure, dictated by organization's policy ranging from 5 percent of the total cost or time of the project to 10 percent, based on the overall uncertainty of the project.

Fallback Plan

The project manager should also decide upon a fallback plan.

- A contingency plan serves to handle specific actions when an opportunity or a threat arises. It gets invoked the moment a sufficient warning sign (risk trigger) is triggered.
- A fallback plan is used to back up or compliment a contingency plan. It also helps to manage the residual and identified risks.

Risk Register

Project teams should maintain a risk register and update it regularly for the following elements:

- Identify the type of risk
- Description of the risk
- Impact on project
- Assessment of risk (likelihood and seriousness)
- Grade (combined likelihood and seriousness)
- Change from the last review

- Date of the last review actions
- Mitigation actions (preventative or contingency)
- Responsibility for mitigation action(s)
- The cost to mitigate the risk
- Timeline for mitigation action(s)
- WBS

REGULAR MONITORING AND IMPACT

Along with risk identification, it is also important to monitor the risk on a regular basis. The following chart can be used as an example to perform a risk impact analysis and arrive at a possible solution.

SLR no	Risk event	Probability of occurrence	Magnitude of impact	Score probability × magnitude	Risk response	Description of response	Risk owner

INTEGRATED PLAN

There is the talk of government appointing Combined Defense Staff (CDS) who will guide all three chiefs of the armed forces for an integrated plan of air, land, and navy attack. In any war or project, integration of all functions is of utmost significance for success.

A project manager must be aware of the activities of each stakeholder and should be able to coordinate all the activities in a single integrated tactical plan. However, he should keep in mind the visual workflow and the order in which the events are connected.

In the armed forces, there is a lot of coordination done at the formation headquarter to combine the task and activities of each unit in phases and mark them in the battle plan or sand model room. All functional stakeholders' activities are centered on the main battle plan of the deliverable. For example, if there is a plan for the infantry company to capture the enemy bridge by D plus 3 days, although the focus would be on capturing the bridge, the supporting plans of artillery, armor, and other fighting and service elements would also be developed in the sand model room to make an integrated plan.

In a similar way, an integrated project plan involves the alignment and synchronization of the activities of all functional departments in an organization. However, a proper visualization, discussion, and agreement from each department is required to arrive at the integrated plan.

Visualization Method of the Integrated Plan

We can use the disruptive method to visualize the complete schedule and network of project activities linking all stakeholders' milestones to form one integrated plan. For example, in the 12.5-km cross country run at NDA, one has to visualize that he has to complete that run in 35–40 minutes, which involves planning to reach milestones on the route amidst ups and downs of the slope.

- **Know the result first.** In a project, it is necessary to create a definite time frame to meet schedule. The schedule period should be enough to accommodate any unforeseen setbacks so that we do not miss any activity of any functional department and experience losses.
- **Setting a target.** While planning a cross country run, the approach should be to fix the distance and time between each milestone and try to attain that by planning when to jog or speed up.

    Similarly, for a project, the necessary work for each department is set with a month/week/day's target to reach milestones. This plan ensures that the functional departments take responsibility for their planned work and that it is not carried forward to the next day.

    The pace is to be set with stamina in mind. While running the cross country, the breathing should be consistent to match the performance every 10 minutes, and it should not hamper performance.

Similarly, in a project, use performance markers that delineate a lower bound of acceptable achievement. These create productive discomfort and must be challenging (but not impossible) to achieve in difficult times.
- **Self-imposed constraints.** Most of the times, we get tempted to go full throttle when we see a downslope while running and forget that there is an upslope coming ahead. The aim should be to hold yourself back even if the going is easy.

  In a project, we should not get excited about an easy goal; this frequently leads to missing out small essential things that deter us before we ever reach the milestone that we are after.
- **The schedule must be within our control.** To ensure a good performance in the run, one needs to plan for his own goals, as the plans imposed by somebody else would eventually prove to be less effective.

  When we create a project plan ourselves, it gives us a sense of autonomy, which is highly motivating and gears us to put in all efforts to reach the milestones in time.

OPERATIONAL INTEGRATION OF FUNCTIONAL DEPARTMENT

A project manager must be able to concurrently link the necessary activities from different departments to prevent delays. A few departmental activities have been listed as follows.

- The material department places order of long lead items
- The construction department stats support infrastructure at site
- The project team ensures parameter studies like soil testing or environmental issues
- The engineering department starts drawing and basic planning

In the battle plan there is the main attack plan with other supporting plans around it to create an integrated plan. In a similar way, while preparing a holistic construction schedule, the committed deliverable would form the primary basis of planning, and other plans for engineering and procurement will support the main plan. The logistic schedule and its correlated activities must fit in with the construction schedule. The material should reach according to the efficient logistic timeline that must match the exact construction progress.

The interface between the engineering and procurement functions with another deliverable of fabrication shop floor and later on the sites needs to be established. Both engineering and procurement departments have to finalize the following with the construction department:

- Requisition for the purchase of material to be made in time. The project manager should assess the actual period of procured items, and if it is not matching with the construction schedule, that would have to be adjusted later in table float. It will avoid VUCA delay. There should be no lag between the request for quote and actual placement of PO and start of work. The request should be processed with the expected delivery date and location including time for logistics.
- The scope of work for subcontracts with suppliers to be finalized. Key procedures and drills or the SOP for delivery of material till the erection part must be made clear to the supplier.
- The equipment aids that need to be hired or procured by the subcontractors should fit the requirement of the construction schedule.
- Normally, there is a lot of delay in activities like the finalization of engineering drawing or procurement of raw material. These activities also need to be driven based on the milestone dates so that a project manager ensures timely engineering approvals for manufacturing clearance and the supplier plans his manufacturing or fabrication completion to match with the construction schedule. Integration

also involves linking the duration time needed for factory acceptance test and other shipping activities from factory to location.
- The seasonal weather issues also need to be kept in mind while connecting the engineering and procurement schedules. There is no point in procuring a material which cannot be used due to rain or bad weather and, moreover, the material may get spoiled. This also highlights the importance of integration of the main plan with the support functions such as delivery and storage.
- There is also an integration needed with manpower contractors for the required workforce. Proper service contracts should be made to ensure early mobilization of the workforce.

THEORY OF CONSTRAINT

In route march competitions at NDA, the runner with weakest stamina was identified and was kept in the front so that he did not let down the rest of the team. Somebody carried his weapon or somebody held his hand, but it was ensured that the weakest runner was focused upon for the overall success. Same is theory of constraints (TOC). Concentrate on the slowest delaying work and plan other factors around it. The slowest work will automatically align with speed to allow others to complete the work in time.

The project manager knows that there will still be constraints between various departments that are likely to cause VUCA issues in scope, schedule, cost, and quality.

In a war, if there is shortage of troops or resources, the battle is not given up; they fight till the last man. Similarly, there is no excuse that a task cannot be done without exploring all the possibilities of adjusting resources and finding a solution within our capabilities.

According to the TOC, the speed of the operation depends upon the slowest activity or the limiting factor which acts as a constraint.

Such bottlenecks must be removed as they are deterrence to the organization in reaching its goal.

- The functional managers in a company can have opposing commitments and restrictions in terms of due date, budget, and content. They give conflicting priorities and promises that have longer lead times than desired. The problems in their departments cascade into adverse effects in the project management cycle.
- **Solution.** Let us try to solve these issues by TOC.
  - **Identify the bottlenecks.** There are internal problems in each department such as engineering, procurement, erection, or execution. One needs to identify the bottlenecks.
  - **Exploit.** A project manager should focus on making quick improvements using the existing resources and avoid blame games. The resources must be used to their fullest potential and the team should be clear about what to produce and in what quantities.
  - **Subordinate.** It is also best to assess the activities of other departments and ensure that they support the functional units.
  - **Elevate.** If there is a resource constraint from another department, then investment should be planned.
  - **Repeat.** The team should move to the next constraint once the current issues are solved. They should also coordinate with several stakeholders to know how they can help in mobilizing resources or funds.

The engineering team focuses on preliminary drawings and execution planning. However, they frequently experience the following constraints.

- **Engineering drawings are not completed in time.** There are pending design changes that delay the work. The delay could be due to regulatory authority approvals or some new features or revisions in the plan. At times, it is also due to conflict of egos between the designers of the customer and supplier or contractor as there is no sign of agreement.

TOC solution. The engineering team should be sure of designs and should be able to clearly define it on paper. They should also provide a realistic schedule plan for the next three to four months as to how the drawing will be rolled out. After that they can jointly scrutinize why the delay was happening to bring transparency in the project and foster collaboration to resolve any constraint of any design.

- **Delays in scope finalization.** The scope is not getting finalized, leading to a chain of delayed events in detailed engineering, field work, start up, and commissioning of the project. The possible reason is that the customer and the team do not have a clear understanding of some uniqueness of the task. At times, geotechnical conditions and variations at the project site add up to more problems and confusion in specifications.

    TOC solution. The project manager should ensure that the project scope has been thoroughly discussed and agreed upon with customer engineering and project teams. There must be open communication and timely approvals to remove any gaps as it helps to shorten the review cycle significantly and cuts down the number of iterations to the bare minimum.

- **Poor engineering.** Poor engineering results in more errors in complete design and are causing rework. Redesigned works eventually lengthen the schedule and lead to cost overruns.

    TOC solution. The engineering teams should conduct orchestrated immersion sessions for the designing team. The junior engineers must get in the habit of collective thinking with experts and discuss different parts and component to create a learning environment. They should also analyze and research the material to link all design parts to perfection.

- **Delays in subsequent execution of work.** The execution team moves ahead of the engineering schedule, which results in the labor sitting idle causing cost overruns.

  TOC solution. A project manager should ensure that 70–80 percent engineering is complete to support the start of execution. Engineering should not be allowed to overlap construction by more than 30–40 percent.

TOC to Resolve Procurement Issues

Equipment procurement specification and construction work packages are procured from front-end engineering design, historical data, and later detailed engineering. The following VUCA issues must be discussed with the procurement team to find solutions in advance.

- **Incomplete or wrong drawing specification.** The supplier does not get timely complete product and project specification from the engineering team, which affects the quality expectation. The challenge is, therefore, to obtain bids, drawings, and the final goods in the scheduled time.

  TOC solution. There must be a collaboration between engineering team, procurement team, and the supplier. The procurement team must get complete assurance from the engineering team. They should understand the scope at their level as a second-tier check of part product list, and the task that needs to be performed.

- **Finding local supplier near site location.** The procurement team faces the dilemma of how much quantity to purchase from the local supplier in remote areas closer to site vis-à-vis an established provider in a metro. They have to also keep the transport cost in mind.

  TOC solution. The procurement team should separate items, products, and services to establish what is explicitly needed from which supplier, keeping the cost of transportation in mind. They should also plan about the work. Example,

there are some structure that can be made fabricated at the site and some structure comes with modular kits that can get transported to site and fitted easily.
- **Delay in delivery.** The project does not meet the due inward dates at which the material is required or the project specifications and quality requirements. The project schedule requirements get hampered with everything falling in the critical path.

  TOC solution. It is best to have a system of regular interval checks of supplier production at their manufacturing premises. A strict follow up should be maintained and the supply teams should be frequently asked to share the product photographs to ensure quality and schedule within cost.
- **Wrong quantity or incomplete list of items.** The engineering team causes overestimation of material required which the procurement fails to control. The quantity and type of material if not fixed lead to overrun in the material cost.

  TOC solution. The bill of material (BOM) quantity should be set along with the full schedules of work and how it will take place. The amount of material should be monitored throughout the project to arrive at the correct estimate of real project works. It is commonly known as the estimated material project cost.

TOC for Resolving Constraint Issues in the Execution Team

A project manager has received the project scope in smaller packages and awarded work to multiple contractors at lower cost (lower unit rates). It increases the flexibility to reallocate the scope if one of the contractors does not perform as expected. Following VUCA issues also need to be addressed:
- **Lack of appropriate funds.** Insufficient cash stability, limited access to qualified human resources, no availability of larger construction equipment, tendency to cut cost, etc.

TOC solution. The project manager must be able to link the schedule with cost and develop monthly cash flow projections in the complete project life cycle.
- **Change in scope.** The work often gets hampered due to less clarity on the scope of work and status of the interim deliverable handed over to the next contractor.

  TOC solution. Client's needs, requirements, and expectations should be identified and understood. The contractor must have a clarity of standards of the interim deliverable when he/she is handing over work to the next contractor. A formal protocol should also be agreed between all parties with zero punch points.
- **Delays in PO and Letter of Intent (LOI).** There is a delay in awarding work to the contractor due to which the deployment at the site is delayed. The commencement of work gets late and project timelines are affected severely.

  TOC solution. The awarding of contract should be time bound and followed up for deployment. The issues related to labor management and industrial relations (IR) should be discussed with the contractor and he/she should be provided with sufficient time to get the necessary work-related documents ready.
- **Resource mismanagement.** There is ambiguity on resource requirement.

  TOC solution. The subcontractors have to manage their labor to get the work done; therefore, it is better to involve them in the calculation of the requirement for direct labor, supervisors, and equipment to satisfy the expected production rates for meeting schedules.
- **Waste generation.** A lot of material gets wasted and lost.

  TOC solution. It is always best to manage warehouses and material flows, keeping them out of the control of the contractor. It also prevents the wastage or theft of equipment.

WBS AND ACTIVITIES

In a tactical plan, all main tasks and their subtasks or activities to accomplish the primary task are listed down. The cost of each work is assessed by the requirement of the number of soldiers that will be used to perform a task. No part of the task is left unaccounted or without any ownership.

Project management also advocates the same philosophy of breaking down the project scope into a WBS and further activities. A manager should work with the project team to hierarchically decompose the work into manageable sections or individual components. A WBS also defines responsibilities and control of project scheduling and facilitates accurate cost estimates.

The level of a WBS is also planned.

- Level 1: Starts with the project name or the name of the assignment
- Level 2: Divides the project into a subsystem
- Level 3: Identifies managerial tasks to be performed to complete the subsystem
- Level 4: Breaks a task into technical subtasks
- Level 5: Creates a work package as the final deliverable
- Level 6: Divides the work package into further components

Level 1 to Level 3 involves the managerial activities mostly at the head office.

Level 4 to Level 6 are all technical activities to be managed at the site.

WBS Dictionary

A WBS dictionary is a document that provides detailed information about each element in the WBS. The basic information needed for a WBS dictionary is as follows:

- Product work package description
- Project work involved to produce the product deliverable

- Schedule activities and milestones
- Dates of product installation or completion of related project work
- Assessment of all resources and labor working hours
- Material handling equipment and time of positioning
- Agreement with contractors and suppliers
- Interdependencies between departments and coordination
- Quality parameters and matrices of the deliverable
- Plan for photographs and testing documents
- Agreement on the acceptance criteria during interim handing over of work
- Analysis of assumption and constraint of predecessor work, customer rules, regulations, and work permit
- VUCA issues and challenges
- Remedial action to prevent that VUCA problems
- Follow-up action to close the issue
- Technical source document
- Any details not entirely covered
- Daily stand-up meetings in the war room to discuss urgent issues
- Manager scope approval from the project manager
- Last updated date
- Next review date

It is good to put a copy of the scope statement and WBS dictionary in the war room so that the project team can monitor it daily and there is an advance visibility about what is happening in each WBS. The team should also list and connect all stakeholders remotely connected with the WBS.

It is important to divide the WBS into activities so that it covers all the required work. There are some rules for making an activity list:

- Each activity must have three aspects—engineering drawing, quality assurance plan, and work methodology.
- Each activity must follow an 80 hours rule which means that the site team or concerned person at the operational level

- should have command and control of the operation, and no single activity should take more than 80 hours to produce a deliverable.
- However, each activity or group of activities at the lowest level should be covered under the decided reporting period whether weekly or monthly. That way the period covered keeps pace with the WBS.
- It is better to identify the issues that would come up for each activity in the plan.

Reverse Brainstorming

It is about addressing the possible problem in each activity by combining brainstorming and reversal techniques. The steps included in reverse brainstorming are as follows:

- Identify the problem or challenge in an activity and write down the problem statement.
- Reverse the statement describing the problem by asking, "How could I possibly cause the problem that derails the project" or "How could I possibly achieve an adverse effect?"
- Brainstorm the opposite problem to generate different solution ideas.
- Let the brainstormed ideas flow freely and do not reject anything at this stage.
- Once all the ideas to solve the reverse problem are confirmed, they should be changed to find solution ideas for the original problem in an activity.

Making a Baseline Schedule

In the army, there are timelines of each subtask and activities that are planned to ensure that the next phase of the battle does not get delayed.

Likewise, in a project, the schedule should be assessed based on the proper allotment of resources for each subtask or activity.

- **VUCA issues.** A project manager is aware of the problems while sequencing the activities. Activities are not planned with attributes of ownership. Too many people are involved, but traceability of accountability is missing.

  In a battle situation, it is important to realize the ground situation before planning the phases of a campaign. Similarly, a planner at the head office must be aware of the issues and problem areas when planning for activities at various levels.
- **Sequencing of activities.** Identify the activities that can be done in sequence or in parallel. It should also be known whether an action or a task is mandatory or of less priority. Experts and experienced members can also be invited to share their inputs about the activities that require crashing or more attention.

  There must also be planning to track the activities that are based on the internal and external support system. These activities must be monitored by continuous contact with people who are responsible for them.

Resource Allotment for Activities

- **VUCA issues.** The resource breakdown structure does not match with the WBS. There are problems in the arrangement of material and resources as per activities. Hence, the work cannot be done fast in parallel, crashing, etc.
- **Resource estimation.** An estimate of activity resources is required before calculating the activity durations. It is better to know first the resources that are available to us within the cost to correctly estimate the duration. A proper allocation of resources in the planned budget would help to complete the action faster.

  The team must analyze the resources and cost for each activity. They should also divide the scope into action components based on the labor involved and match the resource breakdown structure with the WBS.

The labor requirement of each activity is the total number of person-hours it would take for workers to complete a step from start to finish. The data of time estimate can be determined from the historical lesson of parametric or analogous estimation.

Estimated Duration for Activities

- **VUCA issues.** The period of project completion does not assess the actual working conditions. The calculation of duration of events is also not accurate as the resource allocation is done later and not earlier. If the person-hours for work is allotted, then the duration can be more readily ascertained.
- **PERT estimation.** To calculate real values for the duration of events, one can refer to the dates from three sources—contractors, central planner, and our assessment based on VUCA threats. With three dates for each activity, the team can use PERT calculations to find the optimistic, pessimistic, and most likely dates.
    - **Mean expected activity duration** = $(P + 4M + O)/6$
    - **Activity standard deviation** = $(P - O)/6$
    - **Activity variance** = $[(P - O)/6]2$
- **Contingency reserve time.** In a battle plan, the team always has a reserve or a backup in mind. It is basically to cater to anything that might go wrong in a VUCA situation. The contingency reserve time caters to the unidentified schedule risk and is included in the project plan baseline.
- **Management reserve time.** It is not a part of the cost baseline but is an additional fund set aside to cover unforeseen risks that would impact the project ability to meet the target deadline. The use of management reserve will result in a change in the schedule baseline because it is not factored into duration estimates.

Scheduling the Activities with Critical Path

The schedule management WBS gives a rough idea about when each work will start and end with milestones in between. The project team has the activity list, sequencing, resources, and duration; however, they should avoid the following VUCA issues while creating a new schedule:

- The clarity of scope of product and project does not get fully translated into the WBS. Something gets missed, and it puts the schedule or sequence in disorder.
- All stakeholders have different priorities of work with various programs that and this creates more confusion. It is important that they all converge for a deliverable.
- The WBS of a contractor plan does not match with our WBS. They make plans based on their own constraints and there is no certainty about when and how these would be resolved.
- **Network path.** Once the full schedule with milestones has been visualized, a network path is made to show the various series of activities connected in a logical and flowing manner. The next step is to find the critical path.
    - Start with the finding the number of tracks of various activities connected to each other in different sequences, that is, start to end.
    - We determine the time taken by each path by adding up the durations of each of the activities on the path. We can use the PERT method to get an accurate duration for each activity. Critical path is the route that will take the longest amount of time.
    - Every activity must finish on time for the project to complete on time. A delay in any event will cause the entire project to be delayed.
    - An activity or task which is not on the critical path has more leeway and may be slipped without affecting the end date of the project. This is called slack or float.

- o An important point to note is that tasks which are on the critical path have no reserve or spare time, that is, there is no float. These are called critical path activities and can be used to actually identify the critical path during the calculations.
- **Identifying the floats.** The float is the time we can slip in activities before it causes our project to be delayed. The next work diagram deals with the determination of the amount of total float between activities.
- **Total float.** It is the amount of time by which an activity can be delayed without delaying the project end date or an intermediary milestone while adhering to any imposed schedule constraint.
  - o **Free float.** The amount of time by which an activity can be delayed without delaying the early start date of its successor.
  - o **Project float.** It is the amount of time for which we can hold a project without delaying the active project completion date.

The float information is useful and we can use it to organize and manage the project by better reallocation of resources. It also helps team members to juggle work on multiple projects:

Float = Late Start (LS) − Early Start (ES) Or Float
= Late Finish (LF) − Early Finish (LF)

- **Early start.** It is the earliest time in which an activity or successive activities can commence in a network diagram connecting all events.
- **Early finish.** It is the earliest time in which an activity can finish without causing the previous events to slip.

ES and EF provide some leverage to move the start dates for activities without causing problems.

- **Late start.** It is the latest time in which an activity can start without causing any slippage in the overall project.

- **Late finish.** It is the latest time in which an activity can finish without causing the overall project to be late.

LS and LF provide us information about the spare time available between activities.

- **Calculating early and late duration of the project.** There are two ways to calculate the early start, late start, early finish, and late finish for an activity in a network diagram. They are called forward pass and backward pass.
  - **Forward pass.** Early start and finish figures are found by calculating the duration of activities from the beginning to the end of the project.
  - **Early finish:** Early Start + Duration
  - **Backward pass.** Late figure is found by moving from the end of a project to the beginning of the project.
  - **Late start:** Late Finish − Duration
- **Determining the critical path.** The critical path is the path that has the longest duration (see Figure 6.4).

Figure 6.4. Calculating the Critical Path and Float from Network Diagram

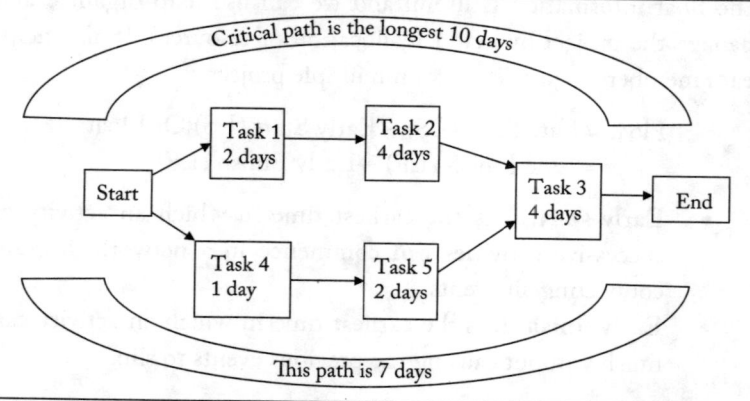

Source: Author's own work.
Note: Attributed to teachings of Project Management Institute. Task 4 or 5 can start or finish with a slack of float or spare time of 3 days, as the total duration of the critical path is 10 days.

- In other words, the critical path indicates the longest sequence of activities from the project start to end. If the activities in the critical path are completed exactly as per schedule, we follow up to ensure that the project is completed by the specified date in future.
- We cannot start new activities until the others are finished. These activities need to be completed in a sequence, with each stage being completed before the next stage can begin. At the same time, we cannot ignore a parallel task or a trivial task in other paths.

Making a Baseline Cost

After scheduling the activities via the network diagram and finalizing the critical activities, the project team must ensure that the cost of activities does not cross the baseline cost given by the management.

In the armed forces, every activity has a cost either in terms of time, money, or lives. Officers are trained from the beginning to save the bullet and use it sparingly and effectively. That thought process carries on with a disciplined use of resources and material. There is also a swift accountability if resources are wasted and an explanation is sought on their misuse.

Accordingly, a project manager must be able to justify all kinds of expenses, some of which often get ignored or are not assessed properly.

A brainstorming session should be organized to develop cost-saving ideas and arrive at a planned cost of the proposed activity. The costs must also be subsequently monitored on a weekly basis during operational planning and execution. The team should decide to do a proper calculation of the cost value of activity using the PERT method. With this, it is possible to get a broad range of rates for each activity.

Material cost. It should be decided if the material should come as reassembled units or in a knockdown condition. This will also determine the cost of other related activities.

Man-hour calculation. Man-hour costing is often wrongly calculated leading to several VUCA issues later. The workforce requirement for each activity is also frequently overestimated and unrealistic. The project team, therefore, should cautiously handle man-hour calculation for a project.

The workforce subcontractor is also unreliable in providing the workforce. There are labor force and supervision including support function work. The man-hours work is divided into two kinds, that is, direct person-hour and indirect person-hour.

- **Direct person-hour.** It refers to the work of people who are contributing directly to the project and construction progress. For purposes of labor, the focus will be on the calculation of direct person-hour only.
- **Indirect person-hour.** It is attributable to all those personally supporting the people who are performing the project work, such as the store, administration, and logistics.
- **Nonproductive hour.** It refers to no work, be it for any reason such as holiday or strike or weather conditions.
- **Standard man-hours (Smh).** These are calculated by dividing bill of quantities (BoQs) with standard productivity rates (SPR). The project team defines all the activities as listed in the BoQs with duration calculation and use SPR as an estimate-based observed data of work and time calculated as average in a different project.
- **Using Smh to determine the project duration completion.** The length of time in which the project would be completed can be calculated using a correlation table decided as per industry standards. For 50,000 Smh, it is usually 6 months, for 100,000 Smh, it is 8 months, and so on.
- **The K factor.** This is influenced by all the factors that affect the productivity. Its average normal value is from 1.3 to 1.8. It can also be < 0.8 or 0.9 if work conditions are better.
- **Calculating direct person-hour.** The Smh factor incorporates the plant design data or the planned inputs from the engineering department. Ground condition influences the

actual condition of work, and K factor designates that direct man-hour is calculated by multiplying the Smh by factor K.

- **The K factor which gives us direct workforce usage is based on**
    - Economic condition of the country
    - Governing industrial rules and union presence and problems associated with it
    - Easy availability of workforce, construction tools, and equipment
    - Climatic conditions of the country or the geographical area
    - Logistic pain areas for raw material
- **Labor rates.** A project manager should be aware of the current labor productivity rates as laid down by the government.
- We now have the following information to calculate the man-hour cost for each activity:
    - A baseline man-hours cost for every activity.
    - Any additional charge of workforce or overtime cost in any activity. In case of crashing, the extra man-hours must be added to the existing cost which has been calculated.
- **Manpower miscellaneous cost.** The project team should consider the following miscellaneous costs related to manpower resources.
    - In the case of organizational workforce, the cost incurred in salaries, benefits, or burdens would be determined.
    - Cost of living and cost of conveyance should be included for the people employed during the activity duration.
    - Cost of airfare and hotel stays along with other site visit expenses of the employees add unnecessarily to the cost. To justify the cost, the teams should agree to introduce the debriefing sessions where anybody visiting the site must oversee the entire spectrum of project functions and note down the points for all functional heads.

- **Cost of tools/equipment handling material.** For every activity, there should be a recheck on the cost of equipment and its need/usage.
  - There should be a proper assessment of the actual needs of equipment of extensive use as it cannot be kept unused. Normally, there is a tendency of demanding new hydra for every construction-related activity but it is hardly used.
  - A driver of hydra is smart enough to save his fuel by sticking to his bare minimum duties and working at a leisure pace. This waste may seem inconsequential in the beginning, but it would eventually hit the cost of the project.
- **Logistic cost.** This is the additional expense in the form of local taxes, or unanticipated cost on the use of heavy haul equipment. Hence, a thorough brainstorming on logistics and its cost with the supplier should be done.
- **Unloading cost.** Once the material reaches the site, the cost of unloading the material with the machines like hydraulic crane should also be planned in advance. Any additional usage of the crane will have to be accounted for. It is also important to follow up beforehand so that the crane is made available when needed.
- **Store and site infrastructure cost.** This does not form part of the activity costing. Hence, one needs to ensure that the capitalized cost and the noncapitalized cost are segregated.
- **Local purchase.** There is some material that is locally expended for the activity. Such cost of material like steel washers' nuts and bolts must be catered for as the local purchase for the activity.
- **The cost of quality.** This includes the specific cost of the quality check, lab test, soil test, etc., that are needed for an activity to be confirmed as a deliverable. It is important to spend on quality rather on the rework.

- **The cost of safety.** It is also most ignored with lack of safety kits, shoe helmets, etc. That can also be part of Capex cost and may include cost of safety equipment, training and also safety officer's salary and living cost.
- **Miscellaneous/Other expenses.** These are unanticipated costs incurred during the execution of the event. We must also add 10 percent overhead cost to the miscellaneous expense.
- **Linking schedule with budget.** The program should be finally connected to the cost. The financial status containing the budget expenses schedule, as planned, should be ready to start tracking the actual and earned value (EV) later. All jobs are unique with different cost compulsion at times and, hence, require specificity so that we get the EV as per the planned value (PV).

Summing Up a Cost Estimate

The operational site team should be very clear on activity costing that will result due to cost overrun at the operational level. To conclude, activity costing would broadly include the following:

Activity I/D description	Duration of completion	Man-hour or direct hour cost	Cost of any equipment	Cost of material package	Supervision cost at site (safety/quality/engineering/administration)	Site inspection visit expense	Additional charges not in plan like Cost of Poor Quality (COPQ). Specify reasons and correction
Total cost of this activity							

- **Contingency reserve.** It is for handling any emergency expenses.
- **Work package cost.** Final aggregated/rolled up activities cost is segregated into various work package activities and is called cost aggregation.
- **Control account.** Work package with contingency reserve totals into control account at the activity level or project level. Here, all kinds of costs related to an activity would be cumulated.
- **Cost baseline established.** This is a summation of control accounts.
- **Approved budget.** This is a cost baseline and a management reserve for unknown risk issues.

Management of Funds

- **Management reserve.** A project manager must keep some management reserve for anything going wrong; he may not disclose the amount, but that figure will be under his control to tide over the urgent issue.
- **Contingency reserve.** This includes the approval of funds of a few thousands that the project manager decides to give to the site incharge to spend in case of urgency, so that they do not have to look back for approvals and hold the work.
- **The discipline of expense.** A cash flow projection should be planned and there should be no delays in the approval of the money spent by the managers at the site. However, it is important to maintain integrity and faith for such decentralization to exist.
- **The value of spending.** The project manager must ensure that there is no disregard in creating basic comfort facilities in working conditions for all the employees. If the team has to do cost control in project, it will control waste and losses but not reduce the employees comforts.

Configuration management. There should be linked configuration to control account with the WBS. Any additional cost above the baseline of an activity should be immediately captured.

IDENTIFYING PROCESSES, PROCEDURES, AND WORK INSTRUCTIONS TO IMPLEMENT THE ACTIVITIES

The scope schedule and cost baselines have to be backed by efficient processes, procedures, and work methods. Tiresome working will only prevent us from reaching the benchmarks. This is the first step to developing baseline quality parameters.

In the armed forces, there are SOPs and drills to execute all activities and ensure everything is in order. The execution team takes off from where the planner team leaves.

Similarly, in a project, one must review the processes and procedures which affect the speed and delivery of his/her objectives.

- **The processes.** It involves any activity or set of activities that uses resources to transform inputs into outputs. It has a defined and necessarily measurable objective, input, output, activities, and resources. It also describes the steps or actions or necessary preparation and checklist the worker has to execute.
    - Inputs/Resources. Every activity has a predecessor activity. There should be proper handing over of protocol that involves sharing of work information, standard of acceptance and clarity of ownership of work.
    - Outputs. These are the results which an activity will produce to be handed over to the successive owner. They must follow the standards or specifications so that there is no rework.
- **Defining procedures (level-2 documents).** It helps to explain how to perform an activity or group of activities, that is, process.

- Purpose of an activity
- Responsibility to do the activity
- Definition of work involved
- Software or equipment/material needed for execution of an activity
- People required for implementation
- Engineering drawing (date of receipt) of the activity
- Date by which all resources are made available to ensure action starts
- Predecessor activity results with correction and handover time
- Date of start of the event
- Instruction to execute an action
- Work instructions to maintain safety during execution
- Documents and MIS format for monitoring and control
- Quality standards of activity
- Reasons with corrections in case of rework and the handover date
- Date of event completion
- Interim handover
- VUCA problems
- Solution and alternatives to resolve VUCA issues

- **Work instructions (level-3 documents).** It describes the steps to perform a task, which is a more detailed portion of the procedure.
  - The purpose of the work instruction: Which activity it covers?
  - Scope: Which part of range it covers?
  - Particular records and proof of work to be kept
  - Responsibility of functions to ensure accountability
  - Tools/Gauges and fixtures
  - Safety requirements
  - Instruction steps to execute the work

Improving to Idealize the Process

Some processes are tiresome, bureaucratic, and time wasting with a lot of nonvalue added steps. It is better to have a review of such methods also to get the ideal process. The steps listed further are followed to create an idealized system for any process.

- **Formulating the mess.** Identify the internal and external factors that can self-destruct the project and understand their causes of occurrence.
- **System analysis.** Make a process flowchart to identify various linkages of departments or their interfacing arrangement.
- **Obstruction analysis.** Address the nonvalue steps or other work culture habits that obstruct the progress of a project or resist change (e.g., conflicts and customs).
- **Reference projections.** Visualize the future process assuming there are not many changes in project requirements. It will produce "how and why the organization will destroy itself" and prove to be a significant change to ensure the success of the project.
- **Presentation of the mess.** Compare the old and new ways of the process. If there is no change, then the chances of self-destruction of a project are more.
- **Ends planning.** Once the change is confirmed, decide upon the steps and best practices. It is an ideal process design that helps to make the project more lean and robust. It also determines the gaps to be closed and prevents self-destruction.
- **Means planning.** Define the action steps and practices to avoid self-destruction.
- **Resource planning.** Identify the resources needed to implement the changes or action plan; they can be personnel, money, materials, or services. It will also involve facilities and related equipment with necessary information, knowledge, or understanding and wisdom needed. Also, determine how and when to deploy or use them.

- **Design of implementation.** Put a decision or plan into effect with clear, delineated responsibility for every individual. It is also best to make a time schedule for each task and allocate resources for the tasks to be carried out.
- **Design of controls.** Ensure monitoring and control of all steps in the process so that an idealized system is maintained.

PLANNING BASELINE QUALITY FOR THE PROJECT

The army maintains high level of standard in any work they perform. It is primarily due to continuous training for improving skills and regular, timely feedbacks.

Likewise, in any project, the quality team must be very proactive for quality verification before and after the supplier dispatches the material. The team should also maintain quality audits and timely correction of flaws to avoid receiving the punch points from the customer during the project closure.

There are, hence, several issues that affect the profit margin of a product:

- Once the quality inspection at the supplier shop gets over, the product items must move immediately for its usage, otherwise it will get spoiled and deteriorated in storage. No ownership will replace the material if the material gets destroyed after the mandatory inspection is over.
- To reduce the cost of material, the supplier often misses out on the proper primer and painting of the product. They also sometimes ignore proper transportation bracket in the lorry which results in damages and loss of paint quality in the product by the time it reaches the site.
- The material that has been handled shabbily in transportation is made to look presentable with some patch work. At the

site, work gets affected, and delay of replacement is not accepted.
- There is a lack of supervision in test trials and no awareness of quality test parameters.

A few quality management aspects have been discussed as follows.

- **Quality of product.** Reassess the quality process at both the ends, customer's and supplier's. This will ensure a standardized quality throughout the life cycle of the product from raw material to the finished product.
- **Test certificates with product.** Monitor the time gaps between each supplier quality test certificate and ensure that the teams check the product before its actual use. The trail test of equipment by our own team is critical irrespective of a test certificate.
- **Quality of packing and transportation.** Whenever our team goes for a supplier quality inspection or a test, they should also discuss about the logistics with the supplier. The product special packing and loading preparation should also be decided.
- **Component checks.** For every product and project process, there are quality controls and SOPs. These are structured steps specific to components and should be verified and rechecked.
- **Finalize quality metrics.** It is also better to have an operational definition that describes the product/project attribute along with a quality control process to measure it. These process parameters should also be known to the contractors and supervisors, for example, on-time performance, budget control, defect frequency, failure rate, availability, and reliability.
- **Improving quality.** There are many processes that hamper smooth project management. In order to ensure quality of a process, we must eliminate the nonvalue adding steps that slow down the process.

COORDINATION WITH SUPPLIERS AND MANUFACTURERS

The baselines of scope, schedule, cost, and quality would be achieved only if we have the right suppliers and contractors to help us in the project.

In the armed forces, there is a culture to deal with the supplier and manufacturer with total transparency and honesty and a culture of building relations and reliability. The supplier and manufacturer, therefore, take pride in working for the armed forces.

As an example, when the Parliament attack happened, the Indian Government ordered the quick mobilization of Armed Forces to attack Pakistan. The war was codenamed Op Parkaram. The army engineering team had a very short time to put the off-road equipment as worthy for war fighting. The team had to ensure all equipment lying off-road for months for want of spares were made serviceable in 24 to 36 hours. The Government had given clearance for funds to procure and make the equipment available, and the challenge was to make it happen.

In this emergency, the suppliers rose to the occasion by establishing a network of spare parts providers who were based from central India to desert borders of Rajasthan. The engineering team could get the material even en route on the train. A few other suppliers also moved along with the units to set up a support system for the requirement of spares and material in tents in Jaisalmer town.

To summarize, if the suppliers are treated as team members, they will surely rise to the occasion when the need arises.

Site material management. Once all the activities are listed in a network and a schedule is made, the challenge is to ensure the delivery of material at the site in time by suppliers. There are many problems with suppliers and manufacturers as listed below that lead to complexities in any project.

- Equipment and materials are not purchased at the best available cost, resulting in cost overrun.

- The material does not meet project specifications and quality requirements. There is the cost of rework of painting again or repairing some bend or damaged portion that was missed out while capturing the cost of poor quality (COPQ). The disputes settlement is also very slow.
- The inward schedule of material at the site does not meet the required delivery dates by the site. The material readiness also does not match with site work. Subsequently, this causes the supplier to face the problem of storage as his material does not move out and his payments are delayed.
- The site team also gets under pressure to inward the material. They have to invoice it to the customer and get payments so that they can further pay to the supplier. Due to all the unforeseen delays and lack of storage space, the material gets spoiled.
- The procurement repeatedly gets purchase requests (PRs) of wasted material, which creates a cycle of waste and excess material.
- There is materials' price escalation cost overrun due to a long construction period. The material which has been purchased at a lower cost earlier often gets purchased at a higher rate later due to the extended period and price escalation. The high incidence at repurchase causes cost overruns.

To solve the above-mentioned problems, one must improve the team's ability to anticipate needs and forecast conditions to plan and schedule. A lot of time is saved when the buyer minimizes the technical queries to prevent delays. There must also be streamlined business processes (internal and external) to place PO and E-sourcing.

There are a lot of professional interactions involved in building supplier relationships:

- Personal involvement of supplier ensures that the items reach safely and in time.

- The supplier and buyer function as a joint team that actively engages and supports each other in response to unforeseen events. They have a common conflict resolution strategy to address each other's problems in a time frame.
- There are times when resources may have to be shared to increase efficiency. The loading/unloading team or transportation resources are shared frequently.
- The supplier and buyer have contact points of key persons and are clear about the responsibilities that lie with them.
- There should be regular monitoring of the partnering process with definitive key performance indicators (KPIs) and matrices.

Selecting the best subcontractors. The contract labor is the single largest cost component of the construction project ranging from anything between 50 percent and 70 percent of the main project cost. Labor can make or break the job depending on the management of workers and contractors.

- The work construction scope must be divided into packages or further subdivided into work subcontractor packages (WSPs). All the work should have recalculated man-hours according to Smh.
- The contracting and material procurement team should extend the contract of the producer of equipment to also manage the installation of the equipment. That way if anything goes wrong, the Operation and Maintenance (O&M) of the producer will get it rectified and there will be less exchange of blame between the producer and any other subcontracting team.
- There must be an identification of the scope of work where reliable-third party contractors will be needed. As an example, for the civil, electrical, and insulation work, the special machining and specialty welding works are outsourced.
- **Subcontractor evaluation.** There should be an assessment of subcontractors to check their performance and productivity

using the agreed workforce for every activity. They must also have the capability to get or manage labor and resources especially during the peak period.
- Evaluation checklist by the contracting team.
  - **Seek qualification of the subcontractor project manager.** The subcontractor needs to be qualified enough to execute the work in project management principles.
  - **Gather feedback.** Assess data and type of work carried out by the subcontractor, along with the size of their central contracts.
  - **Avoid further subletting.** The selected subcontractors should not be allowed to lease their work to other subcontractors and the subcontracting should be kept to one level only.
  - **Work methods defined.** There should be clarity on site procedures, quality procedures, work methodology, documents of the plot plan, data sheet, specification, etc.
  - **Manpower planning.** They should provide workforce deployment schedule with phases of work, split by trade and functional role. They should also provide indirect person-hours to support the direct person-hours work.
  - **Equipment handling machine.** The requirement and rate of usage of vehicles and construction or machine-handling equipment should be specified and confirmed of being properly maintained. The list of documentation of vehicle and workforce as required by IR and safety team should also be provided.
  - **Mobilization and demobilization plan.** It specifies about the temporary facilities and labor camps to be scheduled.
  - **Anti-corruption policy.** The contractor ethical policy should match with that of our company.
  - **Safety culture within their team.** Assess their capabilities to provide safety rigs and training for workers.

- **Quality training program.** It is important to know how much the supervisor is trained for leadership and experience of handling all labor.

• For an item that gets lost or damaged, the contractor tries to claim via the customer through an insurance scheme. If there is a rework or extra work due to the inefficiency of subcontractors, there is a lot of ambiguity about who will pay. It is, therefore, better to transfer the accountability to the subcontractor to ensure his full involvement in completing the work.

    - However, it is our duty to also support the subcontractor and understand their problems. We can jointly assess the site conditions and ensure standards of labor working conditions. We can also mutually discuss the responsibilities to have a better clarity regarding the ownership.
    - Reviews and approvals must be given timely, and everybody should be aware of the performance and acceptance criteria of the deliverable. There would be disagreements or problems for which a dispute resolution process or an escalation/schedule matrix can be established.

• **Insurance.** The cost of resolving unexpected losses have to be claimed by way of insurance. The customer provides insurance for himself and for most of the contractors and subcontractors on site.

    - This is also referred to as the warp-up policy or owner-controlled insurance program in which the savings in the premium are incurred by one party.
    - However, the subcontractors should have a clear understanding of process and procedure and documentation involved in owner-controlled insurance. Timings, documentation, and photographs to surveyor are imperative for getting timely insurance.

Risk	Detail/ Description Date of reporting	Probability and impact	Resolution	EPC contractor	EPC subcontractor	Customer	Insurance	Lesson/ take away	Additional cost incurred

MATERIAL LOGISTICS AND STORAGE PLAN

Logistics remains a significant challenge to bring material within time, budget, and with expected results.

- **Project logistics.** Unlike in armed forces, project logistics is a neglected function in corporate projects, but those companies that focus on these aspects thrive by cutting losses. There is always a significant interface problem to link project schedules to the supply chain that causes a risk impact on material availability and project plans. Some of the problems in logistics are discussed as follows.
  - Proper vehicle size is not catered. Over dimensional or large transport mediums are used for smaller loads. Space in containers is not fully utilized due to which additional vessels are required, thus, increasing the cost.
  - At times, over dimensional cargo vehicles are not easily available and it causes a delay in the cargo movement for any reason which leads to an overall increase in the project cost.
  - Improper packing and loosely fitted items cause damage to the material resulting in rework.
  - Transportation may also be hindered due to the rules and regulations related to specific operating times on a particular route. Different interstate taxes have to be paid which also creates a burden on the transporter.

- Problems that occur while material inward.
    - Project sites need proper and reliable storage of material, and that is rarely available on site. A million-dollar worth of equipment and material can be at the risk of damage due to the ingress of weather.
    - A defective material that is returned to the supplier fabrication shop or manufacturing works causes project delays. The WBS or critical path is severely affected due to the nonavailability of material.
    - There is a lot of variation and correction between the schedule delivery plan and the availability of site storage. Since the plan is not regularly updated, the additional material that arrives on the site often creates wastage.
- Problems in storage plan.
    - There is so much material that is not part of schedule and it keeps getting accumulated. That needs additional space and increased cost of material handling equipment.
    - Changes in material supply, product orders, customer forecasts, or staffing resources can have a significant impact on project schedules to accelerate or delay project delivery. It results in missed milestones, or rework, and cost overruns.
    - In many cases, material availability will change as the project proceeds. Shipments may be delayed, reduced, or may fail incoming inspections. These changes can derail a project.
    - Also, plan changes may significantly change material need dates. For example, a delay in the critical path may push the need date for a particular material. This need time has to be reflected in the supply chain if the alignment is to be maintained.

Methods to improve. The best way is to plan to get material as per sequence of execution to ensure the minimum of movement and handling.

- **Coordination of transportation.**
    - The buyer team, before asking the vendor team to include the cost of shipping, should have data for bargaining from the market. The team should assess the unit cost, time, and availability of the type of vehicle, and the bulk density and criticality of goods transported.
    - The project manager should even see the possibility of picking up the material under their logistic department.
    - The team should ensure incorporating storage requirements in vehicle design specifications and prevent over dimension vehicles to be used against a regular size vehicle.
- **Have a good material coordinator.** The project manager should decide to keep a materials' coordinator who would oversee the delivery of material as per needed requirement. He will give signal/warning to suppliers for arranging transportation. He will be completely responsible for the following issues:
    - Planning of site activities
    - Deliveries of materials to the site
    - Some changes to the detailed design
    - Rework during the construction stage
    - Site working conditions
    - Transportation of materials within the site boundary
    - Avoidance of stocking on site
    - Avoidance of wastage of materials
    - Avoidance of missing deliveries and returned goods
    - Decreased damage during construction
    - Directing the site team
    - Organizing waste disposal
    - Coordinating the use of standard materials handling equipment
    - Organizing weekly meetings to schedule materials deliveries

- Monitoring the delivery of sensitive materials
- Evaluating changes in the master schedule
- Taking action if changes in material supply are required
- Ensuring proper timelines of the logistics

- **Coordination of subcontractors, supplier, and manufacturer for the inward planning of material.**
  - The project manager should call the subcontractors and make them interact with the designer team to confirm and agree on a buildability approach. The aim is how to minimize production/fabrication at the site and transport modular kits on the site.
  - It should also be decided that there would be sharing of management information system (MIS) data of the status of work with internal manufacturers/suppliers. The production of that items can also be halted as space is a constraint at supplier's end as well.
  - All should agree to the schedule of inward of material as per the WBS to prevent wastage or loss of time.

- **Storage plan**
  - To enable the complete delivery planning, the project manager should ask his team to prepare the storage plan package-wise.
  - The store team should have some advance information in the form of a look-ahead plan for the time of the arrival of all packages. The team should ensure that storage is ready for incoming material and assists in the utilization of space.

TEAM MANAGEMENT AT HEAD OFFICE

Team management is necessary for a project just as much as it is for any organization. The project manager should know that one odd representative from Engineering, Procurement, Construction, and

Planning would be attached to his team. The Quality, Safety, and Store team members should also be connected.

There should be a clearly defined role and command control for each person. A lot of team-building exercises are conducted in the armed forces to integrate a new outfit.

Project team management. Likewise, the challenge is integrating the project people into a team. However, the project manager should know that there will be several problems that will have to be overcome:

- The team is not clear on command and control issues. They have dual reporting and are confused between two bosses, that is, functional boss and projects manager.
- There is a conflict of loyalties between a permanent structure of the organization and temporary attachment to the project team.
- Delays by respective departments are not accounted for. Functional HOD blames the project team and vice versa. The team is often under conflict.
- New team members who join have their ideas of expectation of delivery and execution. Consequently, there is disagreement with the preexisting team members. They see each other as threat in terms of acquiring more space and role.
- There is no proper handling/taking over if a team member is leaving the project or changing over to another project.
- Functional managers often move team members without informing the project managers and vice versa. Suddenly there is a vacuum with no carry forward of information of any pending task to be completed.

Disruptive Methods

The project manager should go to the respective functional HODs. They must mutually agree to use each team member with a shared vision of the company project. The aim is to use each team member according to his/her strength and focus on his/her weaknesses with proper training and mentorship. The team members' roles and responsibilities are also defined.

A good dual command and control interface under both functional heads and project managers should be also streamlined. There should be clarity on a decision-making matrix for departmental issues. A time frame should also be agreed within which disputed points have to be resolved. This helps in progress of work.

Tuckman method. The project manager should remember the well-known Tuckman method which every new and old team member has to go through.

- **Forming.** The team members are made to interact with each other. They are usually polite to each other initially and try to know each other and the task ahead.
- **Storming.** This is the tricky part of group development where the internal struggle for power starts.
    o First, it starts politely with rational disagreement, refusing to see each other's viewpoints. Each other's boundaries are stretched and challenged for more space. Everyone thinks that their contribution is the most important, and if given more space, they will deliver more.
    o The project manager decides to allow them to find their way and assess for themselves how much they can drive each other.
- **Norming.** The project manager decides to take them for an outdoor training exercise where they would perform tasks together in small teams.
    o He contacts one of his ex-army friends who is running such capsules of outdoor training in Lonavala hill station. The team participates in many group activities including trekking and starts appreciating each other.
    o He makes sure that the people who were constantly having issues of the power struggle between themselves shared the same tent and worked together in the camp.

- **Performing.** The project manager knows now that the team members are clear in their role, responsibilities, and interconnections and will start performing like a winning team to get timely results.

Ground Rules of Working

The project manager should lay down some ground rules about how the team members will behave, conduct, and commit to each other.

- **The habit of commitment and feedback.** There should be an agreement on engagement with each other and feedback of action. If a promise is failing, there should still be mutually agreeable new timings.
- **Decision-making matrix chart.** The project manager should also formulate a decision-making tree for issues. He should make clear which issues the team hierarchy will solve and what he will micromanage himself.

COMMUNICATION MANAGEMENT AT HEAD OFFICE

Issues should not only come up in the weekly or monthly meetings, as that would cause more delay. Instead, a daily update on the progress of the project helps solve issues as and when they happen.

In armed forces, there is a culture of daily reporting by the ground operation commander to his next level giving details of what all happened. The project manager remembers how evening reporting is a ceremony and an event every day where even formation commander gives a report of his complete formation to the next level formation commander.

Project communication. Unlike in armed forces, the culture of feedback of any activity from one level of leadership to the next level is diluted in corporate projects. That is why maximum issues remain unsolved and decision-making is slow. Now, with the ERP and Oracle system working, there is a lot of focus on information on almost every event. There is no dearth of information. The issue is how to use that information. Following are the issues that need to be addressed:

- Many times the reports and returns are duplicated. The same report is received from different sources and keeps getting shared among stakeholders.
- There are also some reports within departments that do not get shared with the other departments. There is so much secrecy within departments that it seems some independent, secret mission is on, forgetting the fact that there is one common project where all are stakeholders. Critical interconnection gets lost as departments fear that some kind of delay in information of their own deliverable will put them in a bad light. They are reluctant to share their work information, and that creates a big vacuum.
- There should be less number of reports but it should cover all details and be shared with all departments. Any department should have the right to point out weak signals as that signal will be the indicator that something is going wrong which must be corrected.

Solution to improve. Identify the information needs of all stakeholders in the project. Have bare minimum reports, but those that are suited to more audiences at the same time. Define the form of MIS report, photographs needed, video conferencing, or daily telephonic reporting. Define who will deliver the information and its frequency.

- **Regular cost reporting.** The project manager should have regular reporting on the following:
  - Reasons for changes in the baseline.
  - Variance analysis reports for improving/preventing it again.
  - Status of contracted work versus uncommitted work.

- Schedule slippages, reasons, and cost impact with COPQ.
- Evaluation of budget expenses and auditable documents.
- Review of pending logged issues of risk that could change or increase the cost.

- **Regular schedule reporting.** He should also have scheduled reporting.
  - Review of backlog and look-ahead report.
  - Aligning it with updated master schedule.
  - Details of unfinished work and finish dates after due consultation with subcontractors.
  - Aligning it with pending resolutions and resources.
  - Having a relook at the critical path and addressing issues if changed.
  - The project end date should be verified, and all resources and solutions should be aligned with it.
- **Lesson-learned report.** In armed forces, there is a debriefing after every action; it is called an after-action report. Similarly, as shown in Table 6.2, the project manager should seek a lesson-learned report after every milestone/phase change in the project life cycle. The processes should be evaluated to remove nonvalue-adding steps in the planning to execution stages of every activity.
- **Dashboards.** The project manager should also meet with the IT team to decide on dashboards for top management. This will enable real-time information so that execution is visible. Also, dashboards are easy to monitor and control.

Table 6.2. Debriefing Report

Category of WBS	What exactly happened and how it was executed	Recommendation	Best practice take away

Source: Author's own work.

SAFETY PLANNING

The project manager should hold the opinion that safety like quality is everybody's responsibility. He should implement OSHA guidelines in letter and spirit.

In the armed forces, safety in work, be it handling weapons or driving transport or any work, is adequately monitored by leadership at all levels. The leader ensures making drills and following SOP for every work. He/she also ensures accountability by regular surprise checks and audits if the SOP is not followed. Recalling an incident, after a road accident caused by some driver, the Commanding Officer of the unit was also called to give a witness statement and explain what steps were ensured to verify driver training. In other words, leaders do not escape questions if something goes wrong even at lower levels. Safety is the prime duty of every leader to ensure it happens down the chain.

Safety in project. To maintain same safety standards, the project manager also should have qualified safety officers posted at site. However, he may face the following issues which he should tackle by raising the level of the management.

- Funds are not planned in time for the release of safety equipment. To solve this, he should ensure the following:
    - The cost of safety should be covered as a separate cost under training and site overhead expenses.
    - The budget should include the cost of one safety officer and at least one or two trainees in a large project. The yardstick is one safety officer for every 75 craftsmen. Any project work having more than 25 workers and a duration over two weeks should have a safety officer.
    - The budget should also include training cost by a specialist and to buy proper personal protective equipment (PPE), safety belts/tools, and gloves/helmets/goggles, etc. The subcontractors should also be made clear that they will enter site only with PPE inspected.

- Training needs are not addressed in the beginning. The safety officer is himself not trained, and there is a lack of ownership.
  - The project manager should ensure that the safety officer should report to the head office. That will enable him/her to ensure the safety of site against any lapses or loose norms by the site incharge.
  - The projects manager should ask the safety officer to plan a training lecture for people to anticipate safety issues. This will prevent any stoppages of work and risk to lives.
  - The safety officer should own the accurate status report even if gets unpopular as people may not like it. The project manager should make sure that the safety officer would be the one who will call the shots to ensure that all comply with the safety rules. Nobody including the project manager should ever question him if he stops any work owing to safety issues.

PLANNING CHANGE MANAGEMENT

In a project organization, especially matrix setup, there are so many approvals needed for a simple thing. That is why when there is a change in plan, the delay is mostly due to many technical leaders trying to add value to review and file documents leading to bureaucracy. The project manager should avoid this.

War-gaming always caters for the unexpected during execution with an alternative and contingency plan. The rules for taking decision are mostly with the ground commander. It is trusted that whatever decision he will make will be in line with the next leader's strategic aim. It is also more efficient as a single person, say a CO, is making all decision and at a speed that aids in conducting operations.

Handling the Change in Projects

On the contrary, the baselines for scope, schedule, cost, and quality are confirmed in the tactical plan. The project manager makes a matrix chart specifying who will approve a change in the project at what level.

He/she identifies other members and stakeholders who need to be involved in specific change activities. He/she also clarifies the decision-making time and methods of communication. The procedure to monitor, analyze, and control the impact of the proposed change is also agreed upon by all stakeholders.

RED TEAM FOR EVALUATION

In war-gaming, there is always a red team, that is, the enemy who is tasked to find gaps and loopholes in the blue team's plans. That way the plan of the blue team keeps getting better as it is finally vetoed by the enemy mind-set.

Audit of the Plan

The project manager should call the red team! In armed forces, the red team is the mock enemy who is tasked to break into our plans and defeat us. That way we could identify the gaps leading to VUCA situations. It is warlike situation, all brilliant minds asking another team to beat their plan before they get to the target area.

Similarly, the project manager asks his red team to dig deep further for an issue that may pose a future risk. He should make his team line up all threats and risks that remained unsolved after the meeting with the stakeholders. It is best to have a complete situational awareness into the potential mission ahead.

The team should break the purpose apart from looking for more weakness and plan for redundancies. The team should keep peeling into layers until they do not have anywhere to go. Once the team has got backup for every item on the must-have listed, they are ready to move onto next phase.

Reassess resource deployment. The team should identify people and services and backup and administration along with other resources. They should match these assets up with threats to have a quick response to any change in the situation.

Plan reserve at site. The project manager mentioned in a war we do not attack without reserve and the reserve is employed where the enemy is making inroads into their plans. In a similar way, the project team also has to prepare for reserve labor and funds and keep them on standby to ensure that approvals do not delay the work. Some examples to plan alternatives are as follows:

- Who is the standby contractors if the main contractor leaves the job in between?
- What if labor union issues come up?
- What if there is a mass leave during festival season?
- Customs laws and rules regarding commercial shipments are different for each country. It is better to earmark reserve fund for such contingencies where cost of shipping exceeds than what was planned earlier.

Planning for emergencies. The project manager should insist that the contingency plan should be detailed. The team can start by breaking down the WBS or activities into its smallest components, then can rank those elements by their importance, and work out the response. With the scripted response, the operation team can save time rather than running like a headless chicken.

HOW IS RACE METHODOLOGY BEING ACHIEVED?

- **Rapid work.** Collaboration has solved most of the constraints in functional departments. They are also aware of process, methods, and work instructions. The subcontractors and suppliers have been chosen to be reliable with an explicit contractual agreement to share the risk of LD and delays.

- **Absolute scope.** Every department is aware of the activities and breakdown of its tasks. The deliverable has been clearly defined at every phase so that there is no miss-out.
- **Class quality.** Quality matrices and expectations of the deliverable in every activity has been set. The expectations are to avoid rework with proper supervisions.
- **Economical cost.** Every activity has been linked to cost. Baseline value has been fixed. If there are any overruns in cost, that will be noticed.

TAKEAWAYS

It is essential for a detailed thinking and coordination of functional and other stakeholders to plan. A couple of thought processes have been discussed. It helps in proper WBS planning along with deciding the schedule, cost, and quality baselines. An integrated plan with improved processes is the key to a successful tactical plan.

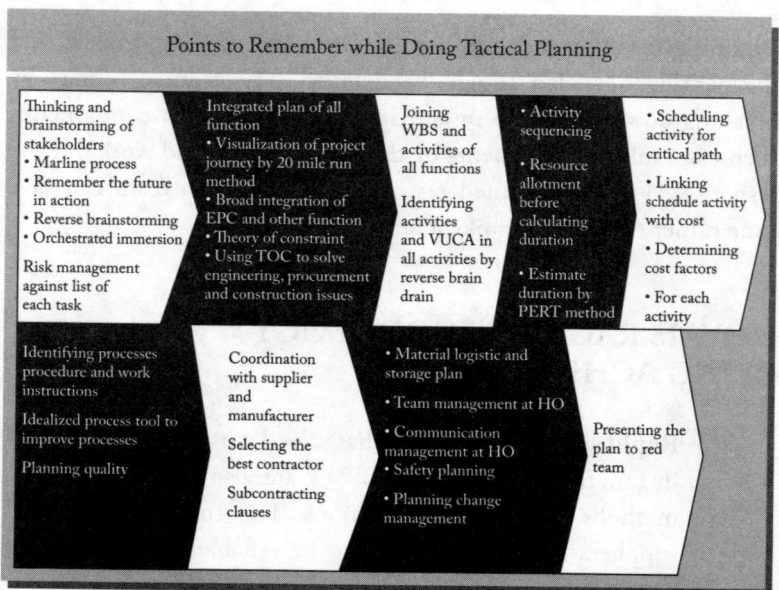

CHAPTER 7

Operational Planning to Prevent VUCA

*Working with users will help
us to respond to their needs*

—A. Wang

Operational planning is the last leg of planning undertaken by frontline or lower level managers. The focus is on driving the schedule plan with specific procedures and processes. It ensures availability and integration of production, equipment, personnel, inventory, and operations of business. Let us discuss an example to understand the different phases of planning.

The Jan Dhan Yojana launched by Prime Minister Narendra Modi is an ambitious plan for the poor of the country. The strategic plan of the Prime Minister was to ensure that the poor have basic bank accounts that would also allow an overdraft facility of ₹5,000 and a RuPay debit card with an inbuilt accident insurance cover of ₹1 lakh. The planning for the next phase is to start microinsurance and pension plans.

It is a good strategy to bring the underprivileged under the banking financial umbrella. It would provide a means for people in the rural areas to start saving and moving away from traditional modes of saving such as buying land. It would also increase the country's capital formation. Moreover, it should allow people to get credit loans without falling into the crutches of moneylenders. It would also allow government schemes to reach poor people with bank transfers that are accountable and traceable, thereby ensuring that the money meant for them is not hijacked by corrupt middlemen.

The tactical plan in this case of the RBI management is to provide banking service in rural unbanked areas under financial inclusion. The accounts are "no frills" accounts with either "NIL" or minimal balance. It also reduced the formalities of a KYC account for the rural folks.

OPERATIONAL PLAN

The dream and vision of the Prime Minister were made possible by a team of banking and business correspondents who took banking to the doorsteps of rural households. They were the real foot soldiers who took technology to the remote corners of the country.

The media and political parties scoffed at them as there was no money but a futile exercise to open an account for the poor. But when demonetization happened, black money hoarders tried to use these account holders' accounts to deposit millions of rupees. Some of these accounts came under CBI surveillance and some accounts' balances soared because of these deposits. They even got relationship managers earmarked as their accounts had now become VIP accounts.

But this aside, how did the operational team operate? They worked in the fields through mobile vans equipped with hardware, moving from villages to villages. They were provided information and communication technology (ICT) to carry out transactions for the smart card holders at their doorsteps through biometric authentication. They also established kiosk that provides cardless solution; account holders could operate the accounts by account numbers as well as Aadhaar numbers.

In other words, operations were carried out by the fast-moving team in liaison with the tactical and strategic planning team at the head office. So what are the ingredients of an operational plan?

BASIC INGREDIENTS OF AN OPERATIONAL PLAN

The young major arrived with his men at his camp early morning at 0400 hours. The dog which he had adopted, Pedro, was happy to see him. His buddy helper was waiting for him with a cup of tea and hot water.

Last night was a terrible firefight but a successful one. They had laid ambush on hard intelligence against some terrorist in the dense forest. Three terrorists were killed, and weapons with a lot of other stores had been recovered. They had waited for a couple of weeks to lay the trap for the terrorists. They were lured to come on this track making them believe that they were safe by making a lot of noise on other tracks as diversionary tactics.

The officer's routine was mostly night operations with his men, and in his absence, during day time he had given the administration responsibility of his camp to his trusted junior commissioned officer. He used to leave every evening with his men by 8 pm after darkness, do patrolling or lay an ambush, and arrive back to his camp by 4 am. After coming back, he used to catch up on sleep and then the first thing he used to do was check on administration safety and welfare issues of his camp with concerned stakeholders by walking around every inch of the camp.

It was followed by a detailed debriefing of his operation the previous night and planning for the next operation, that is, counterterrorism activities with other stakeholders in the headquarter. Any resource issues were coordinated to ensure all activities are adequately supported.

Now, the operations are in a hostile territory and likely to be controlled by a lot of people at the headquarter. That is when VUCA problems start arising when the operation is dictated by a bureaucratic executive who is not clear about the ground conditions. To ensure that real workable solutions are implemented against any internal or external VUCA environment, leadership at the site with a winning team is of utmost importance. Allow them to adopt the simple approach rather enforcing them with complex solutions.

The essential ingredients of an operational plan are primarily leadership at the site, a winning team, ensuring proper administration, safety, hygiene, etc., to operate. Regular planning on a daily basis for the next sets of tasks, and most importantly having a proper debriefing of the day-to-day routine affairs is essential. There could be a lot of decentralization and convergence of planning with other functions. Day-to-day operational planning by leadership at the front end enables schedule to be modified as per the operating situation to obtain results within the cost and quality parameters.

FRONT-END LEADERSHIP

Junior team leaders lead operations from the front. Hence their selection and training is of utmost importance.

In the armed forces, apart from young officers, the JCOs are extremely self-driven. A JCO handles all aspects of camp management, security, and discipline apart from training the cadets and coordinating all the intelligence collation. The JCO also debriefs the officer in charge about the day-to-day matters and about the plans for the next move.

Site leadership in projects. Similar kind of leadership is expected from the site incharge. He/She should lead the execution work of the project by workers and other engineers. It is better to choose a wise junior leader. The site incharge should be a person who has learned the way up doing various duties at the site or shop floor. The skills arm them with better assessment or judgment of an issue considering all perspectives.

Leadership Skills Needed at Site

- **Self-driven.** Site leaders should be acutely aware of the job at hand and should constantly update themselves. All managers should be conscious that whatever they do, they have those quality instructions at the back of their minds. The team should be movers and shakers to solve VUCA issues on their own without looking back. They must keep moving on site to foresee VUCA problems and take preventive action.
- **Team management.** The site leaders should be very efficient in controlling the junior team and getting in the trenches with them to work. Then only they will come to know the positives and the real weak spots of the team members. Accordingly, they can also train the staff to solve VUCA problems quickly without much supervision.
- **Learn to appreciate.** The site incharge must share the praise of good work done by junior engineers or workers and not take the credit for it. That way the operational team will work with more trust as their work is being recognized and they will get their due.
- **Transparency and accountability.** Internal control should be built at site work by following SOP, drills, and safety checks to prevent VUCA. At the same time, an accountable culture should be cultivated so that all team members are ethical and transparent about all expenses at the site.
- **Emotionally stable.** The site incharge must also have a balanced emotional quotient. It is fine to let the site team know how he/she feels. At the same he/she should be able to diffuse the tension with a good sense of humor. Keeping things "light" aids productivity. If one has to fly with the eagles, then one must "think lightly."
- **Feedback to head office.** The site incharge should hold nothing back from the project manager and top management in the review. Stating facts and not giving excuses and

exposing all warts and pimples at the right time will help save the company's reputation. There should be learning from reviews if it is based on facts and that is a way to prepare for future VUCA issues.

IMBIBING SKILLS AND CHARACTER IN TEAM

A group of soldiers in an army is a set of people aligned together toward a common goal. At times in counterinsurgency, a hostile population surrounds the post, and a terrorist attack is always imminent. It is, hence, important that everybody is highly operationally trained. The team is alert around the clock to attack any terrorist that tries to enter the camp. Everybody carries a weapon all the time even while attending nature's call or while sleeping to tackle any VUCA situation from terrorists. There is a lot of rehearsal for quick natural reaction to fight with speed and effectiveness.

On similar lines, in a project, a lean and trained active team is the best. Too many people at site create confusion and chaos. Every member of the site team should be a solid contributor; an all-rounder can fit in different tasks along with a specific work. Every person should have a sense of mission and understanding of priorities.

The following qualities are desirable in a project team:

- **Candor.** In the armed forces, it is said that men in the field cannot mess around with little white lies, hidden secrets, and little games. Similarly, communication among team members on a project or with their head office should be clean, simple, whole, and accurate.
- **Commitment.** It is first to your team, then to the site crew, then to the site incharge, and then to the organization. Trust and security are the central foundations for teamwork and coordination.
- **Decisiveness.** It is studying your alternatives to do a difficult work and carefully selecting the best course of action keeping the safety of people and material in mind.

- **Dependability.** It is doing those tasks that you have been told to do and those that you have promised to do in a complete manner.
- **Competence.** It is the basis for the confidence which establishes commitment since pattern and strength of trust and mutual support are formed by where power lies and in what degree.

A few tricks for a winning team:

- The crew can be given caps with the word RACE written on them to remind everyone to work with speed, absolute scope, quality, and economically.
- Write the team's mission on a chart and paste it where everybody can see. For example, if the mission is to get a bonus from the customer, then it is understood that to get the bonus everybody has to work hard.
- Post the vision statement at the site and head office so that the team sees it at all times.
- At some sites, people have innovatively used tricks such as whoever fails in the commitment or does not meet the deadline will get sweets for everyone. This reminds the person of the failed commitment and allows for some fun and sweets to be distributed.
- Games and movies at weekends help in clearing tension between team members to some extent. Birthday announcements on the notice board for everyone from the site incharge to the labor involved and a small 10-minute celebration at the end of day lightens everybody's mood.
- Best worker award for the month among labors and best safety award among contractor supervisors can be instituted.
- Resolving pay issues or any HR issues among all site team members.
- Training lecture or sharing of work experience can be organized for all team members.

- Mock drill of safety, evacuation, etc., can be held to determine the performance of the team and how each member contributed.
- Cleaning the site along with firefighting practice every week or fortnight can be organized.
- A payment system for three months should be followed. All the contractor bills are to be submitted in the first month. The second month is the processing period, and payment should be issued at the start of the third month. The bill submission should be error proof and cleared in the first processing only.

Support the team with clear role and training:

- **RACI chart.** A winning team functions best when it is clear about its role. Have a RACI chart for every team member which defines the job description, that is, technical duties and work methodology including nontechnical skill requirements.

Activity	Responsible	Accountable	Consultative/Informed

- **Training of operational teams.** Train the blue-collar workers or unskilled workers for the job as well as for multiskilling to use them in emergency VUCA situations. A certificate can be given at the end of the training to boost their self-esteem and confidence. An example of such training is a welding or rigging certification. Similarly, training of supervisors is also important.
- **Work methodology.** In the armed forces, good JCOs set an example for the soldiers to follow. The site supervisor should also be trained in lean methods and material management to prevent waste and ensure correct and accurate use of material. The method of work and the quality parameters can be printed on small pocket cards that are easy to carry on the person. It will ensure that when in doubt, the supervisor can look up the work methodology and be sure so that no rework is required.

- **Establish KPIs.** It is for third-party vendors and contractors as they would need to be aligned with the main project team. Monitoring of labor is another crucial factor as contractors need to provide labor on designated dates to avoid delays. There should be a backup plan also for every team member's absenteeism or a reserve contractor for providing additional labor if they are needed.

CENTER OF GRAVITY OF THE OPERATION

Center of gravity is what Clausewitz called "the hub of all power and movement" on which everything depends, the point at which all our energies should be directed. In counterinsurgency operations, the center of gravity is the valley with a thick jungle covering the tracks coming from the enemy side. It facilitates the movement of terrorists coming into the Indian Territory. Once the terrorists cross this jungle they would easily merge with the local population therefore more patrolling is required there and if an ambush has to be laid, then the jungle in the valley should be the center of gravity for such operations and that would control VUCA conditions.

Likewise, the site layout where the project is to be executed is the center of gravity and should be the complete focus of every management executive either in the head office or at the site. If the site location facilitates easy administration and foolproof safety and security, there will be ease of operations. However, some VUCA issues can prevent proper project work such as:

- Approval of budget to establish the site is delayed for any reason. Either the customer has not given an advance, or our system transfer takes weeks and months.
- There is no proper layout of the site. The roads and tracks are not adequate, and traffic comes to a standstill especially during rains. The material gets dumped all over the place leading to safety issues of both material and manpower.
- The material is shifted haphazardly and then damage starts. Accumulation of waste is another factor that can be avoided.

- Safety issues among workers are ignored, for example, labor working without proper training in safety and security gear; sometimes women workers complain that wearing helmets and gloves or shoes is cumbersome.
- 5S and regular cleaning of the area do not take place; the place very soon gets out of control.
- The initial living condition of people gets ignored; attention is not paid by contractors to the labor colonies as they want profits by preventing essential amenities. Hygiene and sanitation plan is also ignored. The place gets littered with scraps, wastes of all kinds, leading to the outbreak of diseases.
- Security of material against theft; there is no proper boundary fence for material, making it susceptible to all kinds of mishandling.
- In summer conditions, the temperatures soar high and thus dehydration cases increase. Labor working at heights is most at risk if not properly trained and lifeline not suitably erected.

Essential Information to Establish Site Center of Gravity

The project manager should assess the following information to establish a good site:

- Weather conditions and the cycle of monsoons and temperatures with wind direction during summers and winters.
- Road, rail, and air used for smooth supply chain movement and for the movement of people. Public road and public transport arrangements.
- Location and type of water resources and sewer lines along with waste water discharge.
- Security, especially in insurgency areas.

Site Layout

The following considerations should be kept in mind for the site plan:

- Dividing the space in the site for inward stocking and appropriate utilization. Storage needs have to be considered in a phased manner for the material that is going to come inward.
- Job office location and layout to be formalized. Shipping containers to be used for offices.
- Plan for fencing and security guards against theft. CCTVs to be fitted.
- Soil testing is part of the site project work and should be done through proper lab procedures.
- Existing drainage system connected to the main pipeline should be cleaned. Additional drainage work to prevent flood and loss of material.
- Proper route inward and outward for heavy material and small transport. Plan for regulating traffic and proper records of inward material and resources to be maintained with the timing of entry and exit.
- Earmark fabrication yard and good electrical connections, tools, and fixtures with scrap disposal arrangements. It should be preferably near the site erection work to save transport cost.
- Scrap management and waste disposal area and arrangements, keeping in mind environmental conditions.

Administration Arrangements

- All the subcontractors should be fully deployed with complete legal and IR documentation.
- The labor colony should be comfortable with hygiene and sanitation facilities. Their living areas and working areas

should be segregated and movement to and fro should be prevented.
- Mess, toilets, a first-aid room with a doctor or nursing facilities, and recreational facilities will go a long way to keeping workers motivated. Glucose and water arrangements, rest, and recouping medical facilities should be created.
- Training and measures to prevent fire hazards should be provided. Lecture on safety working and equipment should be organized.
- Proper security verification of employees and transport with the discipline of traffic should also be addressed.
- Civil administration approvals in environmental clearance and safety audits should be completed.
- Power connection with short cables should be made systematically. Map of the existing plant or infrastructure layout to ascertain underground pipelines or cables should also be ascertained.
- Communication tower and approvals should be taken timely so that regular communication and ERP starts.
- A tool store room should be made from where special purpose tools are issued on a daily basis, cleaned after work, and kept safe. The necessary basic tools are allowed to be held with workers. The tool store manager should be responsible for taking requirements of special purpose machines and dividing the usage time between different users as per the priority of the WBS.
- The requirements of material handling equipment like Hydra should be collated a day in advance and time should be fixed for its various usages like unloading/loading of equipment or shifting to site work. The aim should be to use the Hydra to full capacity by dividing work as per priority. An idle equipment incurs cost as the contractor driver apparently tries to save fuel.
- Safety and condition of material handling equipment, tools, and belts should be assessed every day.

- Proper daily maintenance of equipment after work, such as air compressors, step-down transformers, and fabrication welding machines should be there with light fixtures, etc.

Material Storage Planning

- There is always a space constraint at the site. The material that is to be inwarded has to match with the sequence of the WBS.
- It is better to use an ERP system to allow material inwards. If the material is visible from the supplier's end to transportation to its usage, better storage and preservation can be planned.
- Store infrastructure should be completed within three months and it should be ensured that necessary resources such as tarpaulins, concrete sleepers blocks, outer area, and proper soil foundation to store material during rains are also done. Maximum material gets damaged during rains.
- Inward and outward documents of material movement should be done so that there is a proper record of what has come and what has gone out for any work or due to issues to the site construction team.
- Storing material properly and recording the location ensures easy traceability. Experimenting should be done with bar code and radio frequency identification (ID) methods of supply tracking and management.
- Timely information of proper tonnage and timing should be send to the site. That will enable timely positioning of the special tackle tools and equipment needed. It will help in coordinating the flow of materials as per the capacity plan.
- A separate scrap yard facilitates cut pieces to be stored after fabrication work. They can be reused but proper record entries should be made.
- It is best to make subcontractors also establish their own storage rooms at site and consumables issued to them in advance. They can store them, and site engineers can track

the usage. Further, the workers can get consumables issued directly.
- The central store can track surplus and take it back from the subcontractor. This allows the reduction of real movement in daily transportation and a system of Kanban can be established to restock the subcontractor store from the main store. A proper reordering system can be followed and usage can be tracked.

Safety Aspects

The safety officer is positioned at the site to analyze the risk associated with all kinds of operational work on a daily basis.

- A safety officer should ensure that all workers are following drills and SOP as per work requirements, such as:
  - Working at heights and near pits or trenches
  - Using a scaffolding
  - Electric fitting work
  - Machine and Hydra movements
- Training for the workers by specialized agencies and a safety exercise every morning should be conducted; it should be a repetition of instructions. If the workers hear the instruction every morning or they take turns to read these out to everybody, the workers will start living the safety education every moment.
- Training of OSHA should be made compulsory. OSHA Act covers most private-sector employers and their workers. There are several training, compliance assistance, and health and safety regulations which are also audited by OSHA auditors. It also ensures proper documentation and records of the working condition.
- Compliance of other factory and labor acts that are related to injury and illness that require medical treatment should be ensured. Record of these incidences is often compared

to person-hours during the jobs, during the year. It gives an indication of safety standards.
- Insurance premiums should be paid by subcontractors or the team and customer as decided. It enables a family of an injured or dead employee/worker to get compensated adequately in an uncalled incident.
- Proper fencing for the area out of bound should be displayed, particularly when people are working at heights. Posters and written cards in a language the labor understands should be put along the dangerous site locations.
- Most importantly, accountability culture of supervision of safety has to be established. Most accidents happen because the site incharge does not ensure the checklist of the workplace. Daily rounds should pinpoint issues of security overlooked by supervisors. The safety protocols should not be compromised.
- An ambulance and tie up with a hospital nearby should be arranged. First-aid kits with medicines should be kept for emergencies.
- Use of machine for handling Hydra equipment should be under surveillance. There is regular inspection of wire rope and lifting belts. Test certificate of Hydra is verified. Analysis of lifting calculation, weight marking on equipment, compared to load carrying of Hydra machines should be done.

CONTROL AND COORDINATION AMONG ALL OPERATIONAL STAKEHOLDERS

For any operation to be successful, it is imperative for all stakeholders of the strategic and tactical plans to be in sync; otherwise, there will be different responses to the same VUCA problems.

While decentralization is advocated in operations, it is important that for the success of the operation, a proper coordination with the head office is done to understand the tactical and strategy plan. In counterinsurgency operations, the intelligence is of utmost importance and should be shared and coordinated between different teams that are operating in the same terrain. However, at times, due to unnecessary secrecy, timely intelligence and information are not shared among security forces and that helps the terrorists in getting away. So that is why coordination is important.

Operational coordination. In a similar way, there are many stakeholders working to support the operational team. All stakeholders at the site and head office should align with each other for better coordination and faster work.

Interaction with all the subcontractors and suppliers is required to mutually align toward the project goals. A complete understanding of the contract should be established. All should be informed of the time-related clauses and baseline schedules.

The process of financial closure after certified deliverables should be defined. The completion date is linked with the payment condition. Incentive plans based on the achievement of certain milestones is also discussed. Any exclusion or specific constraints applicable to Extension of Time (EOT) should be on the record. There should be reportable visibility that the contractor team was not responsible for seeking more time to do a work. That will ensure fair play while billing for the work.

Resource management. The operation's success is dependent on how resources are managed. All site engineers should have resource management capabilities. They should have an accurate understanding of resource availability in current and future workloads. They should learn to work around constraints and they should be able to make an informed decision on fluctuating needs. Supply and demand should be aligned to optimize critical resources. This will help move from reactive to proactive management.

Internal Teams for Coordination and Monitoring

- **Monitoring manpower capacity.** There will be a fluctuation in workforce needs with variations in the WBS due to any reason. The project manager can assign the administration

manager to assess the monthly requirement of the workforce. The administration manager can attend meetings to review status changes and ensure alignment of supply of workforce as per requirement.
- **Monitoring supplier and subcontractors.** The buyer and engineers always get to know procedural and cultural problems in supplier and remote subcontractor teams. The site team should help the supplier and subcontractors with that kind of support to move the project forward.
- The material planner for the site has to work with the supplier to synchronize their supply deliveries with the WBS.
- The site engineers also should analyze subcontractor performance and delivery capability and execution.
- The site incharge should ensure that daily planning is related to progress with visibility and synchronization.
- A feedback mechanism should be put in place through assessments to validate schedule performance decisions and activities.
- Schedule subcontractor coordination meetings should have a specific agenda with interactive, honest communications. There should be objective evaluation and open communication with subcontractors regarding what is bothering them.
- It is always better to discuss mutual support with them to align the schedule and coordinate the project. It should be discussed with them how they can break bottlenecks and mitigate the risk increasing cost or causing delays elsewhere.

Issues in Operational Environment

The success of the operation depends upon continuous awareness of what is going wrong and what can prevent our success.

Company commanders in the armed forces regularly assess local conditions. It helps them anticipate issues that will come up with different stakeholders, that is, local people, politicians, and other friendly security forces deployed in the area. Likewise, project managers should instruct operational teams to regularly analyze any issues that might be left/overlooked by functional HODs or not thought of by the team in the head office. The operational team is best placed to assess conditions firsthand and plug any gaps.

- Site engineers and planners must be able to accurately predict potential stakeholder impediments to teamwork by analyzing who is not able to meet their commitment or timelines. Reasons should be analyzed through a continuous feedback loop. That would counter any unforeseen delays using some alternative actions. In their daily rounds and interactions, site engineers or planners must identify what obstacles could come up on a day-to-day basis and make alternative plans and solutions to minimize the potential impact of an immediate risk.
- Engineers and other planners should not allow any adverse stakeholder ability to influence project mobility. They have to put in place proactive measures before any stakeholder causes any negative impact. This may include a bit aggressive action to align him by a constant feedback loop. If prevention fails, then it is best to maneuver negative forces by straightaway bypassing routine bureaucratic channels to avoid impediments to project mobility if this is viable within the scheme of the maneuver. At times, it is best to offset any risk givers in the form of stakeholders causing obstacles/impediments by any means. Start going to their bosses or escalating timely or coordinating beforehand so that there is an open support.
- The site team should ensure survivability and other protection measures that will deny any VUCA problems the ability to inflict more damage. The response should be according to the extent of harm. It must be scalable, flexible, and adaptable to problems that will come. It includes a well-developed information system in place to see the effect.

Reassessing Local Threat and Intelligence at the Operational Level

- The local problems that affect the daily working routine are financial threats by a key supplier/contractor, social risks, political risks, environmental issues, or regulatory problems.
- It is good to do a risk analysis of the project and ask questions like "What opportunities are available?" "What are the benefits?" "What are their risks?" "What consequences?" You could describe them with "If…, then…" statements and group them under categories, such as funding, safety, schedule, and so on.

After that the team should address the issues that increase the level of risk. The team should assess both probability and impact of risks and forecast the expected value to mitigate it. They should also prioritize the values and develop candidate management actions to enhance opportunities and reduce risks.

OPERATIONAL PLANNING APPROACH

- In the armed forces, operational commanders are given enough autonomy to plan the ground-level operations. The headquarter at the battalion level and brigade level continually review and update the company commander on terrorist information that they get from various intelligence sources and satellite communications. That enables him as the company commander to modify his approach to lay an ambush or send a patrol party in his area by the company operational planning.
- The operational plan ensures that every day there has to be a particular task which the team has to carry out and give a feedback about how it was aiming to the overall objectives. The plan of daily activities and sub-activities comes from the site team. That way the site team took responsibility of the

daily plan as it was also more realistic as per actual conditions. More about this has been discussed in last planner method later in this book.

The operational decisive points (milestones). The schedule is divided into certain decisive points called milestones.

- In between each decisive point or milestone are several nodes along the LOO.
- Each node has several linked activities in sequence as per the event list made during tactical planning and lined with the node by an operation identifier.
- Each work attribute is defined in precise detail. There should be a job description for each event. The task description should also be in sufficient detail to ensure that the project team members understand what work is required to be completed.

Resources identified for every activity or work. The site incharge and site engineer should make an operational plan for each event.

- Who will do the work?
- Location of the activity to be done?
- Resources needed for doing the activity?
- What will be the sequence of the event in the schedule development and handing over parameters?
- What is the deliverable that should fall within quality parameters?
- What defines the business as part of the accepted deliverable so that it is not repeated as rework?
- What are the list of milestones/decisive points to be achieved?

Ownership of activity. To have clear ownership of each scope of work at the operational level, it is important that the site team is made aware of the following aspects:

- Vision, mission, and objective of the project and broadly the strategic and tactical plan to achieve this.

- Every member of the site team should have a broad understanding of the contract clauses and quality standards to achieve it. It is also better to be on the same page with the customer about what exactly is the scope at every stage of the work and have a clear understanding much in advance to iron out any issue of work that is not included in the scope.
- The beginning and end of work should be clear for each subcontractor. For example, once the mechanical subcontractor's work complete and the electrical contractor's work starts, there should be clear handing over of each subcontractors' work, where it begins and where it should end. The contractors also have issues of removal of debris, the safety of material, and upkeep of 5S. These matters should be addressed in the contract scope so that they are owners of such responsibilities including storage of material.
- Rework and delayed scope penalties as combined and joint ownership between the concerned stakeholders should be addressed, so that no contractual clauses of scope and final deliverables are missed out.

Activity methodology for each worker and supervisor. Nothing should go wrong while execution; hence, the following needs to be ensured:

- The scope of contract should be drilled down to each supervisor and labor. Each engineer, supervisor, and worker should have the clear orders of work that is expected out of them.
- The team should also ensure that the scope and deliverable are as per drawings and contractual obligations.
- All steps needed to achieve scope should be rechecked by doing a general reverse brainstorming with workforces so that they can think of problems and solutions at the same time. Real innovative solutions come from the site team.
- Each worker should know his scope of work that should finally add up to the overall day's scope of work regarding quality delivery time and cost parameters.

Identifying LOO/critical and noncritical path. The project manager should have a schedule that defines the LOO and that connects the various milestones. The operations team should monitor the critical path and prevent it from going wrong.

Connecting the LOO with the line of efforts (LOE) of other functions. The LOE is the action of support sources that help in achieving the range of efforts. For that all functions have to deliver in time and ensure there is a convergence of their particular operations to make the LOO.

Simultaneous operations. To achieve LOO and LOE, it is important that all functions in the project work simultaneously to ensure that their department deliverables converge at a point and result in the main project deliverable.

CONVERGENCE OF OPERATIONS

Project Convergence Plan

The operations team should identify LOO, LOE, and decisive points in project work to establish the end state condition. It also helps in ensuring smooth support services. The next step is a convergence of LOO with LOE as follows.

Convergence plan ensures external or internal activities to be synchronized. It is related to timely providing an engineering drawing and ensuring availability of material, parts, and equipment. All these must meet in a single location at the same time. The document delivery schedule of the engineering drawing release date should match the material procurement delivery time. For timely construction work to start, the dates for manpower availability and positioning of resources like material handling equipment should also match with dates of engineering drawing and material delivery period. The contract labor is also kept in the loop of convergence of engineering drawing, resources, and material. The workflows and processes along with logistics should align with the schedules of all departments.

- **Convergence with engineering.** To finalize drawings of the product and various project activities, convergence with the engineering team is required. Timely construction approvals have to be tracked for the manufacturing schedule.
- **Convergence with procurement.** Requisition for procurement has to be monitored and updated as per plan. The team also has to be assisted in making scope contract for suppliers so that there is no ambiguity in what is to be delivered as per specifications and drawings. The bid must be clearly understood by all. It should also specify any transition work to be done if one supplier is handing over the product to another contractor/supplier. The scope must also cover the transportation and packing clauses, and the amount of preparation needed. The loading and unloading charges and material handling normally are with the site team, but at the supplier premises, it will be within the supplier scope. Clarity should be there who will do repainting/retouching and who will bear the cost of repair if anything gets damaged or if transportation is in the supplier scope.
- **Convergence with the supplier.** The manufacturing supplier needs engineering drawing and clear procurement documents to start production. The supplier's plan for his engineering and product completion has to match with the project schedule. So liaison and efforts have to be done to align the production schedule with delivery dates of the project at the site. A chaser can be appointed for this purpose to coordinate the documentation, files, or any other issues. This has to be resolved between engineering, procurement, and manufacturing stakeholders.
- **Convergence with the manufacturing shop floor team.** Visits to the manufacturer plant or shop floor of the supplier is necessary to have a good understanding of the

manufacturing processes and how timelines and quality could be integrated with the project. Establishing contacts with the shop floor people and keeping their mobile numbers to get updates on the stages of the product delivery can be helpful. The appointed chaser can give updates on the progress on the product. The aim is to have milestones identified during the production stage by tracking to avoid delay.

- **Convergence with the project fabrication team.** The product or raw material delivery from the supplier should be linked with the fabrication schedule of the project at the site.

    o Coordinate issues of labor/material handling equipment/space management/overall work breakdown, the structure of erection and construction schedule. The team should also have regular weather updates and be tuned into the monsoon forecast as well.
    o In the case of inevitable postponement of any activity, there should be enough time to adjust or be flexible to coordinate the delivery with the next schedule.
    o Mobilization of contractor employees and equipment to handle fabrication should be coordinated with inward delivery from suppliers.

- **Convergence with the logistic team.** The team should drive the logistic plan in coordination with the project progress and with the production schedule of the finished product at the manufacturer's end or delivery of raw material at the site. The logistics officer has to coordinate the movement of equipment, material, and people to and from the work site.

    o Due to fixed high daily costs of operation, proper timelines and work output has to justify the cost. This accountability of everyday work can be ensured only if it is linked with engineering procurement.
    o If the material is not used by the team in time or not used correctly, the stuff keeps getting stored and unused material leads to storage utilization and wastage/spoilage issues.

MAKING THE SCHEDULE TIMELINE LEANER BY CCM

In the armed forces, the headquarter would give a broad weekly plan to go on a particular route for patrolling and ambush. However, the commander on the ground knows exactly which route to take to save time, and he utilizes that buffer time for some other task where results were difficult to achieve.

Resolving schedule constraint by the critical chain method (CCM). Identically, in projects, a full tactical schedule baseline plan is decided at the head office and is sent to the site team for operational execution. The site team starts the work and finds that there is a significant gap in the proposed schedule at the head office and what is going to be followed at the site. It concludes that the critical path is 100 percent incorrect. The critical path calculated at the head office is overestimated because of the following reasons:

- The wrong estimate of task duration will have a significant impact on the critical path. The software cannot judge human efficiency. Central planner, while making the tactical baselines, is not aware of how a team can work faster if ground conditions are good. So the planner overestimates the duration.
- The planner may have added contingency allowances in the duration due to industrial strikes, rain, and test failures but he missed that it was a good weather or strike was resolved in time. All this will facilitate speedy work and team will not need the extra time allotted for the task.
- There are many tasks that can be done parallel which may not have been taken into consideration by the planner.
- There could be a job that is resource dependent and resources may not be available.
- The planner also missed out the fact that at the site there are multiskilled and more experienced people who can work faster than others.

Therefore, the operational teams should handle the actual operational schedule planning by the CCM and last planner method. These methods are part of the TOC to actually determine the true fate of the project.

CCM to Replace CPM

CCM gives importance to the task completion date and allows for interim milestones in between.

Figure 7.1 shows any task duration on the x axis for the outcome on the y axis. In an ideal scenario, the job should get completed in A duration. However, the head office planner, while making the schedule and deciding the critical path, assumes that a lot of things will go wrong. So instead of thinking about A duration as a real success, he extends the period towards the right infinite. It is a long tail extending from B to C.

Now the planner has given enough leverage to the operational team to avoid any time extension issues, and he knows that even with a major disaster the executive team can complete the work comfortably till C duration. The site team will surely achieve 95 percent of the time duration till C, and the management with the client will also be happy.

Figure 7.1. Stretching of Time Duration from A to C

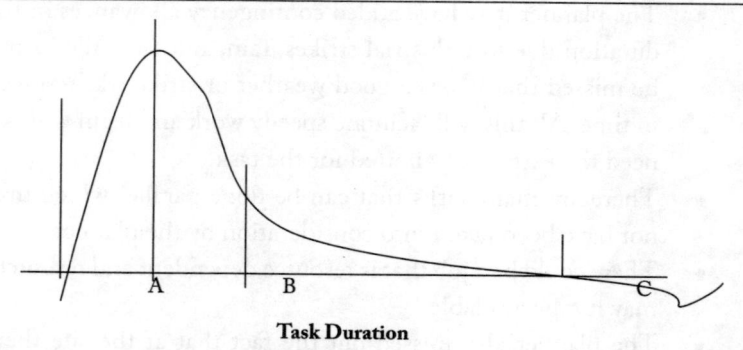

Source: Author's own work.

A project manager, however, knows the best estimate of completion, that is, B is achievable, but the planner tries to build a buffer with time C for catering to resource contentions or multitasking issues. The project manager knows that it is a comfort zone to work in C duration and still look good in the eyes of the management.

The project manager knows from experience that if resources and time are best utilized, they can shorten the critical path method (CPM) duration. So he motivates the operational team to confirm schedules in actual, that is, in time B, and not unnecessarily extend each task to make a comfortable zone of estimated duration to be time C. The challenge is to disrupt the master schedule plan by being ahead and building reverse pressure on the head office to catch up with the operational team.

There is further scope to reduce the duration as per the actual site conditions that are more favorable. That reduction is moving timeliness from C to B. This is the operational time duration which will be less than what the time estimate planner at the head office attempts to build into a critical chain schedule.

- The project manager can instruct the operational planner to reduce all activities to B and take for granted that it is the duration estimate giving a 50 percent probability of achieving this.
- In other words, if a resource is given this duration as an estimate, he will have a 50/50 chance of finishing on time.
- However, to cater for the additional time needed after 50 percent of length, they also add buffer. The buffer is the portion of the time saved by moving from C to B task estimates. It is aggregated for all activities at the end of the schedule to act as an overall "shock absorber" for the entire project. This aggregated buffer is called the "project buffer."
- The team operational plan adds back buffer from the delivery date into the schedule at the strategic point. The size of buffer accounts for uncertainty in the duration of the chain of activities leading up to that buffer. Once buffer program

activities are determined, planned activities are scheduled for planned latest start and end dates.
- In other words, the CCM is now a modified form of the CPM at the operational level.

Whenever the armed forces attack, they factor in reserve time and reserve forces. Similarly, in a project, the project manager advises that a buffer period be used to eliminate the concept of float or slack of individual activities in the critical path or noncritical path.

The team takes 50 percent of the time expected in the critical path by the planner as additional buffer for the critical chain path. The buffer which is extra time taken from all different activities and is spread throughout the chain provides the cushion for delays in the schedule activities. Buffers are not a padding and are planned and inserted to minimize known risks. Buffers are planned activities to manage uncertainties. Since the buffer time is pooled from various activities and spread over places, it is easily borrowed by any activity if the activity is delayed. The project manager analyzes the remaining buffer to find the status of the project.

Difference between Float of Critical Path Method and Buffer of Critical Chain Method

As per the definition of buffer in the CCM, it is not zero on a key chain or any other chain, whereas we keep float on critical path as zero. The CCM develops a schedule by assigning each activity to occur as late as possible to meet the end date. Buffers can be divided into three categories: project buffer, feeding buffer, and resource buffer. The float can be either total float or free float.

Project buffer. It is placed at the end of the critical chain and prevents the target end date from slipping.

Feeding buffer. These are placed at points, not in the critical chain but feeds into a key chain. These feeding buffers protect the critical path from delays in noncritical paths.

Resource buffer. These are reserve resources to carter for any resource limitation that might cause risking the critical chain and further delays at any significant milestone. It helps in solving resource issues whenever the resource is causing problems of delays. This buffer can be a human resource or any equipment (see Figure 7.2).

Converting Critical Path to Critical Chain

There are advantages of switching from the CPM to the CCM. The time which was reduced to 50 percent works as the buffer for the entire project. This total safety margin becomes the pool reserve. The time duration from other shorter branches is also halved and consolidates as the feeder buffer to immunize the critical path from any negative variance. In one sense, the feeding path has its safety margin and unless it is not exhausted, the activities in the feeder chain will not affect the entire project or activities in the critical path.

The advantage is that we start a task as late as possible, and we complete it in half time or less time before the buffer is used. The lag between start and end helps in reducing the time for work in progress (WIP). A WIP is always costly and serves to bog down workers. The same reduction we apply on feeding paths so that a feeding buffer is optimally one-half the length of the previous feeding branch. Finally, the schedule planned by the head office which also has a critical path is cut from C days to a total of B days by the operation team as they know the ground conditions and will use them to advantage.

Figure 7.2. Types of Buffer in Critical Chain

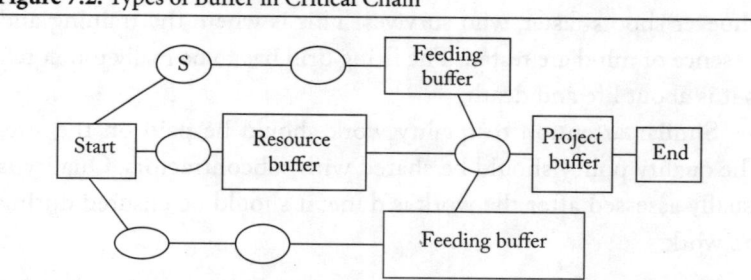

The buffer accumulated will be used for individual tasks, complementing each other by early completion, and allowing the spare time to be collected for some delayed task.

Additional Sills to Keep the CPM Under Check

Move tasks that involve risks closer to the start of the project. If it is known that there is a particular work that will inevitably be delayed, then that should be shifted closer to the start time. Another way is communicating in advance to the stakeholders; if our critical path is delayed for the task, keep the stakeholders in the loop and make them responsible and accountable through review meetings. Laxity in work should not be tolerated and it should be discussed upfront. If the delay is unavoidable, a mutual decision should be made on late delivery or to reduce the scope of the work to be on time as the critical paths will be impacted.

Thus, the CCM ensures that the operation team has a challenging duration and also a buffer which it can use anytime. It also ensures that the project gets delivered on time and within the planned budget.

QUALITY IMPLEMENTATION

In the armed forces, bad quality work results in the loss of life. While the wait in the jungles in insurgency areas goes on for weeks or months for terrorists, it is the only fraction of a second when one comes across the terrorists. At that moment, it is either him or us, whoever shoots faster, who survives. This is where the training and presence of mind are tested. The firing drill has to be really top notch as it is about life and death.

Similar attention to quality work should be paid on the site. The quality policy should be shared with subcontractors. Quality is usually assessed after the work is done; it should be ensured during the work.

A site quality policy should have the following:

- Quality control procedures to be disseminated at the ground level.
- Quality instructions to be in compliance with contract documents.
- Updating of new applicable drawings and documents.
- Activities performed according to proper execution proceedings.
- Next phase does not start without the previous one verified.
- Responsibility for the quality of each task is clearly identified.
- Control of the quality identification of incoming materials.
- Surveillance and monitoring of work process.
- Communication between personnel involved in quality and those involved in material control and construction.

The following inspections and test documents are essential:

- The daily progress report (DPR)
- Excavation and layout measurements
- Test certificate
- Fine aggregate and coarse aggregate inspection
- Reinforcement steel inspection
- Cube test and compressive strength
- Concrete reinforcement bars inspection
- Drawing file
- RA bill file
- Legal documents of the contractor
- Concrete pour card file

CONFIRMATION OF PLANNED COST AT SITE

In army operations, there are fixed troops and resources, and one has to be judicious to employ them within planned numbers so that there are some left to keep as reserve also. There is no scope of any wastage of manpower as a lot of duties of administration, security, and operations are done by the same men. In a similar way, at the project site, resources should be used judiciously by doing a cost break of the resources. That way we will always be monitoring costs when additional resources are needed.

- **Planned cost.** Each activity and sub-activity have a costing. These costs with schedule are rolled into a control account at the tactical level. The aim is not to exceed this cost without proper justification.
- **Cost break up.** A lot of estimates are created at the head office as these items are centrally procured or are viewed as long-term spending. However, depending on the effort of each sub-activity, it is better to also give a proportionate weight of business value to each sub-activity. That way the team is also aware that if any activity is delayed as compared to others, it will affect the overall cost.

Man-hours weighted of each activity in a WBS. It ensures that weighted value of each business is in proportion to its impact in the WBS. Each activity person-hours is thus calculated. Like for Activity A, the budgeted person-hour is 200, similarly for Activity B, it is 400, for Activity C, 300, Activity D, 100.

Budgeted WBS 1,000 man-hours	Person-hours budgeted for each activity	Weighted in overall WBS
Activity A	200	200/1000 × 100 = 20%
B	400	40%
C	300	30%
D	100	10%

EV of man-hours. When the execution of an operation starts, the team calculates how much value was accomplished at a given point in time. It is the budget associated with the authorized work that has been completed at any given time. For example, when Activity A is 25 percent complete, it would have earned 50 man-hours.

HOW IS RACE METHODOLOGY BEING ACHIEVED?

- **Rapid delivery.** The convergence plan is providing simultaneity of operations at all levels and in all departments. All functional departments know the convergence date and point when their deliverable is to meet with another staff. There will be hence no delay.
- **Absolute scope.** Each activity has a proper owner and process so that there is no step missed out. There will be less chance of incomplete work.
- **Class quality work.** Each activity has a defined parameter and matrices. No action is started till the previous activity is not confirmed as an accepted deliverable, so that there are no rework.
- **Economical cost.** In operation, sudden issues come up that increase cost. There is constant vigilance to prevent any cost escalations.

TAKEAWAYS

Operational planning centers around the site incharge and operational team in the forward area. They converge all activities from all stakeholders at the site so that all activities take place simultaneously.

Operational Planning in VUCA	
• Operational leadership and team skills	• Convergence of operation
• Site as center of gravity of operations	• Making the schedule leaner by CCM
• Control and coordination among operational stakeholders	• Quality implementation plan at site
• Operational planning approach	• Confirmation of planned cost at site

CHAPTER 8

Execution in VUCA Conditions

Play by the rules but be ferocious

—Phil Knight

A FLASHBACK OF A QUICK EXECUTION OPERATION

Battle of Dograi

The colonel was participating in a canal crossing exercise. The colonel had done his training in the 3 Jat Battalion in 1989 and had read the complete history of the battle of Dograi which was fought by the 3 Jat Battalion. This was one glorious battle between India and Pakistan fought in 1965.

Between Indian and Pakistan borders, there were various obstacles made to prevent mechanized forces sweeping across the Punjab plains. These obstacles were in the form of canals or ditch cum bund (DCB) obstacle in the form of linear defense. When war broke out, India wanted to capture the GT road leading to Lahore. Pakistan had made a canal as an obstacle called the Ichhogil canal.

The 3 Jat Infantry Battalion was under the command of 54 Brigade/54 Div/11 Corps. The formation was given the task to secure the bridges on the Ichhogil canal primarily and advance to Lahore. The strategic aim of the 11 Corps Commander, unfortunately, could not muster in a proper tactical plan of 54 Brigades or 54 Div. As a result, they could not provide proper backup or support to 3 Jat Operations. 3 Jat had made a surprise attack on Pakistan and had crossed the canal by heavy fighting and had secured the bridgehead. The battalion had achieved the lodgment against the heavy resistance of tanks and air attack of Pakistani counterattack. There was heavy fighting to execute the task.

However, 3 Jat after the battle phase, was waiting for replenishment, ammunition stores, and reserve support troops to sustain the lodgment against Pakistani counterattack. A VUCA situation happened, and they could not be supported by 54 Brigade/54 Infantry Division. The logistics could not cross the canal in time. Reasons were aplenty, but finally, after achieving the initial operational success, the 3 Jat battalion was ordered to withdraw. It was a tactical blunder by the brigade/division and a lot of blame game followed later. In other words, from a victory situation, the battalion was withdrawn by higher headquarter orders simply because leadership failed to provide reinforcements and logistics in time.

First lesson in execution. A VUCA situation may arise due to the inefficiency of the higher headquarter failing to provide support and logistics in time. Clarity of the situation with proper communication and timeliness of support teams is needed from the higher headquarter to support execution by the operation team.

However, the 3 Jat Battalion under the great leadership of Lt Col. Desmond Hyde was asked to capture Dograi in an overall plan to again get a hold on the Icchogil canal. This time Pakistan was well prepared with additional reinforcement. The operation involved attacking in the built-up area of the town Dograi; the 3 Jat Battalion fought fiercely to capture the town but with heavy casualties. 3 Jat again withstood the VUCA counterattack from the Pakistani side and suffered heavy casualties of soldiers and officers, but they sustained this *time and did not withdraw. The battle of Dograi was so intense with hand-to-hand combat and bayonet fighting at the last stage. It was one of the bloodiest battles fought in the Indian Military history. 3 Jat sealed the victory but with a toll of martyrs. There were 58 killed and among them were 4 officers, with 157 wounded on the Indian side, while on the Pakistani side the toll stood at 300 dead and 108 captured. The Battalion got 4 Maha Vir Chakra (MVC) for the battle and a host of other honor awards.*

Second lesson in execution. Leadership and aggressiveness to sustain against any VUCA condition is the hallmark of success.

After this incident, the crossing of canal operations and DCB was given utmost importance in training. The canal is an obstacle laid by the enemy with their force on the far bank in bunkers in defensive positions. If it has to be crossed for further attack in the enemy hinterland, the crossing will require timed steps in sequence. It requires specific procedures for success because the water obstacle prevents common ground maneuver. The speed of crossing is important as they have to neutralize the enemy tanks which are positioned on the enemy side of the canal. The bridge is laid with speed. The infantry battalions and armored tanks cross over under heavy, intense fire support of air and artillery and dash toward enemy bunkers. However, the support troops and logistics follow in sequence as they are also needed to sustain troops fighting in the front.

This is the challenging part which was not followed for 3 Jat, that is, timely replenishment. Any crossing involves the movement of 20,000 troops with entire logistics, heavy guns, etc., all in two hours. This is organized by the Obstacle Canal Crossing Organization (OCCO) and it ensures that the drills of execution are set and fine-tuned.

There is now a regular canal crossing drill and exercise conducted every year by the Indian Army to be ready for a warlike situation. In an exercise in 2005, the Formation Head Quarter team led by Brigadier B. K. Sharma had scripted the entire drill and operation to be executed by the last man. The officers and men were encouraged to memorize a series of programed steps to the last detail and where they will be at every minute of crossing the canal. They were expressively forbidden not to go beyond any level that was not authorized or told by the senior staff. All had rehearsed the movements timed with precision. They had to ensure that everybody crossed the barrier with drills encompassing surprise, timing, and intricate planning. The precision of movement would be achieved despite enemy gunfire across the canal. There was a race between the attacking force crossing the canal and the enemy trying to withhold by fire. Additional force may also need to be called for to stop the attackers. Speed is critical lest the enemy is successful in dividing the attacking force into two halves.

The third lesson. Each step of execution requires detailed planning, speed, control measures, and different technical support.

The fourth lesson in execution. Timing is crucial for execution. There are no second chances to correct a mistake; this also means empowering junior leaders to make decisions in case of emergency.

The fifth lesson. There are scripted action and response for any emergencies and problems that may arise.

The same execution philosophy can be used for corporate projects. Execution of any large-scale project needs:

- Exemplary leadership, grit, and determination
- Planning and aggressiveness
- Timely support from strategic and tactical plan to get the operational plan executed
- Allowing the operation execution team to take decisions
- Teams having complete information about the project, with resources to use and how
- Very tight timelines which should be adhered to
- Immediate response and quick solution to any unforeseen VUCA problem

READINESS FOR PROJECT EXECUTION

The site-in-charge must ensure that conditions are decisive for speedy implementation. Manpower, equipment, and material support should be arranged according to a plan before execution starts.

- The support infrastructure and backup teams should be there. Any lapses will reduce the momentum.
- Everybody should be aware of the end state and quality expected with timelines.
- ERP and project management software should be the center of gravity that will drive the cohesion of activities.
- The lines of operations should be known to all stakeholders and team members; these are the route to the objective.
- Each sub-activity or task should be sequenced and synchronized based on their interdependencies. It should be flexible and based on time and future effects considerations.
- Each phase should be earmarked, and proper hand over to next step between each team should be ensured.
- Each activity should have contingency planning build into anticipating changes to the situation opportunities and reverses. It provides alternatives to achieve certain conditions within a phase and sequels. It also provides alternative options for the next step based on the outcome of the current phase.
- There should be timed operational pauses in execution to ensure regrouping or reassessment of what is not going right. It is basically to regain or strengthen a hold on the imitative and increased momentum.
- There will be moments when things are not moving; this is the culmination point. At this stage, it is best to hold on to the situation without further degradation. A pause or reinforcement should be taken to counter any vulnerabilities.
- The tipping point should be prevented, that is, any action where equilibrium is disrupted should not be allowed.

DETAILED TEAM BRIEFING

During war planning, there is a lot of brainstorming and walkthrough of the battle plan to identify if any aspect has been overlooked. After that, the briefing is to the minutest details to every soldier by the commander. Everybody is aware of their task and timing. They are also conscious of the drills and methods to achieve the objective with minimum loss of lives.

Visualization of the Task in Projects

Similarly, project managers must encourage engineers to do a visualization of the mission for the next day. They must walk through every step of the mission to see if it works. They can test their plans, identify any flaws, and make note of any resource or time constraints. It is good to involve the site supervisor and labor team to get a buy-in from everybody that the mission for the day is achievable and well thought of. There should be a primary objective and also a secondary objective for the day's work that has to be accomplished.

Microlevel Plan

After the macrolevel project visualization, the junior engineers must make the microlevel plan for execution. Execution cannot be left to chance without discussing with the people who are going to do the action part. It should include:

- Deciding the action steps
- Allotting responsibilities for these action steps
- Listing the requirement of resources and support needed
- Discussing VUCA issues that may come up
- Analyzing stakeholders support

Briefing by engineers to the supervisors:

- Brief about the mission—clear and precise.

- Set accountabilities—each person should know their responsibilities.
- Answer every question—clear every doubt.
- Ask for ideas at this stage—an entirely new viewpoint might emerge.
- Get everyone to write the key descriptors and measures of merit.

Operating conditions prevalent during execution:

- Junior engineers and supervisors should monitor operating conditions such as environmental factors, economic situation, technological changes, new laws of compliances, weather forecast, and constant recurring factors that need adjustment.

Real-time visibility during execution:

- All engineers should ensure a system of monitoring for the ease of command and control. Visible problems are the shortest route to understanding and deciding the corrective action. Use ViewPoint Visual Portfolio Board that helps in clarifying issues with anybody in the entire organization. Allow team members to expose problems in an objective nonthreatening way. Prevent information overload and ensure a feedback that everyone can see and understand. Get an agreement on solving a situation, monitor the project, and take the right action to move it close to completion. Get everybody on the same page by displaying data recorded on charts and boards with latest timelines and decision matrix.

EMPOWERING THE TEAM

There is no looking back when the sky is blazing with fire power. The junior leaders have to be allowed to take quick decisions to keep moving forward against all the odds. The juniors then take ownership of the results. Also, empowerment allows the team to share the burden of the project with the project leader.

- **Using the MBO technique.** Management by objectives technique can be used to align everybody with team goals. It should be translated down to functional unit goals and further to individual team member goals as well. The goals are documented (typically on a quarterly schedule) and reviewed/regularly revised (usually weekly) in detail. Every manager and all individual contributors draft their objectives to fit with the level above while adding more detail and assumptions to represent their particular contributions. Each objective needs to include assumptions, measurement means, and verification methods. Joint commitments should be negotiated among the parties to arrive at the same objective statements. Team goals are best negotiated with the team leader in a consensus-driven session.

The team should take responsibility to produce results, at any cost against any problem. There is one battle every Indian should read about, that is, Battle of Razilanga on November 18, 1962. It was fought by Major Shitan Singh and his company to halt Chinese advance and momentum. The stand-off of 13 Kumaon with 5,000 Chinese was at such a heavy price that it changed the course of the war. Out of the 120 men and officers of this Company, 114 died, however five were taken prisoners as wounded and they all escaped.

The unit had a choice to retreat but if something has to be done then it has to be done with an impact that the world sits up and takes notice of it. The company decided to take on the Chinese, even if it was the last man and the last round to get the best results as possible. The Chinese were forced for a truce after they suffered so many casualties of their own and the war ended. The movie *Hakikat* was made in memory of this battle.

EXECUTION STARTS AS PER BRIEFING

Planning and execution scripts are the same; there is no variance. Everybody performs their particular tasks in training, thus making it their second nature. Reliance on scripted response means a less delayed solution in a battlefield situation. It means synchronized combined arms coordination and tactical maneuver on the battlefield. With the same intentions, the supervisors and blue-collar workers go through the working drill which they are trained for. The orders for execution for the blue-collar workforce are simple:

- Do work as planned.
- The work is to be done as per briefing.
- There should be no gap in understanding and action.
- There are to be no glitches or any line.
- The work has no extra scene, simply do as briefed.
- There is a checklist for everything.
- When an activity is completed, perform a quality test of the deliverable.

SYNERGY DURING EXECUTION BY USE OF ERP

The crossing of Canal required a lot of synergy of operations of different organization and units. Air and artillery synergized supporting fire. If it is delayed or missed it will lead to the massacre of infantry who are crossing on boats. Any BMP or Tank that is not able to pass in time will give an opportunity to the enemy tanks hitting the infantry.

Synergizing Departments for Execution in Projects

ERP can be used effectively for coordination. The following terms are used in ERP:

- **MCI:** Material Control Index
- **DCI:** Document Control Index

- **CPR:** Construction Progress Report
- **DMIS** is the safe repository of all documents

Material readiness. The site incharge/store incharge should be informed by an inspection release note by QC that the material has been inspected at the supplier's end. It has been found fit in quality inspection for dispatching it to the site. This will give a warning to the site team that some material is likely to come. It is yet to be dispatched.

Updating the WBS. The site incharge/store incharge will also be informed by the site planner about the material needed as per the WBS. If there are changes in the conditions of circumstances, the WBS gets modified. This could be due to the release of late engineering drawing which the planner will check from the DCI or for any other reasons. There may be some delay in the material needed for the earlier planned WBS.

Look-ahead report. The site planner will continuously update the site team and head office with the look-ahead report. It shows the work to be done shortly. The critical path also changes due to any change in resources, manpower, any drawing delay, or any other reason.

Backlog plan. It is a pending activity for which material, drawing, and resources are needed. Accordingly, the site planner should change the schedule in the execution progress report.

Prevent waste. The Store in Charge and Site in Charge will assess the requirements of material that is to be brought from supplier shop/factory and compare the quantity and type of material if it is matching with the look-ahead and backlog plan. They will accordingly modify the requisition for material to be inward. The look-ahead and backlog report should be discussed every day in a stand-up meeting for 15 minutes.

They will raise the issue of storage or early inward of material via a site action report (SAR) and commissioning action report (CAR). They will confirm if any material is likely to come but not needed as per the CPR approved by the planner.

- They will mention in the SAR and CAR that such material will get spoiled as the site does not have space and storage facilities.

- The team at the head office will decide what should be the alternative solution. They can inform the supplier to hold the material for few weeks at his premises. They can plan some alternative storage either at the site or nearby when in transit or even delay production at the shop floor of the supplier.
- The aim is to try and send the material to the site when it is needed the most and prevent building up of inventory that will only get spoiled.

Coordination of reports in ERP. The MCI/DCI/CPR status update should be shared with site team and store team every day. Even if there is no change in status, it should be informed. These three documents coordinate the drawing, material, and construction activities together for making the site work an integrated platform.

Use of DCI. It can be used to contain daily photos, and these photos can be connected to drawings and specifications for more learning. All CAD drawings can be stored and, in fact, site engineers can access all project drawings from mobile devices and facilitate work on the site.

The SAR and CAR have to be decided within 24 hours. The team can use 3D drawing for the resolution of SAR and CAR issues and solve punch point recommendations and related documentations.

Material safety. Material cost is 80 percent of the expense of the project.

- The inward of the material should also be inspected by the site engineers. The package-wise storages would be earmarked by the store incharge for proper preservation and upkeep. The material should be fitted with barcodes for its stocking and secure traceability.
- The store incharge should update the inventory stock in ERP and the site receipt note should be generated. This is a signal to the buyer at the head office that the supplier can be paid.

- The store incharge should issue the inventory on ERP on a requisition generated by the site engineers. This requirement should be cleared by the section incharge a day before so that on the day of issue the material is released without wasting time in tracing it.
- The store incharge should also carry out a perpetual inventory count on a regular basis to verify the correct status of material and its condition.
- During inward, any material that is found to be incorrect or less should be raised by the store incharge in the material discrepancy report immediately for the buyer to get it streamlined with suppliers.

TRACKING SCOPE, SCHEDULE, AND COST OF WORK

When troops are crossing a canal amidst enemy fire from the opposite bank, the time is premium. There are no second chances to go back and finish the job. Every situation is critical and has to be done in that sequence. Any delay in any work will cause loss of lives. So there is constant tracking of time and scope of work at every stage that should be as per plan in the war room.

Likewise, in projects we can follow the COW Method to track scope during execution. The work should always be progressing with frequent hiccups, and contingency action should be taken. The project manager is advised that it is better to start following scope activities-wise within schedule and cost. One of the methods to track scope is the COW method. The scope task details should be written in cards and put on the wall, connecting with other tasks (Figure 8.1).

- The COW technique consists of interconnecting the tasks (cards) to reflect the optimum order of tasks and their interdependencies. The team hangs each work package on

the wall, by project phase, and interconnects them using markers or yarn to reflect the interdependencies.
- There is a 5" × 8" project planning form for each task. There is a yarn or string for interconnecting the cards and ample walls to hang and arrange the cards.
- Among the benefits of this interactive, visual procedure are:
    - It encourages participative decision-making.
    - There are fewer excuses. The task is on display every day with all actions to be done by a team member.
    - The engineer at site comes and shows his card that is to be followed.
    - Risks are shared by all team members as all are assessing each other's card.
    - When the work is over, it also displays quality results on the card.
    - Most importantly, there is joint team ownership of the plan.

Figure 8.1: Pasting Cards on the Wall with Interrelated Task

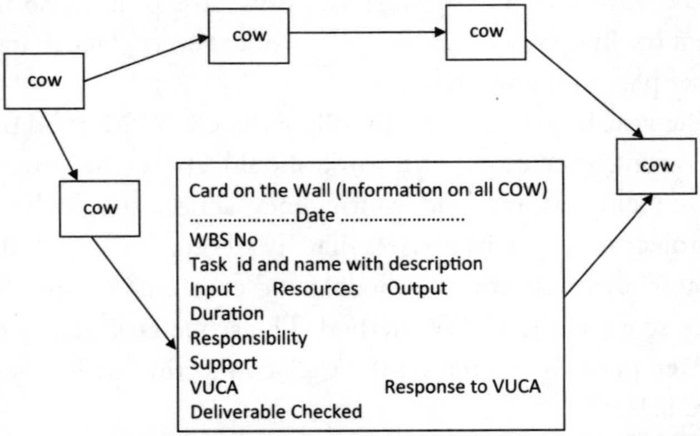

```
                    COW ──────────▶ COW
                   ▲                    │
                   │                    │
       COW ───────┤                    ▼
                   │                   COW
                   ▼
                  COW ┌─────────────────────────────────────┐
                      │ Card on the Wall (Information on all COW) │
                      │ ...................Date ................ │
                      │ WBS No                                │
                      │ Task id and name with description     │
                      │ Input    Resources    Output          │
                      │ Duration                              │
                      │ Responsibility                        │
                      │ Support                               │
                      │ VUCA              Response to VUCA    │
                      │ Deliverable Checked                   │
                      └─────────────────────────────────────┘
```

Source: Author's own work.

Calculating Earned and Actual Cost

The team should be calculating three values on a regular basis:

- **Planned cost of activities**
    - Get total budgeted man-hours of the project.
    - Divide the total estimated man-hours of the project into WBS man-hours.
    - For each WBS, get budget manors for each activity.
    - Find the percentage weighted of man-hours of each activity in the WBS.

- **Earned cost of activities**
    - Find the percentage of work that has been completed at any given moment in time.
    - Convert the percentage of work completed to received value at any given moment in time.
    - Calculate the EV of work for each activity as per the formula mentioned above.
    - Add all EVs and that provides the received value of work for a WBS at any given moment in time.

For example, when Activity A is 25 percent complete, it would have earned 50 person-hours. Please see the following table.

Activity	Person-hours budgeted activity	Percent complete at a given moment in time	Person-hours earned	EV
A	200	25%	50	5%
B	400	35%	140	14%
C	300	60%	180	18%
D	100	70%	70	7%
Total	1,000			44%

Person-hours earned = Multiplying the percent complete with budgeted person-hours for each activity

EV = Multiplying substantial percentage complete by the weighted proportion of business in the WBS

or

EV= Man-hours earned divided by budgeted value multiplied by weighted percentage of that activity in the WBS

So the total EV of work done by the WBS = 44 percent

- **Actual value:** It is how much was spent at a given moment in time. It is a realized cost incurred for the activity during a particular period. It provides the amount of money spent on a project to date. In other words, it is the actual cost that is incurred in accomplishing the EV work calculated earlier.
  - Log all man-hours as a discipline for each activity.
  - Total the man-hours actually expended.
  - Calculate the man-hours expended as per the formula in relation to the total budgeted man-hours.
  - That will give how much person-hours have been spent against the EV at any given moment in time.

Activity	Actual person-hours expended in doing the activity
A	60
B	135
C	200
D	65
Total person-hour used	460

Total man-hours spent = Actual man-hour expended divided by budgeted man-hours = 460 divided by 1000 = 46 percent.

It means that for 46 percent of person-hours spent 44 percent of work has been earned.

SUSTAINING SPEED OF EXECUTION BY THE 20 MILE PRINCIPLE

When an operation starts, there is no slowdown. The speed is sustained during execution. The speed of establishing the bridge on the canal is critical. Otherwise, the force will be cut in half with the main fighting force ahead, and logistics and engineering with main tanks and guns left behind.

The book *Great By Choice* by Jim Collins talks about the 20 Mile Principle. Jim Collins brings the characteristics of the "20-Mile March" to life through the distinct stories and strategies of the explorers Amundsen and Scott, who each sought to be the first to the South Pole. Jim Collins shares what the two teams did. Amundsen and Scott were on their way to the South Pole. The weather was awful and danger was everywhere. What did they do? Both Amundsen and Scott applied different strategies. One team's strategy was to complete a 20 mile march daily, no matter the weather. No matter what, they would walk 20 miles a day. That team was led by Ronald Amundsen. The other team would use good weather to their advantage and sometimes went 40–60 miles in a day. When the weather was bad, they would use that to their advantage too and rest warmly in their tents. Robert Scott led that team. Equipment and kills did not matter. Both had the same equipment, the same skill set, yet only one of them made it; the other unfortunately died. Who do you think made it first?

A lot of people might think that Robert would have made it. The team led by Roland Amundsen that marched 20 miles a day every day got to the South Pole first and more importantly, lived to tell the tale. Robert Falcon Scott and his crew were found dead the next spring. Why?

Any work requires resilience; problems will always be there but that can be resolved by advance thinking, planning, and ensuring that all are aligned with the work on hand.

If one rigorously pursues performance parameters that have to be achieved, all things will inevitably fall in place. Instead of finding a comfort zone in other stakeholder delays, one must learn rigorous follow-up and close the issue. At times, it will require cover-up by doing work with extra man-hours and trying to catch up on schedule.

ENSURING QUALITY OF WORK

If a modular bridge is to be erected for carrying tanks and guns, then the bridge should be strong, otherwise there can be a loss of people and equipment. Even the tiniest of the quality issue can jeopardize the whole operation.

That being the case for projects also to prevent rework and to ensure quality during work, the correct interpretation of quality matrices and standards of the deliverable by the customer should be shared with all. It has to be broken down in the languages to be understood by workers, ensured by supervisors, and checked by engineers at site. It requires ground rules to be followed during the execution of work. It involves individuals taking responsibility to make every activity happen as per the required standards.

- It is better to stop work if there are quality issues of workmanship and material, instead of overlooking it and carrying on. Every activity is connected, and if some activity is not done properly, it will surely catch up later where rework will be involved.
- For every activity, as per various brainstorming discussions and lessons learned of pitfalls earlier, the checklist of how an activity is to be executed at each substage is revised and handed over to supervisors and engineers. The aim is not to repeat old mistakes and ensure the correctness of steps to be executed. This will provide a large decrease in COPQ.
- The contractors and his team have to be trained and made conscious of not taking any shortcuts while executing any activity. That will save a lot of additional cost in engineering and fabrication errors or block any welding leaks later.

- There should be adequate protection against poor weather to ensure that the quality of the essential material is maintained till its fitment.
- Communication across the team is essential. The technical team must have quality critical technical information to remove any guess work.
- Workers should be involved with work processes and supervisors must ask them to explain in daily rounds; they will start owning up the processes.
- The quality engineers must be on site and not in the office; he should be taking notes, photographs, and guiding the workers to do the work correctly in the first attempt. It is much easier to do the work properly the first time than doing rework later.
- The quality engineers and other engineers must also follow the standards regulations, codes, and policies with procedures set by the quality head at the head office.
- The head office should regularly review data sent by quality engineers, ensure facilities like radiography, ensure and nondestructive test are done on material that is going to the site.
- There should be third-party inspectors also to test and check the standard codes and regulations of the work to be done at the site. Advance satisfactory arrangement to organize such tests should be made to avoid any inconvenience to inspectors and keeping the workforce waiting, sitting idle.
- Items that are imported must also be checked for any faults or problems, and replacements should be raised in time as it takes time for items to be imported from other countries. That will save time.
- All record-keeping of quality documents should be in electronic data folders in the data management system for proper safety.
- It is also better to keep the customer involved in quality by sending him/her photographs and quality data at regular

intervals. The customer gains confidence, and a rapport is established with the customer project manager that on-time delivery and quality will be ensured in work. It is also worthwhile to have an understanding of the customer to have interim deliverables so that handoff is easier during the closing of the project.
- The quality person usually checks issues after the work is completed, while he could have verified the same mistakes when the work was going on. So the quality person should always be with site team on the ground and keep seeing things, ensuring prevention rather than correction later.

SCRIPTED REACTION TO OPPORTUNITIES AND RISKS

In every operation, when there are some hurdles, there are also scripted reactions. Every member of the team knows what is to be done. If there are any risks or changes due to VUCA, each team member should also know the response in such a scenario.

Response to Hurdles in Projects

Owing to VUCA situations that may inevitably happen, the project manager must update the risk register as per risk categories and assess it qualitatively and quantitatively. Thereafter, risk response should be discussed and carried out to reduce the impact.

During execution, it is also imperative to decide if the risk response is appropriate and all stakeholders are responding or not. It also helps to establish if any risk has to be closed or new risk has to be added.

A contingency reserve for the project is reassessed depending upon the old risk that is closed and the new risk that is added. During the course of the project, it is easy for opportunities and threats to slip inadvertently. Therefore, the team should keep a lookout for risks and consequences and assess both probability and impact, forecast the expected value of the project, and prioritize according to the expected project value. The team should also estimate the cost of both immediate and contingent actions. They should also look at the mitigation leverage, that is, compare changes to the expected value against action costs. Based on the above, the team should decide on actions required and obtain concurrence and then document and incorporate decisions in all planning.

ENSURING SAFETY DURING EXECUTION

There is a very high level of safety and security cover inbuilt when going into war. There will be causalities in war, but there will be no casualties due to avoidable issues. This is made possible by checks and rechecks of every safety aspect.

The project manager and site incharge should ensure the following safety aspects in projects:

- The safety officer should begin the day by giving safety instructions to workers.
- Subcontractors and supervisors should regularly assess their safety equipment, such as belts, buckles, and other safety kits which can get perished or worn out.
- OSHA regulations should be followed in letter and spirit along with documentation.
- Regular verification of the medical condition of employees, especially those working on heights, should be done.
- There should be a concept of safety card which has dos and don'ts printed and issued to all employees and also visitors visiting the premises.
- Training should be put foremost; supervisors and managers should be trained, attendance should be made compulsory for such training, and it should be recorded.
- Regular checks for issues of alcoholism and substance abuse must be done among workers, and defaulters should be removed from the site.

- It should be made compulsory that the site team and safety officer should send near-miss reports every week as that will encourage them to see things carefully and submit a report about how they prevented an accident.
- God forbid if an accident happens, the first things to be taken care of is to ensure the accident victim is provided first aid and hospitalization. For that an ambulance or a vehicle should be kept on standby, with a nearby hospital designated. The fist-aid kits should always be inspected for the availability of latest medicines and tools.
- Aftermath investigation should be fair and transparent and remedial measures should be taken up and implemented.
- Regular safety walk linked with GEMBA walk (a Japanese term, meaning "the real place") by site incharge and safety officer should be done to ensure that there are no possible VUCA accidents waiting to happen. In fact, the customer safety officer should also accompany so that a joint issues and support system for each other can be addressed.
- During execution, work methodology of an activity should be clearly spelled out and discussed so that all workers and supervisors are aware of any dangers lurking around and preventive actions may be taken.
- Regular firefighting practice with fire emergency evacuation should be done. It should be ensured that the fire points are always well-maintained with sand, buckets, fire beaters, and extinguishers. There should be updated list of duties of a firefighting team and evacuation team. The emergency exit routes should be planned.
- Have a contractor's safety management evaluation checklist that should be completed by the contractor before he is allowed to work. The safety aspects should be discussed with the contractors during the contract discussion stage only. They should also be evaluated later.
- The workers should be made aware that they are the first line of safety themselves.

PEOPLE MANAGEMENT DURING EXECUTION

Team management is most crucial. It is good to set some ground rules for the site crew:

- Zero tolerance to rude and abusive behavior against any employee. Their egos and self-pride, their state or religion or background should be respected. No offensive remarks should be hurled at anyone.
- Every worker at the site is the project manager's responsibility. Regular visits should be made to the labor colony, and hygiene and privacy should be ensured in living quarters that are there for families. The subcontractor usually ignores the discomfort of the labor colony.
- Make eye contact with workers and acknowledge their presence. The project managers and supervisors can sometimes have meals with them.
- Management can be done by walking around. GEMBA walks are the best, and you get the firsthand feel of how work is happening. It signifies that the work will be visible. So when leaders walk around, he can see the VUCA problems and can take corrective actions on the spot.
- Workers who are doing a right thing should be rewarded and they should be made to feel good by appreciating. Regardless of it being a small thing, it needs to be done. Employees are unique resources that can do wonders with training, appreciation, and welfare.
- There should be involvement in safety or technical training with the workers. Feedback and work out session should be organized with them on problems at site or work. Quality and safety should be made an obsession and some training lecture should be held every day.
- Regular salaries with the provident fund should be given and there should be checks to make sure that the subcontractor is being fair and not making profit for himself.

- It should be ensured that as a leader, you respond to a person who has called you or emailed you for any issues. Workers and supervisor should be encouraged to follow the communication hierarchy system and it should also be seen that people in authority are responding. Moreover, they should be encouraged to walk up to you anytime for any ideas or best practices to be conducted. Put up a suggestion box and discuss points monthly.
- While dealing with a difficult worker, it is best to deal with him in private addressing his problems about what is causing his behavior. If he is a real troublemaker, there is only one solution; keep him off work and ensure he is not contributing to anything lest he spoils. Arrange his exit as fast as possible.

RACE

Finally, we get to execution, all plans made from strategic to tactical to operational gets translated to results. The results of what we are expecting are as follows:

- **Rapid delivery.** We have thought of all possible issues that can come before the start of execution and have catered to them. There will be no breaks in actions. Every member is aware of his role; drills are set. The SOP is read and it is ensured that it is followed. Everybody is committed to what has been decided for the day or week by the Last Planner Method.
- **Absolute scope.** Every task or activity is tracked on a daily basis by cards on the wall that give a clear visibility of what is being done or anything missed out that has to be followed up later.
- **Class quality.** Every activity has a matrix, and labor supervisors have cards of quality parameters. The quality is being drilled down to the lowest level so that nothing is done wrong by the actual team that is now doing it.

- **Economic cost.** Every activity has a baseline cost of different components, but the major part is the man-hour cost. That is monitored against work done. If there are significant gaps of man-hours spent against the EV, the reasons are addressed and corrected.

TAKEAWAYS

The execution takes place by the synergy of an operation controlled by ERP. Sustenance of a fixed amount of work with a scripted response will ensure success.

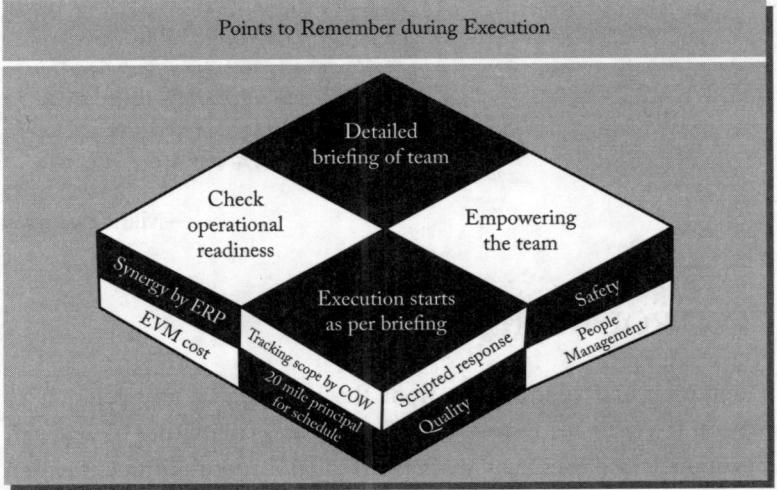

CHAPTER **9**

Monitoring and Control

> *Always acknowledge a fault frankly.*
> *This will throw those in authority*
> *off their guard and give you an*
> *opportunity to commit more*
>
> —Mark Twain

CONTROL BY HEAD OFFICE

Monitoring and control start from the initiation of an operation or project. It continues during the planning stage and later along with execution. It also continues in aftermath till the operation/project closes.

The commanders at all levels in the armed forces have the knack of seeing and understanding things and issues that are actually on the ground. This is because the commanders themselves have had served in the same conditions as a junior rank officer and, hence, known as a senior officer what his junior officers are undergoing.

On the contrary, the biggest problem today in projects or operations is having such managers controlling projects or operations who have served only in soft appointments in head offices from day one. They lead projects without having seen problems that occur in the field. Hence, they are not able to anticipate a VUCA problem. The companies should make it compulsory for a project manager to first work as a site in-charge and having led a project on the ground. There is no better training than being in the trench with the boys.

So the first lesson to monitor and control any project or operation is to always have someone in charge of the team who has himself experienced all issues of a project and knows very well what is an actual problem and what is an oversight that has happened on the ground. An earlier experience helps to foresee in advance what can go wrong.

VISIBILITY OF EXECUTION

For every step of the operation, there is a quick feedback, and in fact, in the age of real-time communication, there is now a full visibility on how it is going. Real-time visibility monitored the surgical strike by Indian troops in Pakistan or the Osama bin Laden strike by the US forces in Pakistan and allowed control in a time of changing situations. The complete execution was live-streamed in the highest office for leadership to see what was happening.

The first raid was code-named Operation Neptune Spear, against the code name Geronimo for none other than Osama bin Laden. The monitoring and control of the whole operation started from the initial planning stage and continued during execution and even in the aftermath.

In the initial operation, the CIA used installing spyware and tracking devices on targeted computers and mobile-phone networks including human intelligence network to get clues of Osama bin Laden, later the planning was done by the use of satellite imagery of his house. They also prepared the pilots with mission simulators and used drones to analyze the data of place including weather conditions. Even during the raid, live streaming of the raid was telecasted in the White House where President Obama and others watched the happenings.

During execution when things go wrong, the objective is still achieved.

In this case, one helicopter was forced to crash-land, but that did not deter the team from entering the compound, carrying on with the raid, and killing the target. The raid was intended to take 40 minutes; it took 38 minutes. The whole operation was monitored and controlled by the dispatch of another helicopter to evacuate the team. The team, before leaving the site, ensured that they destroyed the helicopter also. Even in the aftermath, the conditions were monitored and controlled from Osama bin Laden's funeral taking place in the sea to his DNA and other identification completed. It was ensured that the death of Osama bin Laden was not paraded as a trophy to incite violence.

Thus, with smooth monitoring and control of operations, a wanted terrorist was hunted down, killed, and his dead body disposed of without more collateral damages or losses to US forces or civilians as a revenge.

The second example is the surgical strike by the Indian armed forces across Pakistan on September 29, 2016, on terrorist launch pads.

We will not dwell upon the execution part, but the execution part was witnessed by the Chief of the Army Staff himself. He was there with others in the operation room in the South Block when the Special Forces Para Commandos from the 4th and 9th Battalions were carrying out the assault across the Pakistan terrorist launch pads and killing the terrorists. Before that also the operation was controlled from the planning stage with satellites images. Point to note is that the situation was monitored and controlled even later with the Indian Air Force and Indian Navy keeping on alert along with the Indian Army to counter any adverse response by the Pakistan Armed Forces. Villages were also vacated to prevent any artillery firing injuries from Pakistan.

REAL-TIME FEEDBACK IN PROJECTS

Equally important is the feedback in real time for projects. When execution is on, it is very much advocated that there is an active surveillance of what is going on by real-time visibility through CCTVs, drones, and other media facilities. That is also followed by an effective method of reports submission. Normally, there is a lot of repeated data, and for it to be pruned, it is better to determine the reality of performance parameters efficiently.

Normally, there are three kinds of feedback submissions:

- **Work performance data.** This is real data straight from ground zero, that is, working site. It involves observation, inspection, and measurement from site quality team and other members related to their functions. It gives an indication how the project is performing about scope, time, cost, quality, human resources, risk, procurement, communication, and stakeholder team management.
- **Work performance information.** The work performance data becomes work performance information after it is analyzed how the information will give clarity on the project. It makes sense to get the real status of the project out of raw data.
- **Work performance reports.** These are an electronic representation or graphical or physical representation of job performance information. These are sent to stakeholders to apprise them of the progress of the project and how variance that is detected getting resolved.

ONE-PAGE REPORT BY THE MANAGER

There is this format made by Clark Campbell which reduces any project large or small, traditional or agile to a one-page document. It reflects both the project plan and performance. This one-page report can be further modified to get a report as per the project requirement as follows:

No.	Monitoring issue		Performance status	VUCA reasons for variation/ not achieved	Correction
1	WBS: Covering period Start date End date				
2	Activity within WBS Start date End date				
3	Earned value calculations Calculation explained in subsequent paras				
	BAC				
	PV				
	EV				
	AV				
	SV				
	CV				
	SPI and SPI				
	EAC				
	ETC				
	TCPI				
	VAC				
	Milestone		Previous milestone Current milestone		
	Specific achievements				
	Deliverable acceptance of scope by quality team or customer				

	Punch points or rework noticed in deliverable			
	Lesson learned of activity or WBS completing/ handover of deliverable			
	Any critical decisions			
	Next, WBS planned weekly by the last planner			
	Availability of material and resources for next week			
	Any issues pending for next WBS			

MONITOR AND CONTROL SUPPLY OF MATERIAL FOR SPEEDY EXECUTION

In armed forces, the winter operations are planned with a constant monitoring of winter stocking of rations and fuels and other stores. Operations and battles are lost if the supply of material is not ensured in time. Napoleon and Hitler both lost their world conquest in Russia because they failed to monitor the logistic and material supply in time for their advancing armies during the winter period.

In a similar way, the project manager and the buyers should ensure that resources are made available timely and the tempo of the operation is maintained. The project manager should conduct a structured review of how well the supplier is delivering the resources. He should also use audits and inspection of contractual terms to see that the supplier is meeting the obligations.

If there are any changes in the delivery schedule or WBS for any reason, there should be a proper change control process. It should also be followed by a change in the delivery schedule of the supplier contractual delivery. The team should ensure that all documents and reminders are also kept in record for claiming any damages or legal disputes with the supplier or contractors. Otherwise, the customer would also charge for LDs.

MONITORING PERFORMANCE PARAMETERS

There is a classic example of a navy battle where all four aspects, that is, scope, quality, schedule, and cost were achieved. The code name of the operation was Operation Trident. In project management language, the scope of the operation was to bomb Karachi oil refineries in the western part during the 1971 War. However, the Indian missile boat had limited radar range and small fuel tanks, so it was not going to meet the schedule, and the cost of losing the missile boat was also too high.

The operation was managed and controlled by Naval Chief Admiral Nanda. On December 4, 1971, the Indian Navy did something more audacious; they towed the missile boats as close as possible to the Karachi Port. Three Vidyut class missile boats, INS Nipat, INS Nirghat, INS Veer, two anti-submarine Arnala class corvettes, INS Kiltan, and INS Katchall were accompanied by a fleet oiler, INS Poshak. They also destroyed Pakistani destroyer PNS Khaibar, MV Venus Challenger, PNS Shah Jahan, and PNS Muhafiz and reached 26 km short of the Karachi port. They destroyed the oil refineries and tanks, and the fleet came back to Bombay without any casualties or loss.

In other words, the scope of the operation was achieved by the Indian Navy with quality firing and schedule times with less cost, all controlled and managed from the start of the operation till the end. In a similar manner, a deliverable can be achieved by monitoring and controlling all four parameters, that is, schedule, quality, cost, and scope.

MONITOR AND CONTROL SCHEDULE

The project manager controls the schedule, which involves the following aspects:

- Identifying opportunities for speeding up the project completion
- Detection and evaluation of risks that may slow down the project
- Analyzing the possibility of redetermining the critical path based on local factors and shortening the critical path

- Additional work to meet the task schedules
- Getting back the lost schedule by fast tracking or crashing
- Getting off the critical path as soon as possible
- Increasing and redistributing resources, such as labor and machines, in tasks for the purpose of crashing to cover up lost time
- Saving own essential resources, outsourcing a few activities
- Focusing on getting work efficiencies by training and motivation
- Bringing transparency and accountability of delays

Resequencing

The project manager should also give freedom to do some resequencing of activities to stay on the course of the master plan schedule. It is an optimization process of the current plan with the aim to protect the critical path. It involves the following steps:

- Reviewing the critical path and near-critical path
- Sequence and duration of activities
- Optimization of changes to execution
- Some activities in parallel
- Increasing resources to reduce task duration
- Changing work course or method

MONITOR AND CONTROL QUALITY

The project manager must insist that his/her site team and young engineers are acutely aware of what quality aspects they should request from the subcontractor team.

- **Quality metrics.** The project manager should ensure that quality matrices as agreed with contractual clauses are monitored and controlled by junior engineers every day.
    - Is the milestone on time?
    - How many defects are noticed in subcontractor work?

- What is the failure rate of any equipment commissioned?
- Assessment of reliability of workmanship
- Meantime failure
- Mean time to repair

- **Quality checklist.** Every engineer should carry in his pocket a list of quality steps to undertake and should assess if it is being followed or are there any variances.
- **Statistical sampling.** The site incharge should choose a small part of the large population for inspection and extrapolate the results of a small lot to the entire population. It helps to determine the reliability of a large total population.
- **Inspection.** The site quality inspectors should examine the project deliverable or product to determine whether it meets the documented quality standards. It helps to convert the work performance data to job performance information to assess the variance in required quality standards.
- **Seven basic quality tools.** These are also used to determine the variation in a deliverable against contractual terms or quality standards. These are:
  - Cause and effect diagram
  - Flowchart
  - Check sheet
  - Pareto diagrams
  - Histograms
  - Control charts
  - Scatter diagrams
- **The audit of quality processes.** Quality requirements are made clear in customer contract documents and also in the firm of codes, regulations, laws, and standards. Our work methodology and checklist made by experience from the earlier site are also there. Now the customer and inspectors want it to be enforced. That is where the audit process steps in and ensures that our quality process is not taking any shortcuts missing out mandatory hunting or measurements.

- It is identifying variance in quality checks in raw material to manufacturing stages to complete product stage, and finally how it was erected or commissioned.
- The results give an indication of the trend in real supply or workmanship or erection work at the project site.
- The auditing team addresses root causes of the quality problems.
- The advantage of a quality audit is to prevent/liquidate damages in the form of rework or delayed work or overruns in cost. The COPQ in the shape of nonconformance eats into the profit margin. Every rework has a cost. Even when these defects are discovered in the warranty period, these is a cost to the project.

MONITOR AND CONTROL COST BY EARNED VALUE MANAGEMENT

This is the most critical aspect overlooked during execution. Everybody's focus is on schedule, and the hidden costs behind meeting the schedule are such that the final cost is increased. Another problem is that during review, managers speak of the percentage of work, which is also not clear. There is uncertainty about how the project is going on compared to the baseline and how the project will unfold in future.

Hence, the deviation in schedule and cost and reasons for that never come out. The project remains on the track. The customer and management are not able to get a correct preconceived notion about the value at which the project will close. There is inaccuracy in those figures as they are unable to get a limited range of values.

The biggest flaw in the project industry is schedule and cost are never tracked concurrently. In any review, the focus is on timelines but to achieve those timelines, how much has been spent is often ignored. That is why the COPQ never comes up.

The biggest example of failure to monitor schedule and cost is Tank Arjun. It is more than 30 years that the tank project is going on without any clear timelines of schedule or cost on research or prototype model and how it will end. Now, the latest status is that weight reduction of the tank has to be done to be deployed ahead. We will not go over the pros and cons of the tank failure but highlight the failure to monitor a planned schedule and cost budget. This is often the case with many government-run projects where bureaucracy because of its lengthy processes and approvals take a toll on the schedule of the project. There are more failures in other manufacturing defense equipment where the list is long.

However, that is not the case always; we have much success also like the Integrated Guided Missile Development Programme and Mangalyaan/Mars Orbiter Mission, which were monitored and controlled and were, in fact, cheaper than the US Mars program. So that means India does not lack in talent or knowledge capability.

Earned Value Management

This method examines the project at each stage or weekly/monthly to track the project performance parameters in terms of schedule and cost continuously. The variances are noted and reasons for the deviations are also analyzed so that corrective actions are immediately taken.

The best part is that the project is assessed in a quantitative manner and not subjectively. There are fewer chances of any misrepresentation of the performance of the project. It is simply the amount of EV by the work done so far in a week's time.

This also allows the project team to microschedule the projects without micromanaging and ensures that there are no overruns in cost and schedule.

Earned Value Calculations

This is a disciplined approach for assimilation of data on schedule and cost. The deviation as shown in Figure 9.1 will tell the real

Figure 9.1. Understanding Difference Among PV, EV, and AC

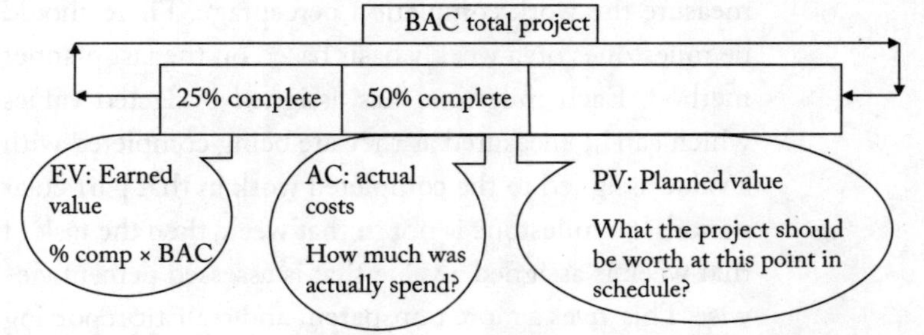

```
                    BAC total project
        ┌─────────────────────────────────────┐
   ◄────│  25% complete  │   50% complete     │────►
        └─────────────────────────────────────┘
   EV: Earned        AC: actual          PV: Planned value
   value             costs
                                         What the project should
   % comp × BAC      How much was        be worth at this point in
                     actually spend?     schedule?
```

Source: Author's own work.

picture of the project and will give a timely warning and corrective solution to close the variances.

- **BAC is budget at completion.** This is the total budget that was initially fixed for the project or activity. Since this budget value is set at the initial planning stage, it is also referred to as the total PV for the project. BAC is the sum of the budget of each phase. The team should track budget for each step and keep in mind the BAC.
- **PV.** It is the budgeted amounts for the current reporting period. It gives us the value of how much was expected to be accomplished at a given time. For each defined WBS element, the budget is decided for resources required to complete the detailed work.
- **Actual cost (AC).** This indicates how much was spent at a given time. The project manager should ask his team to record all direct costs and also generate monthly cost and weekly labor reports.
  - **EV.** The total project budget gets multiplied by the percentage completion of the project. This will provide details of the value regarding the base budget and what has been accomplished at a given time. The EV is based on established measurable, verifiable metrics. The idea

is to quantify what is the authorized work and then measure the work completion percentage. There should be milestones on a weekly basis based on the last planner method. Each milestone has assigned budgeted values which can be measured as they are being completed with a value assigned to the completed work in that particular period. If a milestone is not in that week, then the task of that week is assigned a value that is assessed percentage-wise. This gives a more transparent and realistic reporting of how much work has been achieved in percentages.

With these readily available numbers, the team can do some calculation.

- **Schedule variance.** It is the difference between the current progress and the originally planned development. A negative difference means the task is behind schedule. $SV = EV - PV$
- **Schedule performance index (SPI) calculation.** SPI measures progress achieved against progress planned. The ratio of work performed to work scheduled. $SPI = EV/PV$
  - If the SPI is greater than 1, this means more work has been completed than the planned work. In other words, we are ahead of schedule and so are we too efficient or we have missed something!
  - If the SPI value is less than 1, this obviously indicates that less work has been completed than the planned work. In other words, we are behind schedule.
  - If the SPI is equal to 1, this means all work is completed.
- **Cost variance.** It is the difference between a task's estimated cost and its AC. Negative value is over budget and behind schedule.
- **Cost performance index (CPI) calculation.** CPI measures the amount of work completed at the AC. It is a percentage of work completed per dollar spent.

  $CPI = EV/AC$

- If the CPI is less than 1, we are earning less than the spending. In other words, we are over budget.
- If the CPI is greater than 1, we are earning more than the spending. In other words, we are under budget.
- If the CPI is equal to 1, this means earning and spending is equal. We can say that we are proceeding exactly as per the planned budget spending, although this rarely happens.

Once these values are determined:

— A negative EV simply shows things are not right. The value of the work performed does not match the value of the work scheduled. This is enough indication for the project team to assess the criticality of each behind-schedule task.

— If late works are found to be on the critical path or if the jobs carry a high risk to the project, team members must try to get the new tasks back on schedule.

— The first reaction of the site incharge is asking for additional project resources as there is another reading of cost efficiency. There is no point for the team to pour money in other labor if resource utilization can do the same work.

- **Estimate to complete (ETC).** This is the total cost of the work that remains to be done on the project. ETC should be measured as often as possible to make sure that the expected cost is in line with the established budget. When an original estimate is flawed, ETC is best calculated by analyzing the situation and making a new assessment. ETC = EAC − AC will give us how much projects will cost.
  - **The project has atypical variance.** A project has an unexpected risk or opportunity that skewed the project performance results. If the risk or opportunity is not

likely to be repeated, the variance is considered to be atypical. ETC is the difference between BAC and EV. ETC = BAC − EV.
- **The project has typical variances.** This implies that the differences that have occurred in the project are likely to be repeated in future.
ETC = BAC − EV divided by CPI.

- **Forecasting tools.** EV forecast is different from the preconceived estimate of total cost when a project closes; the difference has to be reconciled. The problems are identified which could be in late submission of drawings or late delivery of material or less labor.
- The rectified measures and commitments are made for future conditions between all stakeholders. There is a revision of the estimate of cost at completion based on performance to date. It also helps in the timely action of funding requirement so that work should not get stalled.
- **Estimate at completion (EAC).** It helps in the forecast of final required costs, based on performance. With this figure, the project manager is able to accurately estimate the total funds needed to complete a project within a finite range of values. The team can assess any time, the actual cost of the project incurred thus far and the estimated cost to complete the remaining work. When BAC is no longer viable, then forecasted EAC takes over.
  - If the project cost has no deviation from the budget or the rate of spending is same and the amount being spent on the project is in line with the fixed budget. EAC = BAC divided by CPI.
  - If original estimates of the cost of the project are flawed, it is best to make a new estimate of the expense of the remaining work to compute the EAC. EAC = AC + ETC.

- **The project has atypical variance.** This implies that the project had an unexpected risk or opportunity that skewed the project performance results. If the risk or opportunity is not likely to be repeated, the variance is considered to be atypical.
  EAC = AC + (BAC − EV). It calculates the AC to date plus the remaining budget.
- **The project has a common variance.** Variations that occur in the project are likely to be represented in the future.
  EAC = AC + (BAC − EV) divided by CPI

- **EAC** is most useful when project schedule is a factor impacting ETC effort.
  EAC = AC + (BAC − EV) divided by CPI × SIP.

- **To complete performance index (TCPI).** It is a measure of the cost performance. This gets achieved with the remaining resources to meet a specified management goal. It is the ratio of cost of remaining work to a remaining budget.
  - TCPI based on BAC= BAC − EV / BAC − AC
  - TCPI based on EAC= BAC − EV / EAC − AC

  Greater than 1 is bad and less than 1 is good.

- **VAC (variance at completion)** = BAC − EAC is an indicator whether the project is over budget or under budget.
  - If VAC > 0, project is under budget
  - If VAC < 0, project is over budget
  - If VAC = 0, project is on budget

- **Performance review.** It compares cost performance overtime/overrunning or underrunning the budget.
- **Variance analysis.** There should be regular analysis on a periodic basis and cause identification with impact

to be determined along with the mitigation plan. Have proper explanation (cause/impact/corrective action) after determining the following:

- CV = EV − AC
- SV = EV − PVC

Percentage of acceptance of variation will tend to decrease as work proceeds.

- **Trend analysis.** This is determined over a period if performance is improving or deteriorating.
- **EV performance.** Compares performance baseline to AC and schedule variance.

Using all the above calculations, the variance can be analyzed:

- What is the problem causing the variance?
- What is the impact on other activities and efforts being undertaken as all are interrelated?
- What is corrective action to be made to negate the difference or reduce deviations?
- What will be the impact on performance parameters baseline of cost and schedule?
- What will be the expected benefits of the corrective and preventive actions being undertaken?

MONITOR AND CONTROL SCOPE DELIVERABLE

Till now the schedule, cost, and quality had been monitored. Now, it is time to ascertain if the deliverables, as agreed in the scope of the contract, have also been achieved. Ultimately, it is the deliverable that matters in a battle.

Take an example of Subedar Bana Singh in Operation Rajiv to capture the highest peak in Siachen. The operation was named after Second Lt Rajiv Pande who had earlier led a 13-man patrol with ropes tied.

Unfortunately, he was killed, but the team had been able to establish a foothold. There were many more unsuccessful attempts, and in the end, a task force led by Major Varinder Singh and a final assault by Subedar Bana Singh got the post amidst heavy blizzard. The whole operation was monitored and controlled by Officer Major Varinder and his brigade commander who gave heavy artillery fire barrage before the attack. In the last phase, when Subedar Bana Singh reached the top, his guns got jammed but he lobbed a grenade, and after a heavy hand-to-hand combat, the Pakistani soldiers were killed, and the post was taken.

There was no compromise on the deliverable. The peak was to be captured, and that was it. There was monitoring and control of the complete operation at different levels, the brigade commander controlling the artillery fire support, Major Varinder Singh controlling the support operation on the ground, and Subedar Bana Singh controlling the last leg and ensuring the deliverable is achieved.

The project team should have a similar spirit. They have to provide a deliverable which is a verifiable product, result, or a capability required by the project.

- The deliverable undergoes internal quality control processes and is verified as being correct. It conforms to the necessary and documented quality control specification, and it becomes a verified deliverable.
- The project manager should ensure that every deliverable is assessed against the expected quality standards. Once they meet the expected standards, they are presented to the customer. The scope validation is for obtaining acceptance of the deliverable from the client.
- The scope is validated using inspection as a tool and comparing nonperformance data and information against customer requirement. The acceptance criteria are to determine if the product is acceptable to the client or not.
- If the customer is happy with the deliverable, the deliverable is accepted and is used as an input into closing processes and work. The deliverable is formally signed off.
- Proof of acceptance is taken on record for closing the project.

MONITOR AND CONTROL SAFETY AUDIT OF THE SITE

There is a regular review of safety and security before, during, and after the operations. This is one aspect which is never lost sight of amidst even thick of the battle. If a situation is becoming a threat to the soldiers, an immediate assessment is taken of VUCA issues, and a safety review result in plan B also, if needed.

Several days before the 1971 War, there was a salient called Boyra in the Indian territory. This area was being used by Mukti Bahini, the Bangladeshi rebel group, to train and launch guerrilla attacks in East Pakistan against the Pakistan Army. To counter these tactics of Mukti Bahini, Pakistan started attacking the Indian territory with Sabre fighters who used to strafe the area with bombs and slip back to the East Pakistan territory. The safety of the Indian Population was at stake.

After a review of the safety situation, the Indian Air Force was tasked to get them within the Indian territory, and time was a few minutes over a 3 km territory in the Indian borders. On one such occasion, the Indian Air Force scrambled their Gnats Aircraft, and they got three Pakistan Sabre Aircraft in the famous dogfight witnessed by civilians also from the ground. The provocation of safety was thwarted timely by the Indian Air Force and the tone was set for the war to follow.

Equally, the project manager during the execution of the project must always keep track of safety and security issues under his/her own watchful eyes and not delegate it, so that timely action can be taken before the situation gets out of hand.

- A safety walk in every nook and corner of the site with all subcontractors and another team will ensure that some subcontractor adopts the best practices. There will be some lapses or gaps that will also be highlighted on the spot.
- There should be compulsory as many "near misses reports" as possible, describing what was going wrong and what remedial action was taken to rectify it. Encouraging "near miss report" will increase safety awareness. If safety trends are measured, the safety will be adequately controlled.

- Proper subcontractor evaluations should be done for the expected safety criteria standards. The aim of each subcontractor safety arrangements and preparedness should be zero injuries. There should be proper ownership across the site. Safety should be everybody's concern.
- All team members should be trained and unique to the safety in the job. Safety written instruction should be displayed wherever possible, starting from the entrance of the gate, with visitors also being a safety card of dos and don'ts. There should be proper communication of safety issues every day for zero injuries which should be the objective at the site.

MONITOR AND CONTROL STAKEHOLDER PERFORMANCES

This is the most important aspect of war or a project. If there is a failure or lack of support or proper planning at the top or senior level, it goes unnoticed. It has serious fallouts also. First, like in Kargil, the lackluster performance of the top leadership of all organizations that were responsible for monitoring the intelligence across Line of Control (LOC) resulted in Pakistan troops occupying height on the LOC. A bloody war followed with a loss of young lives, but what happened to those stakeholders whose performance failed to prevent the Kargil occupation. The bottom line is if stakeholder are not monitored at all level, a Kargil will happen in projects also.

The project manager should establish a culture of transparency and accountability by paying close attention to the following aspects:

- Have individual progress review sessions to assess if all people are aware of their duties. All should be aware of what falls in noncompliance. The excuse of a task not understood and causing rework will not be acceptable.
- Timely reward and recognition of good work should be encouraged. At the same time, there should be absolute

clarity on the consequence for inaction on the agreement, and accountability questioning should happen promptly.

Lt Col. Awasthy could not get honor and reward for his last stand in the battle of Lagyala Gompa in the 1962 War as there was nobody left to cite him and those in the rear could not come forward as their own role would be exposed why the debacle of 1962 happened that amounted to so many lives lost. When 62 Infantry Brigade was withdrawing due to Chinese aggression, Lt Col. Awasthy took charge of remnants of the battalion and others and when they were passing through the Lagyala Gompa monastery, the Chinese ambushed them. The Rajput Battalion could have withdrawn, but they choose to fight it out. All were killed along with the brave CO Lt Col. Awasthy. The Chinese dug a mass grave and buried them till their bodies were retrieved later with gun wound in front and not in back, indicating how they were killed fighting facing the Chinese and not withdrawing.

- All junior leaders should be sensitized to take personal responsibility and accountability for progress.

The project manager should also advise his site team not to accept the generalized statement that progress is happening, instead take a specified date from functional managers and keep following it up.

- Close issues between stakeholders at the earliest.
- Establish a progress measurement system.
- Take pictures from remote locations.
- Send chasers to close gaps with the parties concerned.
- Man-hours spent are an indication of the cost and progress.
- Ensure no over complicating of processes.

15-MINUTE WORKOUT

In the Indian Air Force and Indian Army or Indian Navy flying drills, the most important aspect is the morning briefing. There it starts with information on the weather and the airfield status and later the actual mechanics of the flying sorties and other tactical and operational aspects.

A daily review, workout every day with the team, and the project manager addressing the whole site team once a month are essential. In Army, the CO used to take a Sainik Sammelan once a month. That solved many problems on the spot.

- Agenda of workout every day.
  - Which are the task we are not doing properly?
  - Who is doing what and by when?
  - The work activities, by resource, and the schedule of completion leading to the next milestone and deliverable.
  - What might affect the work—monitor all VUCA issues, which includes having a plan for mitigating or eliminating the risk or issue.
- **Who is depending on the deliverables?**
  - Determine who are dependent on the output of the preceding step.
  - The team members who are to complete their work.
  - Who are the other stakeholders or external entities who are working with the team. It is better to coordinate their deliverable with the team deliverables.
- **Who needs to know what?**
  - Type of communication is the key to all successful projects.
  - New scheduling needs to be updated as a bottom-up exercise activity by activity.
  - The new update reflects the real situation as felt by the people that are close to execution.
  - Identify and tackle those issues that prevent smooth execution.
  - Ensure people who are executing are listened to.
  - Feedback should be provided to functional contributors.
- **Resolving issues during execution.** Some issues always come up during execution, for example, a functional manager

not supporting timely for a requirement from the head office. Thus, the site suffers, and execution also gets affected. The project manager should encourage one-to-one conversation and later use ERP to log an issue.

- **Problem reporting and resolution.** It involves recording an issue in a project which will even remotely result in a VUCA condition.
    - **Incident reporting.** The project manager should monitor all such matters that need to be brought to the notice of the head office related to any loss of material, resources, or any safety issue of the team.
    - **Issues management.** An issue is a point that requires file noting but is not considered a problem or change. It is solvable with or without the project manager's intervention, and the team gets the resolution implemented. There should be timelines for such resolutions.
    - **Resolving issues at the head office.** The project manager should make his head office team chase all the stakeholders for issue resolutions and the resolutions should be communicated in writing to the initiator. There should be fixed times and after the elapse of the same, the project manager should take charge of the issue himself.
    - **Issue register.** The project manager should ensure that his team executive maintains an issue record or system entry in ERP. It is better to record in a document all matters that are brought up by any stakeholder, which are not getting resolved. The top management keeps a tab on its timely closure by preventive or corrective action. The executives also ensures that issue log is sent to concerned stakeholders for follow up, in the best interest of the project. That way, it helps to solve all stakeholder expectations as well.

MONITOR AND CONTROL COST OF POOR QUALITY (COPQ)

There are regular reviews on why waste or losses have happened in armed forces. The finding is usually assessed by a proper court of inquiry if losses are considerable. That prevents something being swept under the carpet and accountability is fixed with losses either to be borne by the state or by the individual. In other words, if the government is spending on the COPQ of any nature, it has to be justified.

Likewise, the project manager must identify the correct definition of waste and losses that are unacceptable to the company. Many times, inefficiency swept under the carpet is never referred to as a loss. People are aware of it, but nobody talks about it. That loss keeps hurting the profits. During the stakeholder meet, there should be a clear and agreeable definition of COPQ:

- It could also be rework done by engineering and fabrication errors
- Quality rejects of material and replacement cost
- Quality declines of welding and rework
- Lack of day-to-day planning that caused delayed work, or material handling equipment lying unused in contractual hours
- Late engineering drawing release
- Inadequate protection for material storage

THE TRUTH BOARD

In the Indian Air Force, there is a magazine in which pilots share incidents of accidents that happened or could have happened. The idea was to share these incidents with other pilots and save lives. It also had comments and reviews of specialists, providing causes of and reasons for these accidents. It improved the overall mistakes in flying drills and also refined the safety policy. This practice of sharing flaws and mistakes also provides guidance in preventing future oversight during the whole process, which is never-ending.

The project manager could have a "truth board" in the head office where team members can post confessions of problems, delays, or cost overruns. There should be no shame or fear as no work is devoid of problems and negatives. The project manager must explain to the team that if weaknesses are not exposed in time by us, the customer will expose it with more serious repercussion of losses. So accept the pitfalls and improve to prevent VUCA issues.

A DELIGHT UPDATE TO CUSTOMER FOR CUSTOMER SATISFACTION

The peak has been won; *Yeh Dil Manage More* were the words of PVC Captain Vikram Batra.

Whenever an accomplishment has been made in a battle, it is transmitted through a colored flare in the darkness of night or by radio or by a flag waving in the thick of battle. It helps to share successes as it builds further tempo for operations.

Project Milestone Feedback

The customer should regularly be informed on following lines to avoid penalties or LD issues later. Isn't this a dream feedback for any customer for getting the report that the team ensured that 100 percent scope of work was achieved by reaching a milestone. It is possible by the following:

- There should be a lot of advance thinking of what can go wrong in a VUCA situation in the performance baseline. Preventive and corrective measures were put in place.

- The team should submit a list of concerns, every week or month, of VUCA issues and how these were addressed to ensure that baseline performances are always kept on track. Each delay that is caused should be measured and corrected as per the list.
- The team should attach the planned, actual, and EVs. They should also show productivity norms of man-hours every week and machinery used to prove that there was very less variation between planned and actual values.

RACE RESULTS

- **Rapid speed.** It was maintained by monitoring schedule through work performance data, information, and report. Critical path was always reviewed, and material supply was monitored to arrive in time.
- **Absolute scope.** It was achieved by ensuring that all deliverables are verified and accepted by the customer. Any deliverable not accepted goes back to execution and gets completed in all aspects. There are no backlogs from any phase.
- **Class quality.** The quality checks were strictly followed to make deliverables acceptable. Regular inspection monitoring of matrices was ensured to make it a class quality product.
- **Economical cost.** The project was monitored by EVM calculations and gaps in variance between planned and actual values were addressed and brought back to performance baselines.

TAKEAWAYS

Visibility of work every day is most important by at least a 15-minute workout. That will help in further monitoring of schedule, cost, and quality to achieve an acceptable and deliverable scope. At the same time, monitoring stakeholder performance, safety, and COPQ are very essential to ensure smooth working.

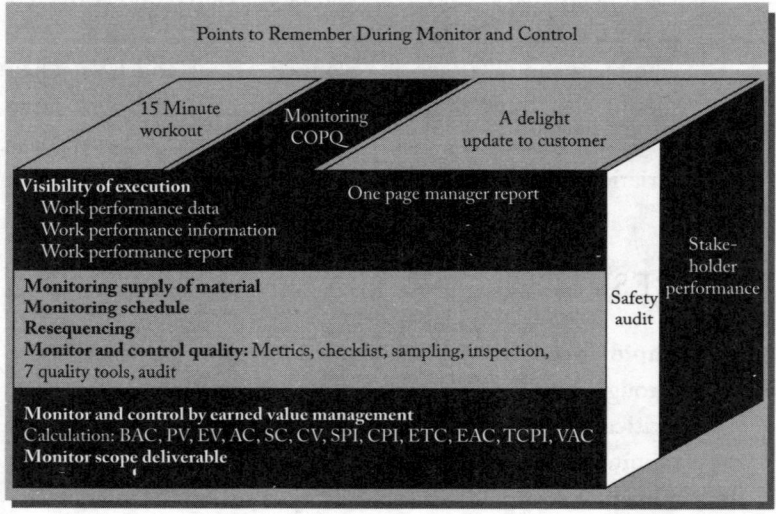

CHAPTER 10

The Hybrid Leader

> *I looked for those sharp scratchy harsh almost unpleasant guys who see and tell you about things as they are*
>
> —Thomas J. Watson

DECENTRALIZATION OF PLANNING AND EXECUTION

There is a new requirement in today's world. It is of hybrid leaders and managers who can do both planning and execution at the lowest level of execution and come back with results. They are particularly needed in the VUCA environment when things can go wrong and there is no time to look back. They have to work with a contingency plan on the ground.

There is a famous true story of an army officer Lieutenant Andrew Rowan written by Writer Hubbard in 1899. It reflects how an individual can make a difference and make things happen without any dependency on headquarters or senior management.

The story is during the 1898 Spanish–American War. There was a lot of tension between the United States and Spain. Spain ruled Cuba at that time. When hostilities broke out between Spain and the United States, President McKinley wanted that Cuban rebels should start a war with Spain. He wanted somebody to deliver a message to the Cuban rebel leader General Garcia to help America in the war against Spain. He inquired from his intelligence head Colonel Wagner, "Where can I find a man who will carry a message to Garcia?"

At that time General Calixto Garcia, a Cuban-born Creole was fighting the Spanish Army in the fight for independence. No one knew his exact whereabouts in the mountains. There was no way any mail or telegraph could also reach him. However, Colonel Wagner recommended a young officer, Lieutenant Andrew Summers Rowan for the task: "Rowan will find Garcia for you if anybody can." And so the President handed this army officer a letter with instruction for it to be "delivered to Garcia."

Col. Wagner's directions were simple "Young man," said the superior officer, "you must carry a message to General Garcia, who will be found somewhere in the eastern part of Cuba. You must plan and act for yourself. The task is yours and yours only." Col. Wagner then shook Rowan's hand and repeated, "Get that message to Garcia."

Without asking any questions, Rowan left to find Garcia. In four days he landed by night off the coast of Cuba from an open boat, disappeared into the jungle, and in three weeks came out on the other side of the Island, having traversed a hostile country on foot, and delivered the letter to Garcia.

Rowan simply delivered the message to Garcia. He did not bother his superior or headquarter. He did not ask what the Cuban General looks like? Who are his contacts? "How do I get there?" He simply took the orders and did what he was asked to do.

Now, for a project, when things go wrong and time is vital for bringing the situation back to timelines and cost, is there a Rowan among us? Is there somebody who can get a message to Garcia without having to do an interrogation of his senior officer first? Is there someone who can get the job done without needing to have his employer hold his hand until the task is completed? If not, the boss might as well do it himself.

Now, this story accidently caught the attention of a writer by the name of Elbert Hubbard who was discussing the Spanish–American War with *his family. Everyone had been cheering General Calixto Garcia, the leader of the Cuban rebel forces, as the key to winning the war in Cuba, when Hubbard's son, Bert, put forth this argument: "In my mind," ventured Bert, "the real hero of the war was not General Garcia, but Lieutenant Rowan, the man who got the message to Garcia." His son's words made a mark in Hubbard's heart. Hubbard wrote the article, "A Message to Garcia" and the edition went to print. Since then this story has done the rounds in many magazines and forums.*

Why are so many people interested in an article about some unknown lieutenant by the name of Andrew Summers Rowan? The reason is everyone is looking for individuals such as Rowan.

In a world where slipshod assistance, foolish inattention, dowdy indifference, and half-hearted work seem the rule, we need "Rowans" who are willing to "do the thing" ... to stand up, take the initiative, and just do it.

Now Ask Yourself "Are You the Rowan of Your Company?"

1. Are you available for assignments, without hesitation, and adaptable to whatever task is at hand, given by your boss?
2. Are you reliable? If your boss asks you to get something done in a timely manner, have it done by that deadline. Often other deadlines must be met down the line, so do not be the weak link.
3. Can you figure out how to get it done on your own? This is a fine line to walk, but the more you can do on your own, the more burden you relieve from your superior. The more burden you relieve, the more grateful your superior will be.
4. Can you take action? So often people get bogged down in the details that they become apoplectic and unable to even start a project. Oftentimes, procrastination prevents even the first step from being taken, which is most often the hardest step to take.
5. Are you diligent? it will show your employer that you do not need constant hand-holding or someone looking over your shoulder to make sure that you are getting your work done.

If you are all the above, then you are the Rowan of any organization that learns to value your kind of work. We have become experts with excuses when faced with VUCA of why we cannot do what we are supposed to do. When execution is on and there is a VUCA problem, can we afford to keep looking to the head office for making decisions? If that is the case, then project or operation will get high jacked. It is okay to slow and feel bogged down by pressure but one must not give up.

In battle or in projects or any operation, there may be times when one finds himself/herself drowning in quicksand, times he has to hang on to make it through, times when he feels so downtrodden, he does not know if he can put one foot in front of the other, but he will not quit. Quitting is not even an option.

A project site team member will always say that he/she will accomplish the task that is set before him/her. A project manager or executive will pursue excellence. Even though he/she may fall down, he/she will get backup. He/she will dust it off, and keep pressing on until he/she wins.

Situation awareness. The first thing a Rowan or hybrid manager, when faced with VUCA during execution, will do is becoming aware of the ground situation. There is a constant inflow of details about the information from ground zero. That helps in quick response and planning a future flow of operation as per changing conditions. A quick estimate of the situation should be taken and the problem acted upon.

PRIORITIZE VUCA ISSUES TO SOLVE THE CRITICAL PROBLEMS

In 2015, an earthquake hit Nepal. Indian Army was on its way to Mt Everest. The expedition was halted, but the Indian Army team focused on other VUCA issues that were building up. Apart from providing medical aid to the victims hit by an earthquake, they salvaged many dead bodies.

Similar is the story of another British Climber Leslie Binns, 42, from Rotherham, South Yorkshire, who was a few hours away from reaching the summit when he saw an Indian woman climber in distress. He judged the situation and made a choice of giving up his Everest dream and rescued the fellow climber by getting her down to the base camp and administering medical aid.

Both these stories will inspire any project manager to identify what all issues and challenges can be controlled and what cannot be. The aim is to do more of what can work on that particular day. The idea is not to allow any workforce or time to go wasted even if there are problems of resources. There is so much alternative work one can do at the site till problems are getting resolved at the back end.

Another key point is to invest in human relationships. The British climber said that no Everest is more worth than a human life. In other words, if work is stalled, use that time in training or doing something for team members or locals and invest that effort which will surely come back in some form later.

PREPARING THE CONTINGENCY PLAN

The first set of plan usually undergoes a change when contact with the enemy has been made. It is not necessary that the enemy will react the way we had decided and thought during the planning stage. Going into any battle, a leader always has four plans, the strategic plan (long-term plan), the tactical plan (whom his different arms and functions will coordinate), the operational plan (how his soldiers will fight it out in phases), and finally there is a fourth plan, that is, the backup contingency plan.

This contingency plan is made but is decentralized allowing junior commanders to modify and execute. Before this plan is set in motion, the reactions of the opposition are always gauged based on many factors such as terrain and resources held by the enemy. Even the profile of the leader is assessed as to how he will react. The policy-makers deliberate how significant the impact of the response will be on the future operations and the overall battlefield scenario.

All things considered, the project managers will face some regular problems which need some change in execution methods. As a matter of fact, many times the situation can change during the execution of a project. For example, reduction in contractor workforce, labor accidents, material missing or not arrived, work stalled because of rains, etc.

As a result, work will stop or slow down despite commitments made using the last planner method. However, one must be ready for changing events during project execution and have a flexible response.

Now, whenever these changes occur, the team should review the happenings quickly. Most importantly, the actual ripple effect of the event should be accessed. It should be seen what the impact of the threat or VUCA will be. It should be analyzed if other activities need to be rearranged. If there is any variance detected in baseline parameters of scope, time, and quality, then impact on cost should also be determined. To ensure this analysis, we will discuss ODDA loop that will help in clear decision-making in the chain after due consideration of consequences and pros and cons regarding disruption in a project.

QUICK DECISION-MAKING AND EXECUTION USING ODDA LOOP

How many of you have seen the movie "Top Gun?" That was the first time as a kid I saw the concept of ODDA loop. Tom cruise as "Maverick" inverted his fighter plane on the Soviet pilot aircraft cockpit. That was one of the most mind-blowing scenes of the movie with Tom Cruise taking the photo of the pilot in the inverted position himself in his own aircraft and showing him a finger. Now that scene showed a remarkable superiority of the pilot in air-to-air combat, always one step ahead of his opponent.

That superiority in situation awareness is the aspect every manager should strive for, to be ahead of any problems or opponents that may come in the way. Now, what are these problems and opponents? There are VUCA issues that need quick and rapid decision-making to reduce the adverse effects that may cause losses of lives and material. If a request for change of any planning step is sent to higher formation headquarter, it is followed up in a time-bound manner, and its impact is also assessed.

However, it is to be understood that without follow-up, things will never move, as there are different priorities of decision-makers who may put an issue at the back burner as they may feel that something else is important. Thus, bureaucracy seeps in. They are the opponents—somebody like the Russian pilot in the movie *Top Gun*.

Under similar circumstances, the project manager knows that there is always a hidden bureaucratic setup in any functional department that is heavy on administrators. They also have to justify some value addition, and hence will ensure that the decision considerations are caught in layers of approvals and excessively complicated processes. It, however, results in extended schedule and cost overruns. Without losing time and heart, the project manager should always encourage his team to use real-time communication to keep updating and revising any plans as per changing environment.

The ODDA loop is one of the methods for quick decision-making methods. The OODA loop was devised by Former US Air Force Colonel John Boyd for decision-making in an air combat. It is always better to be one step ahead of the problems or competition and be prepared to react in anticipation. ODDA helps us to do that.

- **Observe.** Collect current information from as many sources as practically possible.
- **Orient.** Analyze this information, and use it to update your present reality.
- **Decide.** Determine a course of action.
- **Act.** Follow through on your decision.

The team will continue to cycle through the OODA loop by observing the results of their actions. They will assess whether they achieved the results as intended. They will then review and revise their initial decision and move to the next action.

Observe. Like an air force fighter pilot with a full field of vision, the team will capture as much incoming data as possible. The project manager should ask several engineers at the site to assess issues that are directly and indirectly affecting the work. They should also decide the residual effects later on and how many such predictions were correct, enforcing that they should be taken seriously on realities of working conditions.

Orient. It is related to the interpretation of the situation by the team so that they can jointly take decisions. The team should build an ability to analyze and synthesize the data that comes in, and based on the previous experiences deal with the new information that is coming in. The team should understand what is going on and make sense of the ground realities. If they get oriented fast, that will enable them to move faster amidst issues. More than anything, it is also important that all keep reorienting to the situation in the project as new information is added in the observation stage.

Decide. Decisions are the most difficult to make, especially when they are based on observation and orientation, and realization of problems keeps coming. Hence, decisions also keep changing as situations change. New circumstances trigger changes to earlier decisions made and subsequent actions, as team cycles through observation and orientation stages again and again.

Act. The act stage is where the decision is not only taken but also implemented. The team also assesses the effects of the decision made by cycling back to the observance stage. The team then learns about the action influence on the rest of the period, what was missing, or if more measures must be taken. It is always better to assess work rather than wait for fallouts which may have disaster consequences.

The OODA loop is also not a fixed or hard cycle to tell us what to do, but it is a more of the continuous real-time process that keeps telling us to change what we had originally conceived. With this approach, one moves faster through each stage as the situation changes as there is no time to have a bureaucratic process for allowing decisions to take place. That would slow down the process.

The final step is to keep orienting to changing the situation and taking appropriate measures as new information is added. The conclusion is to make a smooth and direct transition between various phases. The team observes, interprets, and takes necessary actions and again sees the effects of the actions, makes changes if needed, and keeps moving ahead. There are no long pauses. Proactive is the name of the game and opportunities are exploited, overcoming any looming VUCA threats.

DEALING WITH CONTINGENCIES

For every situation, there are preplanned responses. It is a matter of choice to drive these responses with a heavy, strong force reaction or divide them. It is situation-based. Like in mountain warfare during the Kargil War, while attacking an enemy who was perched at the top, the enemy used a single light machine gun to target our attacking forces as we were climbing up in mass waves. There were a large number of fatal casualties. Therefore, the second option that the Indian Army used was to have small lean teams attacking from various parts of the mountain. Each team was taking multiple routes to divert the attention of the enemy. There are few casualties, and the enemy reaction is divided.

In deserts, unlike the mountains, it is better to move with the impact of a large force of tanks thundering across shivers the enemy. So it is a case-to-case situation what course of action to take. Similarly, when we are attacking problems in projects, there are many alternative action plans. The team should decide the course of action to cover the backlog of work and schedule. There are basically two methods to close on the backlog:

- **Fast tracking.** It means those activities which were supposed to be done sequentially can be done in parallel now with other activities. It may result in rework, but it can be used to compress the project schedule. It is akin to a lot of small teams climbing up concurrently to tackle an enemy.
- **Crashing.** The team added resources to complete activities ahead of schedule, or simply "throwing more money at the project." Crashing is usually less efficient than fast tracking. It is akin to a complete wave of troops climbing up at the same time to overrun the enemy, but in the bargain there will be losses of own troops also.

The decision-making process. Initially, when things go wrong, the OODA loop is used to observe, orient, decide, and act on which option to take; we can do some parallel activities together or use additional resources to complete the backlog and current activity.

- Analysis of factors to decide the course of action whether to use fast tracking or crashing:
    - Based on commitments got or made with other stakeholders
    - The level of complexity of project schedule and how it will be back on track
    - Existing possibility/margin to compensate delays through particular effort or additional resources with minimal cost
    - Lesson learned from similar projects—how much buffer we can use?
    - Existence of buffers on critical chain
- **Comparison of courses of action.** As the project manager analyzes options to compress the schedule, the possible

impact on resources and project budget should be kept in mind. External perceptive on stakeholders' resolutions of issues should also be sought for. Issues that are not so important and can be caught up later should be identified. Future VUCA issues that may come if current or particular backlog tasks are not completed should be figured out and a calculated judgment should be taken based on that.

- **Fast tracking.** The project manager always preferred fast tracking of activities. It was essential to timely get the additional resources and to close any backlogs by working overtime. There was also no necessity to go through the long chain of unnecessary approvals or processing any irrelevant file, noting sheets for routine expenditure. All such expenses were within the site manager's powers of spending. There are many ways of fast tracking like:
    o Splitting a long task into smaller tasks and making the team focus on small tasks, getting more output in a shorter period.
    o Additional buffer time covers backlogs of any delays in the task.
    o Eliminating less important work to be done later, completes the primary mission, so that the main work gets back on track.
- **Selecting a course of action.** The options are presented to the project sponsor (or the project board) for approval. The final plan should address the following:
    o The schedule has to be realistic for intensive phases of work with resource margins for acceleration/compensation of reduced productivity.
    o The program should be focused on the main activities, with the right balance and sound quality update and change agility.

- To protect the project budget, a single contingency element for such backlog is always added in the order of 5–7 percent of the total budget.

- Conduct of the decision-making process.
  - The project manager should issue new orders during execution. He should allocate tasks and ensure that timelines are given in the LOO.
  - Necessary resources and material should be provided.
  - Standards expected should be of class quality.
  - Each task steps should be identified about how the work will be executed.
  - Supporting functions ensures appropriate LOE to LOO.

The cost of crashing. The project manager at times also has to opt for crashing instead of fast tracking. Crashing always adds to the cost, so the team should follow certain rules when opting for crashing:

1. Identify the activities that are falling on the critical path.
2. The activity will influence future events, and a cyclical delay will happen.
3. Crash from least expensive to most expensive.
4. How much new team or new members will be competent, will they make any difference?
5. Did the team exhausted the option of fast tracking?

Crashing costs are considered to be linear. The project manager should observe the least costly activities of crash cost per week. Crash such activities. It is always advisable to crash the least expensive activities on the critical path first (based on cost per week). Crashing, however, is a risky proposition as there is indirect cost also linked with it like the cost of overheads of site infrastructure, construction equipment, and machinery. There is an always increasing interest on the investment made on utilities, added labor, personnel salary costs, etc.

APPROVALS OF CHANGES

Change Control Board (CCB)

Once the analysis of the situation and ODDA loop has been followed with a choice of deciding fast tracking or crashing, the approval has to be sought from the CCB.

If a change is small, the project manager should authorize the site incharge to make decisions about change requests with some level of authority and keep the project moving.

If the change is significant, then a change request should be raised. All change requests should be recorded in the modification log. All change requests should be given a unique number also on the configuration system. All changes should be managed in a coherent manner, documented, evaluated, tracked, and incorporated into a project management plan.

The control change board comprises of the project sponsor and key members of top management. They hold the meeting on the receipt of change request which is outside the project manager level of the delegated authority.

- **Change control process.** It facilities the interaction between the CCB and the project team to have a mutual understanding of the impact of the modification.
    - A preceded method for file noting and required approval through ERP is assisted for authorizing any change in scope, schedule, or cost.
    - The changes will be raised in the configuration system as increase, record, review, and resolve change requests.
    - Performance baselines quickly become invalid if they fail to incorporate changes to the approved baseline when the work scope has been modified through additions or deletions. Hence, all project change requests must be quickly addressed by either approval or rejection.

- **How change is managed till the sign-off of a deliverable.** The project manager should follow a very transparent system to ensure that work once turned concludes into a deliverable by going through a series of steps.
- **Approved change request.** It represents work to be completed on the project. Once CCB approves the change request, the required work is sent back to planning and execution stages for completion. The work is then checked during quality control work if it is as per change request made earlier. The monitoring and control of all work finally results into a deliverable which is any unique product/result.
- **Validated change.** After an approved change request has been implemented and checked, conformance then becomes a validated change.
- **Verified deliverable.** It must be subject to quality control to determine if it meets quality requirement and should be moved on to scope verification.

Acceptance of Deliverable

These verified deliverable finally ensure that the customer is happy with the results. It also enables obtaining acceptance of deliverable from the customer. If the customer confirms, deliverables are signed off, and proof of acceptance is used as a significant input into work involved in closing the project.

Configuration Management

It controls the change control procedures within the system and provides how different iteration of project and results are tracked and monitored with a unique number of the identifier. It ensures that all stakeholders also have an update of the plan and reference of the expected unfolding of events.

FORWARD ZONE PLANNING

During the Kargil War, the small-team concept inspired the plan at the post to regain the lost peaks that were earlier occupied by Pakistani forces and jihadists. Not only that, but the forward team was also empowered to rationalize the resources among themselves so that all could take advantage of critical resources.

The final allotments of air power, artillery, or armored gun support was considered at the headquarter level, but the actual demand originated in the form of forwarding an observation officer, an officer from artillery who should always be with the fighting troops to request the arty strike. Similarly, there was the ground liaison officer to request the air raid.

The control of supporting resources such as material and logistics was also decentralized as much as possible to the CO so that he does not have to look back for supplies or ammunition or fuel when he is fighting the battle.

Likewise, the project manager should encourage the same concept of forwarding zone planning with his site team, hence the idea of the last planner in forwarding area.

The scheduling process is a continuous affair. The situation for fast tracking and crashing occurs as the ground realities do not matching with the plan. The scenarios are so much flexible, and the situation changes so quickly during tempo of operations. It is best to shift planning of execution now at the site when one is in the middle of the project. It helps everyone to allow the team to take charge of ground operations.

The last planner system (LPS). The broad concept of LPS is as follows:

- It uses the overall project plan as the general frame and ensures that the essence of timelines expected at the head office does not get lost.

- It is more concerned with day-to-day activities of the actual production at the site.
- The planning and execution are managed by a more flexible approach accounting for the real progress of the project.
- All the prerequisites such as resources and material with engineering drawings needed for performing a distinct task are in place before it is assigned to a workgroup.

Define priority areas. The project team should classify the work at the site in the following categories:

- **SHOULD.** Assignments to be done shortly as per the overall project plan. It comes under phase schedule.
- **CAN.** Assignments that have all their prerequisites ready, for example, previous project steps completed, necessary materials are at hand, and the workforce is available. It is under look-ahead plan.
- **WILL.** The tasks that are commenced before the next planning round and form part of weekly plan.
- **DID.** The assignments that have been completed and are viewed as progress tracking.

The master schedule. The master schedule should dictate the theme of the operational LPS. It will set the milestones to be achieved.

Phase schedule. The planning should be done by starting from the benchmark and working backward so that each task releases work to the next task.

- The planner does reverse thinking to select the value adding tasks by working back from the target completion date to produce a pull schedule?
- He calculates the "contingency" period and think of issues where it will be used as an emergency.
- He coordinates a phase scheduling meetings by sticking small notes with task names, and durations are written.
- The direction of these notes is from predecessors in the left to successors to the right.

- Phase scheduling produces better schedules as we plan near action and involve specialist and a team which will be doing the task.

Look-ahead process. These constraints have to be removed in time by the project manager, site in-charge and team by regular follow up with other stakeholders in the Head Office. The team is ordered to perform only that tasks which have no constraints or restrictions of any kind. This ensures there is no waiting time for any resource to come up and there are no unfinished or delayed task later. The onus is, hence, on the complete team to constantly monitor future task to remove all constraints in time.

The current task and forecast could also be used for look-ahead functions. The site planner shapes workflow sequence and rate of man-hours required. He is better positioned to match workflow and capacity needed to do it. He also maintains a backlog of ready work. Finally, he plans detailed plans for how work is to be done:

- **Advantages of a look-ahead schedule.** The project manager was very optimistic of the last planner method remembering the Kargil operation where the young officer did the last minute planning to make things work. It would operate better as a checklist which is cross-checked with the forecast information. It gives an early warning when tasks cannot be implemented according to the phase schedule because of resource problems or conflicts between subcontractors.
- **From look-ahead to weekly plan.** The site incharge now considers targets of the next week selected from the look-ahead plan. The work that is ready is selected from the workable backlog to be completed. The reliability of the weekly program is assured, and if there are any failed assignment, a cause analysis is done to prevent the problem from happening again.
- **The advantage of a weekly plan.** This weekly meeting is different from regular planning meetings for the week ahead. The head office does not dictate the preconceived plan

but the site engineer and site planner select the task to be performed using a "can be done" filter in their selection. This ensures that only "mature" tasks (from the workable backlog) are scheduled. Any task that has unresolved constraint is avoided. The weekly plans are presented as bar charts.
- The pressure is back on the functional HODs to resolve the related constraints with negotiations and discussions to achieve a workable plan and which has everyone's commitment. It also brings the different trade managers together to coordinate their activities over the following week.
- Overall advantages of the LPS:
    - The site team can achieve deliverables faster at a reduced cost.
    - The plan is more realistic and was similar to just in time production.
    - It is the best option when traditional critical path is not working.
    - There is greater collaboration with field personnel and subcontractors.
    - There is alignment from the head office to site engineer now with a weekly plan.
    - The project manager respects the decision of the site engineers to call the shots now.
    - There is coordination with all stakeholders.

Inward of material by forwarding team. The last planner at site ensures that all seven flows—information, plant, equipment, materials, people, etc.—are flowing to the workforce so that tasks can be done when required. As far as material is concerned, the last planner at site ensures the following:

- What is the location of the different goods needed for a certain project task?
- What materials are at a particular place (e.g., site inventory or intermediate storage inventory)?

- What is the location of a certain shipment?
- The on-time delivery rate of a supplier.
- The lead-time of orders (from ordering to receiving of the goods).
- The lead-time of deliveries (from the dispatch to the receiving of the delivery).
- And, if the packages are traced in several locations, the deconstructed lead-times can be used for performance analysis of the supply chain.

The last planner allocates tasks on the finite schedule:

- Removes the material constraints of each task by making sure that the necessary materials are ordered before the functions are allowed to move to the workable backlog.
- Since the functions are positioned on the limited schedule, they can also be used to produce forecasts of future delivery needs for the suppliers.
- The last planner continuously updates a possible schedule for the project tasks shortly based on the progression of the project.
- When having visibility to future material needs, the suppliers can inform the last planner of potential delivery disruptions.
- The last planner can then adjust the task schedule taking the emerged material constraint into account.
- The material needs of each work have to be known.
- The materials required for a task can be thought of like a BOM for a task.
- Transparency to materials in the project supply chain is needed to enable checking whether the identified function materials are available or not.
- When equipped with the availability information, those project tasks in which substantial delays are detected can be transferred to later dates where the delays are satisfied.

Resource rationalization. There are occasions in projects when there are resource conflicts; at times the same resources are to be used in a couple of activities and it is not easy to manage them.

Talking of resource constraint and fighting it out, I am reminded of the Battle of Saragarhi where 21 Sikh soldiers of 4th Battalion of Sikh fought against 10,000 Afghans on September 12, 1897, as one of the world military's great last stands. They were not bothered about resource constraints and defended the signaling post to ensure communication between two forts held by the British. Saragarhi Day is celebrated every year in India and UK and the battle is part of school textbooks.

In projects, during the planning of resource allotment, ideally, there should be an even spread of support in the project life cycle with a smooth increase in early phases of the project and decrease as work gets finished in the end. The support encompasses workforce, material, equipment, cash flow, IT resources, etc.

- **Resource leveling in the WBS.** The project manager uses resource leveling of the workforce to ensure that resources are equally distributed over the schedule duration of the WBS. Here the period is fixed, it is time bound, and additional resources can also be used if needed.

  However, the rule is the best possible use of resources within a time constraint. The method primarily focuses on how much any noncritical activities can be delayed by using their float period to match with shifting of the resources. That way we get an even spread of resources prioritizing the use of same resources first for critical activities and later for noncritical activities.

  The best way for spreading resource allocation is to identify a few noncritical activities in the month and determine their earliest and latest start time and finish time.

  The Float period should be used and resources shifted to noncritical activities a bit ahead or a bit early. Normally, there is a peak time where both critical and noncritical work

is being done and by shifting noncritical activity without delaying the project allows constant resource utilization. That way the team then can focus on the main activities with full loaded resources spread over the entire duration.
- Simple steps for resource leveling:
    - Analyze the complete activity schedule.
    - Assess the critical activity which is the prime focus.
    - Determine noncritical activity also in the same period.
    - Calculate the resource usage for both critical and noncritical activities.
    - Total the resource usage in that particular period which will give the peak or trough in resource histogram usage for all activities spread over the project duration.
    - Accordingly, it is identified which week has high resource usage and which week has low resource usage.
    - The solution is now to shift the resources from the peak period to the low usage period by also identifying which all noncritical activities can be changed to the small peak period but within their free float time.
    - It is also preferred to shift those activities that have no successors and move those activities whose float permits the liberty to shift.
- **Scheduling limited resources.** There are instances when the team finds critical resources inadequate. There are many activities in a WBS occurring parallel with limited resources. So the only way out is to prioritize the side activities and delay the others until the earliest time the resources become available again. At the same time, it is important to ensure that resource limit does not exceed.

    The schedule will grow in more number of days, as successor activities are delayed until the earliest time more resources became available. However, now the resources are only considered upon to undertake one task at a time.

Point to note is that in any cycle the total amount of resources used at the beginning and while the activities are ongoing is less than or equal to the available resources.

MONITORING THE CONTRACTS COMMITMENT

Crashing of schedule. There may be an occasion where the customer is responsible for delays on the site by not fulfilling his commitment of help needed to do any work. The delays could also be due to unforeseen factors like monsoons. Now this backlog of work has to be completed by crashing the schedule and adding more workforce and resources. This additional cost of crashing should be first approved by the customer as part of change management procedure. This sanction of extra spending is a must to avoid any penalties later.

- **Starting and closing of project dates.** The customer may allow inward access to the site late by few weeks for his internal reasons. However, the time of entry has gone beyond the agreed contractual time. That means the baseline schedule and impact on cost due to dates shifted in monsoon or winter have to be taken on record as it will require additional person-hours. The increased cost should be put on records.
- **Work sequence changes.** The work sequence is agreed with the customer and subcontractor. There may be an occasion when either of them wants a change for some technical or resource reasons. If there is additional cost on that activity, be it changes in work sequence, take it in record as change management and cost impact.
- **Lack of support structure to EPC team.** The customer is obliged to provide support like elasticity, water, less interference of union who is working internally, and most significantly, space to work or store material, etc. If these are not being attended to, causing a delay for our subcontractor,

the meetings with the customer and his commitment should also be recorded if it is an impact on cost.
- **The cost of extra material.** If the scope of work is increased, the additional cost of equipment and its storage should also be recorded.
- **If there is rework by a subcontractor.** It could be due to reasons for which our team is not responsible, that cost should be debited to him/her. If there is cost impact due to own failures, it should also be reported to the customer, and we should be ready to add to COPQ.
- **Failure of the project to perform.** At times, we ask the subcontractor to deliver some work by insisting on what kind or size of the material to be used. It has to be either of it. Either we ask the subcontractor for a performance parameter of the system or ask him only to fit a particular type of part that may result in failure. So we cannot pass on the claim to him entirely. It is best to involve the subcontractor and take his/her view during the engineering and procurement stage before we ask him/her to start fitting in the construction stage.
- **Punch points.** If interim handover occurs scope-wise or packages-wise to customer representatives, there are fewer punch points. It is better to plan to handle over with photos and documentation so that any defects that come out during the execution stage are corrected. If handing over is done in the end, the punch points may end up as a major failure and become reasons for claim.
- **Ambiguous clauses and words.** It is also best to have clear understanding of the contract and every word, lest it is used as per convenience to raise a claim.
- **Send regular updates to the customer about any changes with delay reasons.** The updates will show the following:
  - Determination of the actual physical progress achieved compared to that planned
  - Complete development of the original plan

- Approved changes of the critical path and out of sequence activities
- Performance assessment of subcontractors
- Impact of VUCA disruption and how we should prevent further loss by timely assessing it and taking appropriate actions
- Delay analysis to identify causes of delays and impact calculation
- How all risks are to be mitigated

CONTROL OF WASTAGE

The contract was normally in two parts due to tax structure advantages. One is the material supply contract and the other is for execution contract. Normally the material is dispatched directly to the site from the supplier but documents are received from the provider at the head office, based on which the good receipt note is prepared and cost booking is made. The invoice copy, packaging slips, delivery note, etc., are sent for commercial invoicing to the customer. The payment is received either through LC or directly from the client.

At the same time, delivery note, packaging slip, dispatch instruction document, lorry receipt, etc., are received at the site store along with material, and accordingly, after the verification of content, a place receipt record is generated. This becomes the basis for payment to the supplier.

VUCA issues in this system. Normally the billing breakup is always as per the WBS and, accordingly, the material is pushed at the site. More the material goes over the place, and in time, the work speeds up, and better is the invoicing to the customer. That way, revenue generation is aligned up to date.

Problems start when a work is delayed and its corresponding material has already reached the site and the following stage equipment is also on its way. If the team is not able to catch up on the delayed milestone, the articles start piling up at the site. Concurrently, space problems start and if it is the monsoon period, material such as panels or electrical items or insulation material start getting spoiled.

The supplier is also not informed by site team to withhold any future dispatches to site as the site does not have enough space to keep the finished goods. The supplier does not also have any alternative place as their own place is filled up with finished items. The payments to the supplier for dispatches as per contracts have to be done in time as it is not their fault if the site is unable to use the material.

So, alignment of material with work breakdown structure is a must, and one has to ensure its timely utilization to prevent space problems.

HOW IS RACE RESULTS BEING ACHIEVED?

- **Rapid speed.** The work was monitored for any sudden changes, and if any change in plan was needed, it was done with ODDA loop decision-making. The option of fast tracking and crashing was also considered.
- **Absolute scope.** The project planning was finally shifted to the LPS where the scope was more micromanaged to be done weekly with all constraints removed for the task to be done in a week.
- **Class quality.** The quality checks were ensured as per contract clauses.
- **Economical cost.** The cost of crashing was also considered where the effort was to crash only that task which involved less cost. Resource utilization was also done to maintain cost and prevent wastage.

TAKEAWAYS

During execution, there will be changes. Those changes are best controlled by the team at the site using the last planner method and the ODDA loop.

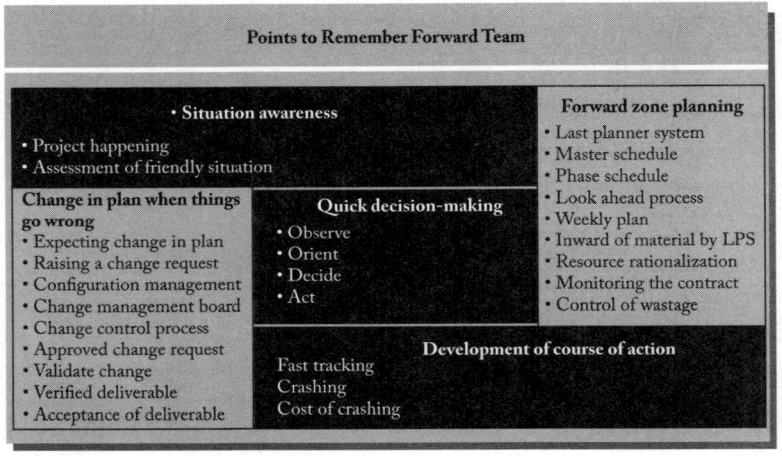

Points to Remember Forward Team

- **Situation awareness**
  - Project happening
  - Assessment of friendly situation

- **Change in plan when things go wrong**
  - Expecting change in plan
  - Raising a change request
  - Configuration management
  - Change management board
  - Change control process
  - Approved change request
  - Validate change
  - Verified deliverable
  - Acceptance of deliverable

- **Quick decision-making**
  - Observe
  - Orient
  - Decide
  - Act

- **Forward zone planning**
  - Last planner system
  - Master schedule
  - Phase schedule
  - Look ahead process
  - Weekly plan
  - Inward of material by LPS
  - Resource rationalization
  - Monitoring the contract
  - Control of wastage

- **Development of course of action**
  - Fast tracking
  - Crashing
  - Cost of crashing

CHAPTER 11

Closing of the Project

> *Don't tell people your plans,*
> *show them your results*

The closing of a project requires the same intensity as is required in planning and execution. No work is less important, although many times when we feel that execution is more important than the aftermath. In a battle, the reorganization phase is most significant when the last phase ends. This is the time when deliverables of the objective are assessed whether they have been secured or not. The next phase is accordingly planned. Troops are replaced by fresh troops and injured are sent to the medical aid post. Ammunition and food packets with water are distributed. In other words, a stock of things is taken for either closing the operation or pursuing the next stage. Normally, in the closing phase, the leadership's focus is on more vital issues for the next phase but there are so many things that team members can do on their own to make the first phase worthwhile.

The movie "Hacksaw Ridge" is a true story of Desmond Doss who refuses to pick up arms due to his Christian beliefs but still goes to the battle as a medical aid person. During the assault phase, the attacking force, of which he is a part, suffers a lot of casualties from the Japanese who are defending the ridge. There are wounded soldiers left on the battlefield as his battalion does a hasty retreat from the battlefield.

Desmond Doss refuses to get down the ridge during the reorganization phase and goes back to the battleground where in the night he rescues several wounded soldiers and drops them by rope from the ridge. He is able to do an impossible task of rescuing so many soldiers and saving their lives singlehandedly without a weapon. His unit gets so motivated by his efforts that in the next phase they win over the ridge in a fierce battle of which again Desmond Doss is a part; he also gets injured during the battle. Later, Desmond Doss was awarded the medal of honor for service during the battle of Okinawa.

Now, this story is of great significance as it shares that how a single, unarmed person saved so many lives because he went about his task undeterred even after others had given up, despite the risk to his life.

REORGANIZATION PHASE

In any battle, once the objective is taken, the reorganization phase starts. It means consolidation of the objective by verifying any lose remnants of the enemy that may stall the taking over of the objective. It involves mopping up the last resistance of enemy and organizing some semblance of order in the aftermath of the battle. It also means taking enemy prisoners and medical aid to enemy soldiers and our troops. A regimental aid post is immediately established. The equipment with guns and armored tanks are also rechecked for the battle worthiness of the next phase. The logistic vehicles come up setting up central administration for the troops.

Similarly, the last leg of the project is a crucial phase where all the loose ends should be tied up. There cannot be an unfinished scope of work. Reorganization or closing of the project involves the following steps:

- **The project commissioning.** The project manager ensures that all parts, components, systems have been designed, installed, erected, tested, operated, and are now in a maintainable condition. His/her quality and commissioning team ensures that the system as a whole with all interconnected software and hardware is functioning properly. It means ensuring that all individual service are working and are in synchronized harmony with each other.

- **Installed checking to remove all punch points.** It is the direct responsibility of the site team to resolve all punch points observed in installation tests, leads to point checks and system checks of all equipment. The quality inspector verifies that the design and proper interfaces between systems are established. All the punch points are cleared. Any deviations with contractor and customer which are mutually agreed should be documented.

    During installation, the static test is also undertaken; the readings give the quality and workmanship level of the facilities. Any lapses or errors are rectified before commissioning readings are taken.

- **Commission system checks.** It is the responsibility of the commissioning team to check all systems, equipment, and monitor how they are working. A walk down of all system verifies that all parts and interfaces are configured and operating correctly. For commissioning of each system, the following steps are observed:

    o The system is taken from static completion to working order by repeated testing and adjusting, keeping the health and safety requirements in mind.

    o The purpose is to achieve the specified performance by proper calibration of the system settings.

    o Data is collected for the time periods defined in the test procedure and verified against scientific model baseline data. Variations are corrected for compliance with all test stability criteria.

    o The performance test results that have been accepted as satisfactory signify the system as properly interfaced with the other systems. It can now take loading conditions also for verifying the stability.

- **Performance tests for plant and equipment.** Upon completion of the commissioning, performance testing can begin. Test runs are conducted with a standard agreed procedure for an individual plant, equipment, and facilities to assess the guaranteed performance. Variances are analyzed and cause of any test anomalies is determined. It is identified and corrected before starting the test or being accounted for in the final test report.
- **Handing over to the operation or production team.** The team that is going to work on the product is trained on the following processes:
    - Process for the planning of required quantity of material
    - Fixing responsibility and ownership to individual machine operators and supervisors
    - Regular plan start-up procedure
    - Normal shutdown procedure
    - Emergency closing procedures
    - Method for increasing the capacity and load production putting machining on full throttle
    - Guidelines for checking safety aspects on peak loads
    - Parameters for stabilization of operations
- **Customer satisfaction with final acceptance deliverable process.** All deliverables produced by the project go through a three-stage process.
    - **First stage:** Internal monitoring and quality control where the project manager takes the responsibility of ensuring that the deliverable conforms to the quality standards (during testing, inspection, commission, and performance checkup). Once all test readings are confirmed, the deliverable is termed a validated deliverable.
    - **Second stage:** These validated deliverables are presented to the customer for acceptance. If accepted by the client, they become accepted deliverables.

- **Third stage:** It involves the agreed deliverables to initiate the closing process and activities finally. The final acceptance requires sign-off between the sponsor, project manager, and customer.
- **Transfer with handing over of spares and assets.** The project manager has a date agreed with a customer to close all the transfer of essential spares and property along with complete ownership of the plant and its related equipment. The transfer should also be a legally binding agreement, and a record should be sent to all concerned. A formal ceremony is organized with the customer, taking charge of the operations.

  Concurrently, all legal administrative and financial with commercial closing formalities are also underway to finalize the transference of ownership.
- **Financial closure.** The biggest problem is resolution with contractors on the delays and rework that invoked penalties, and LD clauses with the customer. The subcontractors somehow try not to hold themselves accountable for customer penalties on delays that are caused by them. The customer holds payments for milestones or deliverables not matching quality and subcontractors wants payment for the work done.

  The project manager ensures to keep the subcontractor in the loop while the handing over of milestones is being done in regular phases. There should be an unwritten understanding that payments for work done by the subcontractor will be subject to quality and schedule contractual clauses without rework. However, it is also important that issues with a customer should not be palmed off to the subcontractor with delayed payment of work which was done satisfactorily.

  Financial closure, hence, primarily involves settling all outstanding bills of suppliers and contractors for the work and services they gave as per the contract. There should be a proper reconciliation of the organization cost accounting system with the project budget. All variance must be resolved

and settled with an appropriate documentary proof before financial closure.
- **Legal closure and time extension with insurance claim resolution.** The customer would be charging LD or time extension claims palming the team with many blames that a certain work was not done properly in time. The best way to prevent all this, which the project manager should do from day one, is to do the document work properly.

    The team should hand over to the client an interim accepted deliverable, take the sign-off, and ensure that commissioning and performance guarantees are matching the contractual obligation. Any change in the work deliverable or schedule or costing should be with customer concurrence and a signature obtained. If these points are taken care of regularly, then there will be no problem of the client charging penalties for delays.
- **Identification of delay.** Delays can be excusable, nonexcusable, compensable, and noncompensable. Excusable and compensable delays are those resulting from risk events beyond the contractor's control and always attributable to the employer. The project manager proves that the delay is not due to the issues on his/her side, but it is due to the client issues. In any case, during the project, he takes the responsibility to mitigate wholly or partially the impact of such delays. Moreover, the project team records the delay impact due to such events.
- **Recording delays.** The project manager records all suspension notices and submits them to the client. The delay notice should provide all relevant information related to each delay event which are:
    - An employer request for change if any
    - A detailed description of the modification and the quantities related to such change
    - Related drawings and specification

- All correspondence (letters, transmittals, and technical queries)
  - Relevant contract clauses
  - Time impact analysis performed to quantify the impact of such delay
  - Estimated cost impact if any
- **Details of all the delay issues identified should be recorded in a delay register.** This document is designed to capture all delays, regardless of how small they are, which could have contributed to the cause of the critical delay incurred. The project team keeps a live register of "early warning notices." That allows both parties to resolve issues in the first instance of their occurrence not using the concept of "wait and see."
- **Contractual basis of the entitlement.** The project manager defines in a separate section of the claim document the contractual basis of his eligibility for ET and states clearly the contract clauses. He reviews all reference materials, such as appropriate contract provisions, construction drawings, sketches, specifications, vendor data, regulatory and administrative codes, field directives, correspondence, and cost estimates. He also prepares an accurate description of the changed condition or the delay encountered.

For more details, he also mentions the parties who were responsible for such change/risk event and also the repercussions. All verbal instructions or those received via emails are recorded and confirmed by the employer in writing. The activities which are impacted are mentioned along with the scheduled start and finish dates for all affected activities. All this record keeping is also shared with the client at regular intervals.

The project manager also describes in detail the action taken to mitigate or recover delays including the sequence of activities necessary to mobilize the required work. A correctly written narrative of the overall time impact analysis is done for the delay. Factual references to contract clauses, minutes of meetings, technical queries, and any written or oral communications are identified to support positions and ultimate conclusions. Weekends, holidays, and any recovery periods involved in the calculations should be included.

- **List of required records to establish adequately establish the substantiated the claims.** The project manager submits the following documents:
    - Baseline schedule from the project effective date
    - The scope of work that was to be executed by subcontractors
    - Planned workforce and machinery resources and its revisions
    - Schedule updates weekly or monthly based on the contract requirements
    - Notices for the delay once the contractor knows about the event, and within the given period as stipulated in the contract documents
    - Schedule revisions indicating changes and the required resources and the impact on the contract completion date
    - Delay analysis of each program, which should be updated weekly
    - Time impact analysis, showing the potential implications of the changes before carrying out the changes
    - Cause and effect analysis for each delay/disruption event
    - Weekly productivity analysis reports
    - Minutes of the daily and weekly meetings (upon request)
    - Minutes of any particular session (upon request)
    - Change of work notices within a given period, as defined in the contract, from the date at which the contractor came to know about the modification
    - DPRs
    - Weekly progress reports

- Monthly progress reports
- Claim register (monthly)
- Delay events log (monthly)
- **Closing audit.** There is a proper reconciliation of the organization cost accounting system with the project budget. All variance are resolved and settled with appropriate documentary proof before financial closure.
- **Administrative and contract closure.** The project manager closes the project with a client once the customer accepts that all work has been verified, delivered, and received by the customer. Any punch points or open issues, barring any economic billing issues, are closed.

  At the same time, the project manager closes the contract with his subcontractors and suppliers as and when their work is finished during the project life cycle. He does not wait for the project to get over, but as soon as the word or deliverable is handed over to the next phase, he/she settles the commercial aspects of the concerned stakeholders.

LESSONS LEARNT

After every battle, there is a record of the lessons learned, so that the next generation of officers understand how the sequence of battle was fought. The pros and cons of each step are analyzed so that valuable lessons are analyzed and recorded for essential learning.

- **War diary.** The project manager should also maintain a war daily for the project on a regular basis. It is the best place and time to capture lessons learned as it is at the moment that the project is happening. It ensures recording of the best lessons learned based on daily experiences, both active and adverse. It is archived for the future project team to learn so that they do not fall in the same pitfalls that occurred in this project.

- **Wrap up session.** The project manager, the project team, and the key stakeholders should also conduct wrap-up lessons. They should review all the documents and quality assurance reports jointly to get a sense of project issues and success. They should ask themselves if the project goals were attained and what needs to be done to meet better goals in the future.

  The objective of the wrap-up session is to assimilate issues that went well as per the vision, mission, and goal and aim of the project.

  It is also to holistically assess what went wrong and what were the reasons with unintended consequences. How the project suffered. The issues that they would deal with differently if they were to do the project again, what they can change if they were to go back in time zone are also jointly pondered upon. Finally, they give a joint recommendation for improvement for new projects.

  What were the VUCA surprises the team came across and how these were dealt with? What were the circumstances that could have been anticipated to avoid loss? Did the team develop any useful workarounds or solutions to problems that cropped up during the project? Preventive measures and best practices derived from the project should be suggested.

  Once all these lessons are assimilated, they should be uploaded in company database for an accessible repository for the experience gained and best practices.

In fact, I happened to read about a successful project which motivated me also to try and close a project within schedule, decided cost, quality, and complete scope. This project was a bridge made in France—Millau Viaduct. There have been a lot of case studies on this bridge. It is a great lesson learned for any project manager to learn how to overcome enormous challenges in large-scale innovation projects. Now, why I decided to mention this project when there are so many such projects that are being run all over the world. It is a simple explanation; the project's management first ensured that the project attains the four performance parameters of timely delivery, controlled high cost, quality, and absolute scope, and they also put efforts to make a case study by recording events and sharing them with the world.

So my request to all project manager, make a case study of your own project and put it on YouTube/the web. Let the world learn the essentials from the experiences of such project managers. Project management is a field where disruptive technology is also making an impact to make the project leaner and smarter against VUCA conditions. The next chapter is on such technologies.

FINAL PROJECT REPORT

Let's take an example of how the final report on the Kargil War would look like. It was the middle and junior leadership that rose to the occasion. The Kargil War would not have happened if there would not have been a realistic VUCA threat assessment and planning at the higher level. The positives were a great interaction between the leaderships of the Indian Air Force, Army, and Navy that formulated the strategic, tactical, and operation plan together with great execution by ground teams and aircrafts, along with monitoring and controlling at all levels. In the final analysis later, Kargil became a military, diplomatic, and political success for India. But we cannot forget the loss of nearly 500 military men and over 1,100 serious casualties. That lesson and numbers should prepare us better for future VUCA wars.

The final project report is a confirmation of the project that has been closed with documentary evidence. It also provides information on project success, challenges, lessons learned, and how transition took place from one phase to another phase. It is a collaborative effort of the inputs of all team members and not a one-sided impression of the good part only. It, hence, shows the truth of the achievements also and any gaps with baseline performance perimeters. It enables analysis of variance (see Table 11.1 and 11.2).

Table 11.1. Root Cause and Corrective Action Recommended for Delayed Schedule

Planned finish date	Actual finish date	Variance (in days)	Schedule on ahead or behind	Root cause	Corrective action
[dd-mm-yy]	[dd-mm-yy]		☐		

Source: Author's own work.
Note: "On schedule" calculation may be within +/– 10 percent of the approved schedule.

Table 11.2. Root Cause and Corrective Action Recommended for Cost Overruns

Approved budget	Spent budget	Variance (in $)	On under or over budget	Root cause	Corrective action
[$ 0]	[$ 0]		☐		

Source: Author's own work.
Note: "On budget" calculation may be within +/– 10 percent of the approved budget.

Identification of changes to the BAC, EAC, or ETC were also observed at a different stage of the project to assess the forecast capabilities. Analysis of the gaps with the baseline is done by identifying the cause of the variance. There is a recommendation of corrective and preventive actions also to prevent such difference in future projects.

Taking Customer Feedback

The project manager also takes a good feedback session with the client throughout the project life cycle. He/She gets updated on every progress and shares every issue and aspect. There is also smooth handing over of the product after proper commissioning, and his/her operation team is also trained.

Obviously, the customer will be happy at the lean work done. The project manager must remind the client of his mission to take a bonus from the client. Ensure that there is a proper felicitation ceremony where customer top management presents the gift to the project manager and his team. The customer will also share the feedback with other potential customers from the same industry and will become an advocate. Moreover, there will be repeat orders from the customer, which is a sign of success.

Apart from the project success, the project manager has to be successful in changing the RPV management in his project. If he improves the RPV, future project and generation of project managers will also benefit.

The project manager must also take a critical customer feedback which is an essential component to improving in a healthy, growing business. If the client team faced any recurring problems, he should analyze them to stop the problems from occurring again and potentially affecting other customers (see Table 11.3).

Party Hard After the Project

Before moving on to the next project, it is important to savor the successful completion of the project at hand. Rest and rejuvenation is required to work hard on the next project. Facilitating the achievers and acknowledging the support received from various quarters is essential to keep everybody motivated.

Table 11.3. Customer Feedback

Success criteria	Meeting customer expectations		Suggested improvements
	Criteria met	Pain area	
[Enter success criteria from project charter here...]	☐		
	☐		
	☐		

Source: Author's own work.

THE LAST WORD

I remember a poem at NDA that sums up the closing of any event or project. This poem by Rudyard Kipling is framed and hung in the each and every cadet's room at NDA. The poem stared at me every day when I was a cadet during my study period and has been a guiding force.

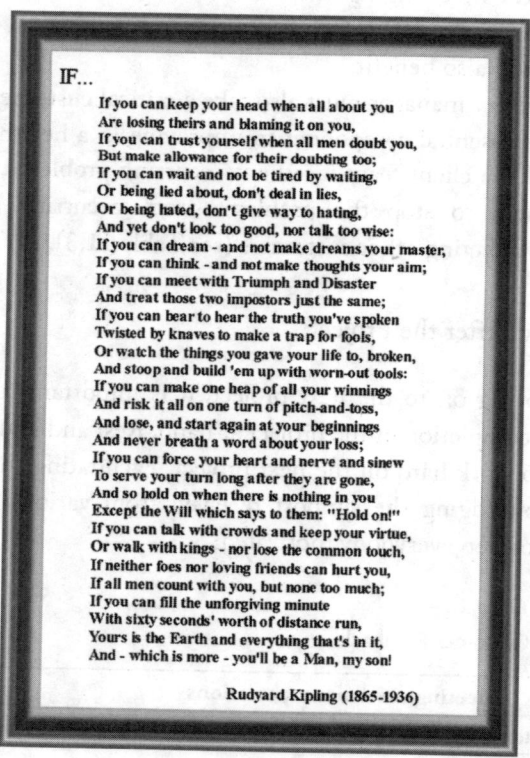

HOW ARE RACE RESULTS BEING ACHIEVED?

Rapid. The commissioning of the product and trails with handing over was completed in time. Other activities like administrative and contract closure were also rapid and an ongoing process.

Absolute work. All punch points were cleared in time, and there were no pending issues left with the client.

Quality. There were hardly any rework or poor quality issues as the interim deliverables were properly checked before being delivered to the next stage.

Economic cost. There were no additional work or rework increased cost. All matters of LD have been resolved amicably and time extension issues were discussed and the client was satisfied with proper documentation.

TAKEAWAYS

Most important activity is to hand over the project without any defects or punch points and get legal and administrative clearance. The lesson learned with documents have to be archived for future projects.

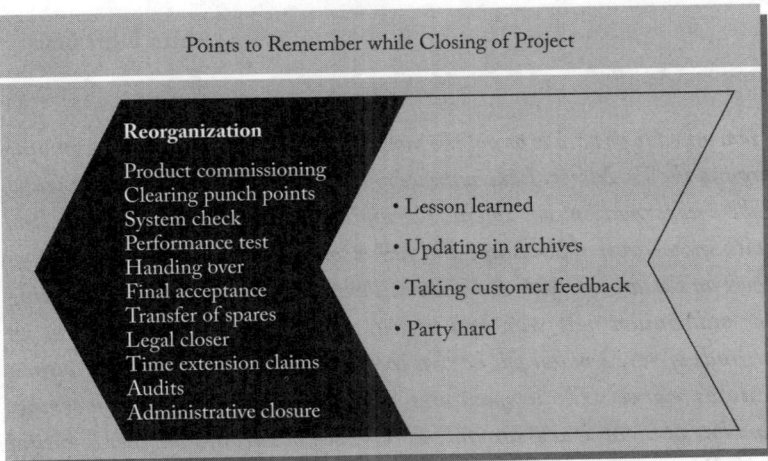

CHAPTER 12

Technology to Help in Countering VUCA

> *Sometimes I think we'll see the day*
> *when you introduce a product in*
> *the morning and announce its end*
> *of life at the end of the day*
>
> —Alan F. Shugrat

He wanted to go back to one of the most beautiful places on Earth—camping around the Tso Moriri Lake with ice and crystal blue sky reflecting in water where ice formation was absent. The night was very beautiful, moonlit and with snow-covered landscape and full moon reflection in the lake. He was there on the last new year eve of the millennium. The world was celebrating the millennium new year, and he was in a freezing environment at an altitude of 4,522 m but felt he was the luckiest guy in the world to witness nature's marvel. The temperatures were touching −10°C early morning, and late at night, it was around −20°C. They had crossed another beautiful lake, Pangong Tso, and the distance to Tso Moriri was 235 km.

The mission was to rescue a team of soldiers who had come there but had met with an accident. Communication was very difficult then, and there were no modern means to assess the real situation. Moreover, the Chinese threat loomed large. The damaged vehicle and radar was also difficult to recover along with aid to the injured.

It is 2017 now and today when he reflects on those days—all on his own with a small team in a snow desert—if the same situation happens today, there is technology to help in VUCA conditions, be it in armed forces or projects of any kind.

There is a designer who will give you complete details of the terrain and road maps with difficulties in navigation or crossing any obstacle by modeling the actual scenario. You can practice your mission drills also. There is all kind of data and even specific information through big data servers connected to satellites and surveillance equipment like drones. With radio frequency identification (RFID) and GPS, you can guide more logistics backup with satellite communication if you get lost. Your equipment and devices will confirm if anything is wrong and warn timely replacement. You can ask for spares through ERP and even get the design or details on your mobile. If there are bigger spares you can use 3D printing on the spot to design and fit the replacement in the highest altitude of the world. There are robots to do the dirty and dangerous work where human life is in danger. In midst of all this, you can send photos of your mission on social media or to your family.

This is a brief of what disruptive technology can do for VUCA conditions. Let's discuss these technological wonders one by one.

SMARTER DESIGN: 3D, 4D, 5D, AND BIM MODEL

In the armed forces, technology has taken massive strides in wargaming. Today one has to put the enemy strength in software, and one gets various scenarios from where and how the enemy will strike and what should be our response. The computer games on battle are just a reflection of the real simulation of the battlefield that can be generated on a console.

In raid for Osama bin Laden, the complete simulation of the raid was practiced by the SEALS. They had undergone complete construction and demolition of a mock-up of the house of Osama bin Laden. Gone are the days where a scheduler or planner would make some plan and present to the client. Today building information modelling (BIM) can integrate design, time, and cost information among all stakeholders from early design to project life cycle and even to the O&M stage and maybe even till the decommissioning stage.

BIM is not a software but is a business process, and it is evolving continually. It is a digital representation of a physical and functional characteristic of a product made by project management processes. Here, all problems are simulated in advance, and the potential VUCA impact is analyzed to solve it as a collaborative affair between all stakeholders.

- A 3D model is being used by engineers for better visual creativity and understanding of designs and activities. They use width, length, and depth in 3D visualizations for walkthroughs and to ensure project coordination for better understanding.
- A 4D model helps in identifying potential temporal conflicts in schedule. Here, the 3D parts or assemblies are linked and connected to the schedule program and sequence in which they will come up. It also shows what all resources and in what quantities will be needed to achieve the timelines. There are prefabricated and modular designs to assist project phasing in the realistic schedule.
- A 5D model has come in to identify costs and model cash flows for each step of construction. The 4D model is now being integrated with charging. We can generate the bills of quantities, and derivation of productivity rates and labor costs to do the complete project.

All these models have helped in reducing VUCA issues by making more accurate designs and increasing collaboration between stakeholders. They have led to precise work without errors as these can be detected in advance.

BIG DATA

Armed forces were early adopters of big data connecting dots to find terrorist movements. Too much intelligence inputs are there on an everyday basis and the real crux to find the actual motives of the terrorist is a challenge. A team of the analysts works full time to decipher the real stuff about what the terrorists are going to do so that they can take preemptive actions. The challenge is connecting the dots. Usually, the terrorists leave lots of signs on social media and bomb-making material on eBay but data is so much that by the time security agencies connect the dots an explosion has happened somewhere in the world.

Likewise, it has lots of usage in project and operations. Big data is a collection of data from traditional and digital sources inside and outside the company. It is a source for ongoing discovery and analysis. It has three ingredients:

- **Fast data.** It provides the ability to see all information in a short time.
- **Big analytics.** It assesses any risk or opportunity and the necessary action needed.
- **Deep insight.** It generates new knowledge and insight in the domain of business.

It has now a lot of use in project management to determine the possible VUCA conditions:

- Allows projects to be kept on schedule and a budget by providing insights based on data generated by various sources, like job sites.

- Timely availability and prices of materials, suppliers, human resources systems, and communication.
- Assesses the current work data as measurable and analyzable to ensure that their product is aligned with a proper commissioning procedure.
- Uses data of similar projects to determine the risk profile and see the trend and predict overruns in cost or delayed schedule. In the movie *Minority Report*, Tom Cruise is catching people before they have done crimes. Basically, he is a red flag to prevent a VUCA situation.
- Helps in improving productivity and quick decision-making. The decisions are also accurate as they are based on empirical data.
- Gives geographically dispersed team members real-time and shared access to the same documents which helps minimize delays. Also, it ensures that all team member use the same information to do their work.
- Documents such as drawings, models, contracts, and procurement materials can be indexed and made searchable for anyone involved.

INTERNET OF THINGS (IOT) IN PROJECT MANAGEMENT

Sensors and actuators embedded in things like battlefield surveillance gadgets send information to the central system for better tracking and analysis of the enemy position. Almost all objects or devices will have an IP address and are connected to each other. It is more or less like a human brain with local device nodes resembling neurons. All are interconnected and generate enormous volumes of data. For example, using a drone flying into enemy territory to understand the communication, and then to tap into data feeds using various techniques and transmit back. The challenge is to filter out redundant data and also protect the data from getting attacked.

Use of IOT in Project Management

Following are the various uses of IOT in project management:

- Control of rates in transportation by placing sensors on transportation vehicles and gathering data by signals to assess the distance covered and how many resources were committed. It helps in making accurate bids.
- Sensors placed on high-value equipment prevent theft and contribute to using fewer security guards.
- Sensors placed in products and real use can help in determining any defects and changes due to environmental conditions. They will tack such defects and inform to the project management system. It will help in further research and development of better material and products and ensure quality control.
- It will help technician also to pinpoint particular defects in big assemblies and proactively take corrective actions on potential machine performance problems. The maintenance becomes proactive.
- Use of RFID in material safety by using RFID tags. We can monitor the tags of many sites from a central location remotely.
- There are self-detecting sensors that can give an alarm in machine and tools when they need maintenance.
- IOT is also useful in deploying devices remotely by the internet in hazardous conditions keeping workers' safety in mind. Accidents from falls, collisions with heavy objects, etc., can be reduced.
- There are wearable devices to monitor the health of workers. These devices also give an alert on environmental hazards and safety alerts. These machines log time for employees and prevent falsification of records.
- There are wearable interface devices like Google Glass to transmit images and access information while operating machines.

DRONES

It is another innovation taken from the armed forces where it is used for better surveillance of the enemy. We keep reading how they are being used in Afghanistan by American troops and now at our borders also to track round the clock activities of the enemy. We can have a similar use of drones in projects. They are very useful for a project for site work monitoring:

- They can be used to capture site terrain and relevant data to make 3D maps. They are useful for analytical tools to make fast and informed decisions and can even conclude how the project will look like. They can be used for marketing and business tools also.
- Drones can be employed for work monitoring in hazardous locations, especially at heights, to identify structurally unstable buildings and even underside of bridges, etc. The images and data that come from drones help engineers to assess faults from homes or offices and get timely repairs done.
- It also contributes to monitoring work across the site and controlling schedule and budget by making work visible and transparent to all.
- Like CCTV it also helps to protect material against theft and trespassing.
- Movement of materials. Amazon has already started using drones to transport goods to its customers; similar work can be done to take content to the otherwise inaccessible site locations with a vehicle.

MOBILE APPLICATIONS

There are battlefield command control vehicles equipped with all latest surveillance and communication systems that get deployed in the forward zone or anywhere in the war zone. On similar lines, there are applications now in communication equipment that help in OODA loop that can observe, orient make decisions, and act as per the situation on the ground. It saves a lot of time by ensuring rapid results in the thick of a battle scene; an example is monitoring reinforcement of troops or casualty evacuation.

There are a lot of applications in projects management software offering mobile versions of their systems for access on smartphones and tablets.

- These ensure the team is working on the move. The employees are having access to the system anywhere, any time beyond typical business hours.
- They can plan their day, visualize goals and milestones, set tasks and due dates, and communicate priorities and offers central to administration and billing.
- The application provides real-time collaboration and problem-solving, thus accelerating project delivery in time within cost. Team members can track performance metrics at all levels.
- There is a lot of cooperation within team and stakeholders for unified work with live updates.
- There is ease of exchange of data with the updated status of actionable execution. It assists in quick analysis and decision-making.

USE OF ROBOTICS AND AUTOMATED DEVICES

There are a lot of trails underway making robotic soldiers and cyborgs replace human soldiers. Robots are used in many operations. They are being used for recce patrols by relying on back information through sensors. They are also used to remove explosives or diffuse bombs and save lives. There are lot of automated devices fitted with sensors to detect motion, gas leaks, any faint sound etc.

The next generation of robots and automated devices are already there in projects. Robots are more useful than skilled labor to enhance productivity and quality work within time and reduced cost. There are improved capabilities for job performance in speed, accuracy, quality, and size of work piece.

Safety can be ensured by deploying machines in dangerous tasks and unhealthy environmental conditions. These are useful where workers find themselves in uncomfortable working positions. Data can be transmitted to the devices by sensors and surveillance aids like drones.

They are also suited to solve the instability situation of the absence of labor force or extra cost where more work may be required. More so, there is less cost of labor mobilization and training or IR issues.

USE OF RFID AND GPRS

Supply chain and logistic movements in projects are often overlooked. The material not reaching in time results in delays and cost overruns. Now, it is possible to track the flow of the finished products right from the manufacturer stage to transit to site and erection/commissioning.

There is a GPS receiver fitted to the logistic vehicle, and the operator can request positioning anytime through satellite navigation. The satellite can also be used for communication with a base station. It is best to use a unit that can support both satellite and GSM/GPRS communication. GPRS is utilized to send the information to and fro from a GPS-enabled device in the remote areas. There is software application at the base station that shows the location of the goods 24/7 on a geographical information system (GIS). Any deviation from the planned route is immediately brought to notice.

RFID are low-cost tags that emit radio waves to automatically identify an object, often by storing a serial number (and any additional information up to 2 MB) on an antenna. There is a transponder attached to each item to be tracked (typically trucks and containers) with active readers installed inside the vehicles and linked to the

GPS/GPRS devices. A receiver emits a short-range alert when the integrity of the bulk has been compromised. Some RFID tags also monitor environmental conditions.

3D PRINTING

A 3D digital model of the item is created using a 3D scanner or CAD. It is a manufacturing process and an additive process where material (plastic metal powder, sheet material, liquid) is laid down in successive layers of the printing medium and fused or joined to create an item. In projects, it ensures better product designs with the creation of new components to allow the client satisfaction of his visualization. Such mock-up identifies flaws and pain areas in advance to prevent any rework. It reduces the time spent on processes and allows massive cost savings and efficiency benefits. There are few errors at the production stage and a quality finish.

SOCIAL MEDIA

Social media is here to stay, and it is better to use it to own advantage in project management for the ease of communication and for sharing media and information of project status update. WhatsApp, Facebook, Twitter are some of the easiest ways. Video conferencing reduces travel cost in the project. Wikis can be used as an online PMO for lessons learned or to build the project life cycle as it happens on the ground. There are endless possibilities, and it will keep improving day by day as new technologies usher in.

ERP ON CLOUD

Traditional ERP have routine problems such as low bandwidth, high latency, and disconnected communications that increase VUCA possibilities where a team can be left unsupported also.

In the armed forces, in the last couple of years, there has been a rapid growth in creating infrastructure of logistic ERP and linking with the battle management system. It enhances quick deployment of operational status by on-time replenishment of needs for combat. Operation Parakram was deployed for 24–36 hours when the Indian Army moved to deserts and border areas from peace locations after the attack on the Parliament happened. Pakistan was caught unprepared with so many forces moved within no time to attack. Now, that occurred not only due to many training drills but also due to the connectivity of ERP and another related systems to bring logistics at par with the fighting capability.

Now, the future battlefield will be in deep deserts where ERP infrastructure will not be possible and cloud will be needed. However, cloud applications also provide complete security to armed forces, ERP, and battle management systems.

Nevertheless, with defense satellites and enhanced security, the dependence on traditional ERP hardware and middleware will lessen. Cloud with safety cover will increase connectivity with noncombat, rear echelon personnel. It will also provide real-time battlefield surveillance and action so that timely support is provided wherever needed.

CLOUD SERVICE IN PROJECTS

Cloud provides shared computer processing resources and data to computers and other devices on demand. It enables companies to consume a virtual machine, storage, or an application as a utility. It saves a lot of costs. Large corporations invest a lot on setting up ERP that needs further investment in upgrades and training and it still never comes around perfecting the user requirements.

The next generation of lean and agile project companies are shifting the ERP to the cloud which is a low-cost, quick-install, highly secure, customized solution. It allows storing large project data and information, which is suddenly available in real-time from anywhere.

The project companies can provide the same service being currently provided by their internal IT team at a lesser rate and more efficiently. They have all functions of project life cycle, namely, project planning, project tracking, project billing, project accounting, and project profitability. There is the better scope of collaboration among workforce to analyze and work on the move.

A new ERP cloud also enables a workforce to collaborate, analyze, and work on the move, accelerating performance and attracting great talent. Finally, a new ERP cloud reduces costs and makes smarter use of scarce IT resources in construction. There is best-in-class service of integrated analytics and dashboards to track status and allow quick decision-making. The users have a clear focus on using those functions that they need to get the work done along with collaboration and interface with other stakeholders.

TAKEAWAYS

Integration of all these technologies will help in anticipation, prevention, and control of VUCA.

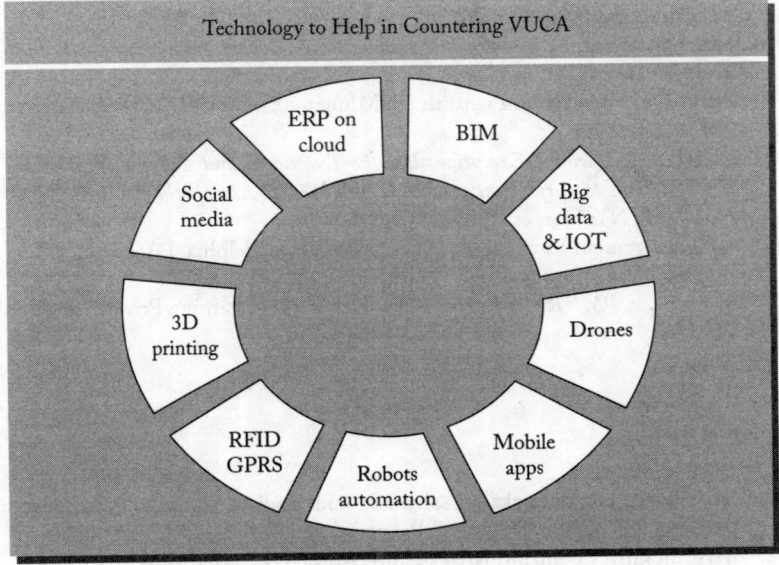

Bibliography

BOOKS

Abidi, Suhayl, and Joshi, Manoj. *VUCA Company*. Mumbai: Jaico Publishing House, 2015.

Black and Veatch. *Power Plant Engineering*. Edited by Lawrence F. Drbal, Patricia G. Boston, Kayla L. Westra, R. Bruce Erickson. New Delhi: CBS Publishers & Distributors, 1998.

Collins, Jim. *Good to Great*. London: Random House Business Books, 2001.

Hessler, Peter G. *Power Plant Construction Management: A Survival Guide*, 2nd ed. Tulsa, OK: PennWell, 2015.

Malone, Dandridge M. *Small Unit leadership: A Commonsense Approach*. New York, NY: Presidio Press, 1983.

Mulcahy, Rita. *PMP Exam Prep*, 8th ed. Minnetonka, MA: RMC Publications, 2013.

Murphy, James. *Flawless Execution: Use the Techniques and Systems of America's Fighter Pilots to Perform at your Peak and Win Battles in the Business World*. New York, NY: Harper Collins, 2006.

Project Management Institute. *PMBOK*, 5th ed. Philadelphia, PA: PMI.

Ward, Dan. *FIRE*. New York, NY: Harper Collins, 2014.

Whitaker, Sean. *PMP Rapid Review*. New Delhi: PHI Learning Private Limited, 2013.

WEBSITES

Agarwal, Rajat, Chandrasekaran, Shankar, and Sridhar, Mukund. "Imagining Construction's Digital Future." Retrieved on April 2, 2017, from: http://www.mckinsey.com/industries/capital-projects-and-infrastructure/our-insights/imagining-constructions-digital-future

Bibliography 281

American Society for Nondestructive Testing. "Codes and Standards Overview." Retrieved May 2, 2017, from: https://www.asnt.org/MajorSiteSections/NDT-Resource-Center/Codes_and_Standards .aspx

Atlas of Public Management. "VMOSA." Retrieved on January 5, 2017, from: http://www.atlas101.ca/pm/concepts/vmosa-vision-mission-objectives-strategies-and-action-plans/

Baumgartner, Jeffrey. "The Best Strategies for Dealing with Disruptive Innovation." In Enterprise Innovation. Retrieved on May 2, 2017, from: http://www.innovationmanagement.se/imtool-articles/the-best-strategies-for-dealing-with-disruptive-innovation/

Beard, Ross. "Customer Feedback: 19 Strategies To Get More Feedback." Retrieved on March 23, 2017, from: http://blog.clientheartbeat.com/customer-feedback/

Capterra Construction Management Blog. "A Guide to the Future: 3D Printing and Construction." Retrieved on April 24, 2017, from: http://blog.capterra.com/3d-printing-and-construction/

Christensen, Clayton M., Anthony, Scott D., and Roth, Erik A. "Seeing What's Next: Using the Theories of Innovation to Predict Industry Change." Retrieved on May 02, 2017, form: http://vedpuriswar.org/Book_Review/Business_Strategy/Seeing %20What %20is%20Next.pdf and from: http://kendlevidian.pbworks.com/f/Seeing+What's+Next.html

Clark, Tracy. "7 Characteristics of the 20 mile March in Schools." Retrieved on February 24, 2017, from: https://tracyannclark.com/2014/11/24/the-20-mile-march-part-ii/

Construction Review Online. "Top Disruptive Technology Trends for the Construction Industry in 2016." Retrieved on March 30, 2017, from: https://constructionreviewonline.com/2016/01/top-disruptive-technology-trends-for-construction-industry-in-2016/

"EPC Contract Structuring Key Legal Issues Damages in EPC Contracts." 5th Annual Senior Management Forum Mumbai April 26, 2012. Retrieved on December 31, 2016, from: http://documents.mx/documents/damages-in-contracts-25-04-2013-epc-workshop-wvj.html

Frieght into Africa. "RFID Cargo Tracking." Retrieved on April 15, 2017, from: http://www.freightintoafrica.com/page/products_and_services_gpsrfid_cargo_tracking_solutions

Global Construction. "5 Reasons Why Construction Firms Need to Start Using Drones." Retrieved on April, 2017, from: http://www.constructionglobal.com/majorprojects/383/5-reasons-why-construction-firms-need-to-start-using-drones

Hall, Harry. "How To Better Your Quantitative Risk Analysis." Retrieved on January 19, 2017, from: http://projectriskcoach.com/2016/03/18/how-to-better-your-quantitative-risk-analysis/

Jang, C. J. "Using Earned Value to Monitor Project Performance." Retrieved on March 10, 2017, from: https://www.cardinalsolutions.com/blog/2012/07/using_earned_valuet

Jenkins, Hodge. "Engineering Standards." Retrieved on May 2, 2017, from: http://faculty.mercer.edu/kunz_rk/documents/EngineeringStandards-for487.pdf

Johnson, Rose. "Tactical and Operational Planning." Retrieved on January 30, 2017, from: http://smallbusiness.chron.com/tactical-operational-planning-18336.html

Kim, Daniel H. "Introduction to System Thinking." Retrieved on November 30, 2016, from: https://thesystemsthinker.com/wp-content/uploads/2016/03/Introduction-to-Systems-Thinking-IMS013Epk.pdf

Koirala, Shivprasad. *"Project Management FAQ."* Retrieved on December 30, 2016, from: https://www.codeproject.com/Articles/29753/Project-Management-FAQ

Kumar, Roopesh. "Theory of Constraints (TOC): Gaining Better Project Control." Retrieved on January 15, 2017, from: http://www.projectperfect.com.au/white-paper-theory-of-constraints.php

Jacob, J. F. R., Lieutenant General. "Freedom in the Offing." *Interview by Ramananda Sengupta of Rediff India.* Retrieved on May 1, 2017, from: http://www.thedailystar.net/op-ed/we-did-not-take-khulna-and-we-did-not-capture-chittagong-yet-we-won-the-war-72964

Mastering projectmanagement.com. "Project Plan Execution." Retrieved on June 12, 2017, from: http://www.mastering-project-management.com/project-plan-execution.html

McKie, Stewart. "Perfecting Project Accounting." Business Finance. Retrieved on January 25, 2017, from: http://businessfinancemag.com/technology/perfecting-project-accounting

Microsoft. "Use Twitter, Facebook, and Other Social Media to Help Manage Projects and Teams." Retrieved on April 24, 2017, from: https://support.office.com/en-us/article/Use-Twitter-Facebook-and-other-social-media-to-help-manage-projects-and-teams-1c9b9c86-e417-4763-91ed-35a5f6e86208

Miller, Michelle. "Stakeholder Mapping for Collaboration: A Tool for Inclusiveness & Diversity." Retrieved on November 25, 2016, from: http://ncdd.org/12354

Mindtool. "OODA Loops: Understanding the Decision Cycle." Retrieved on June 12, 2017, from: https://www.mindtools.com/pages/article/newTED_78.htm

Mossman, Alan. "Last Planner." Retrieved on March, 2017, from: http://www.leanconstruction.org/media/docs/Mossman-Last-Planner

Nagy, Jenette, and Fawcett, Stephen B. "An Overview of Strategic Planning or 'VMOSA' (Vision, Mission, Objectives, Strategies, and Action Plans)." Community Tool Box Retrieved on November 10, 2016, from: http://ctb.ku.edu/en/table-of-contents/structure/strategic-planning/vmosa/main

One-page Project Manager. The OPPM™ Template. Retrieved on March 5, 2017, from: https://www.oppmi.com/OPPM-Corporate-License.cfm

PMI Global Congress North America. "Taking Innovation to Reality Disruption Management." Retrieved on May 2, 2017, from: http://congresses.pmi.org/NorthAmerica2015/program/educational-areas-of-focus/area-of-focus-sessions/session/2015/10/11/default-calendar/taking-innovation-to-reality-disruptive-project-management

Primavera, Oracle. "Earned Value Lite: Making Earned Value Management Work for Every Project." Retrieved on March 12, 2017, from: http://www.oracle.com/us/products/applications/042745

Project Value Delivery. "Crude Estimates of Possible Project Overrun." Retrieved on March 24, 2017, from: http://www.projectvaluedelivery.com/_library/2013-09_Crude_Estimates_Overrun_v0.pdf

Quizlet, Habizine. "Project Cost Management." Retrieved on February 10, 2017, from: https://quizlet.com/36596196/7-project-cost-management-flash-cards/

SAMS 131-101DoctrineFlashcards. Retrieved on February 2, 2017, from: http://www.cram.com/flashcards/sams-13-01-doctrine-2476194

Schoemaker, Paul. "Leading the Vigilant Organization." Retrieved on May 2, 2017, from: https://www.researchgate.net/profile/Paul_Schoemaker/publication/229046527_Leading_the_vigilant_organization/links/0c9605325c13b44447000000.pdf?origin=publication_list

Scientia Iranica. "Influence of RFID Technology on Automated Management of Construction Materials and Components." Retrieved on April, 2017, from: http://www.sciencedirect.com/science/article/pii/S1026309812000727

Seppaneni, Olli. "Production Control with Lean Construction Principles." Retrieved on March 18, 2017, from: http://www.vicosoftware.com/0/blogs/fit-and-finnish/tabid/51274/bid/11046/Production-Control-with-Lean-Construction-Principles-Part-2.aspx

Seppnen, Olli, Ballard, Glenn, and Pesonen, Sakari. "Combination of Last Planner System and Location Based Management." Retrieved on March 20, 2017, from: http://www.nexoncn.com/read/20d80db9314411a81dae122d.html

Subramaniam, Anand. "Earned Value Management." Retrieved on December 30, 2016, from: https://www.slideshare.net/anandsubramaniam/earned-value-management-1784592

Sundarji, General K. "Open Letter to All Officers." Retrieved on May 2, 2017, from: http:defenceforumindia.com/forum/threads/that-famous-letter-from-general-k-sundarji.2927/

The Forum for Growth and Innovation. "Theory: Disruptive Innovation." Retrieved on May 1, 2017, from: http://www.thefgi.net/theory-disruptive-innovation/

United States Joint Chiefs of Staff. *Joint Publication 3-15: Barriers, Obstacles, and Mine Warfare for Joint Operations*. Text Version. Retrieved on February 20, 2017, from: http://www.readbag.com/fas-irp-doddir-dod-jp3-15

US Department of Transportation. "3D, 4D, and 5D Engineered Models For Construction." Retrieved on April 5, 2017, from: https://www.fhwa.dot.gov/construction/pubs/hif13048.pdf

Usmani, Fahad. "Critical Chain Method (CCM) in Project Management." Retrieved on December 20, 2016, from: https://pmstudycircle.com/2014/02/critical-chain-method-ccm-in-project-management/

Vasilash, Gary S. *"Pardon the Disruption."* Retrieved on May 02, 2017, from: http://www.adandp.media/columns/pardon-the-disruption

Venkatraman, Mahesh. "Trends Driving Progressive Change Within the EPC Industry." Retrieved on March 30, 2017, from: http://blogs.ramco.com/trends-challenges-solution-epc-industry-2015

White, Mark, and Cohan, Alison. "A Guide to Capturing Lessons Learned." Retrieved on March 25, 2017, from: https://www.conservationgateway.org/ConservationPlanning/partnering/cpc/Documents/Capturing_Lessons_Learned_Final.pdf

Whole Building Design Guide. "Earned Value Analysis." Retrieved on March 11, 2017, from: https://www.wbdg.org/resources/earned-value-analysis

"It is quite an intellectual masterpiece and a must read for any practicing manager to get nuances of 'big-picture', processes and the stance to keep in day to day management, for success. Delving in depth on stark distinction between 'science-based approach' and 'systems-based aspects', interestingly the author has illustrated the inadequacy of scientific approach in general management, while clearly articulating various systems-based approaches and aspects that can help steer with dexterity in innumerable managerial situations—simple or complex!"

Rajeev Batra
CIO, Times Group

A compelling case for a 'holistic' thinking in organizations!

For special offers on this and other books from SAGE, write to marketing@sagepub.in

Explore our range at
www.sagepub.in

₹395

Paperback
978-93-864-4673-2